W9-CJX-159

ON AMERICA

VOLUME I

NEW TRAVELS

IN THE

UNITED STATES OF AMERICA

JACQUES PIERRE BRISSOT DE WARVILLE

ON AMERICA

VOLUME I

NEW TRAVELS

IN THE

UNITED STATES OF AMERICA

PERFORMED IN 1788

[1792]

AUGUSTUS M. KELLEY · PUBLISHERS

NEW YORK 1970

First Edition 1792

(London: *Printed for* J. S. Jordan, *No. 166 Fleet-Street,* 1792)

Reprinted 1970 by
AUGUSTUS M. KELLEY · PUBLISHERS
REPRINTS OF ECONOMIC CLASSICS
New York   New York   10001

. . . .

S B N 678-00598-2
Volume I 678 04028 1

L C N 67-30855

. . . .

PRINTED IN THE UNITED STATES OF AMERICA
by SENTRY PRESS, NEW YORK, N. Y. 10019

NEW TRAVELS

IN THE UNITED STATES OF

A M E R I C A.

PERFORMED IN 1788.

CONTAINING

THE LATEST AND MOST ACCURATE OBSERVATIONS ON THE CHARAC-
TER, GENIUS, AND PRESENT STATE OF THE PEOPLE ARD GOVERN-
MENT OF THAT COUNTRY—THEIR AGRICULTURE, COMMERCE,
MANUFACTURES, AND FINANCES—QUALITY AND PRICE OF
LANDS, AND PROGRESS OF THE SETTLEMENTS ON THE OHIO
AND THE MISSISIPPE—POLITICAL AND MORAL CHARACTER
OF THE QUAKERS, AND A VINDICATION OF THAT EXCEL-
LENT SECT, FROM THE MISREPRESENTATIONS OF
OTHER TRAVELLERS—STATE OF THE BLACKS—PRO-
GRESS OF THE LAWS FOR THEIR EMANCIPATION,
AND FOR THE FINAL DESTRUCTION OF SLAVERY
ON THAT CONTINENT—ACCURATE ACCOUNTS
OF THE CLIMATE, LONGEVITY—COMPARA-
TIVE TABLES OF THE PROBABILITIES OF
LIFE BETWEEN AMERICA AND EUROPE,
&c. &c.

By •J. P. BRISSOT DE WARVILLE.

TRANSLATED FROM THE FRENCH.

A People without Morals may acquire Liberty, but without Morals they
cannot preferve it.

*Nemo illic vitia ridet, nec corrumpere, nec corrumpi feculum vocatur - - - -
Plufquam ibi boni mores valent, quam alibi bonæ leges.*   TACITUS.

L O N D O N:

PRINTED FOR J. S. JORDAN, No. 166, FLEET-STREET
MDCCXCII.

THE Tranflator is happy in giving the Reader an opportunity to correct the error mentioned in the following letter, as well as to exprefs his obligation to the perfons who wrote it. The note referred to, begins in page 98. He will only add, that he had his information from a gentleman of Bofton, in whofe candour he has the utmoft confidence.

To the Tranflator of BRISSOT DE WARVILLE'S *Travels.*

" HAVING obferved a note refpecting the perfecution of the people called Quakers in New-England, wherein it is af-ferted, that no other perfon fuffered death on a religious ac-count but Mary Dyer, whofe behaviour there is extremely mifreprefented, we called on the Publifher to ftate this matter truly (according to divers authentic accounts), finding the Tranflator had received his information through fome very er-roneous channel.

" It is certain that Marmeduke Stevenfon, William Robin-fon, and William Leddra, alfo fuffered death at Bofton, for no other caufe than their confcientious diffent from the eccle-fiaftical eftablifhment there. Thefe facts are fully ftated in Gough's Hiftory of the People called Quakers, page 391, 404, 473 to 476.

WM. FAIRBANK, *Sheffield,*
JEREMIAH WARING, *Alton, Hants.*

" P. S. We confider the rectifying of the above note, as an act of juftice due to the Society, of which we are members."

PREFACE

OF THE

TRANSLATOR.

NO traveller, I believe, of this age, has
made a more ufeful prefent to Europe,
than M. de Warville in the publication of
the following Tour in the United States.
The people of France will derive great
advantages from it; as they have done
from a variety of other labours of the
fame induftrious and patriotick author.
Their minds are now open to enquiry
into the effects of moral and political fyftems, as their commerce and manufactures
are to any improvements that their unem-
barraffed fituation enables them to adopt.

Many

Many people read a little in the preface, before they buy the book; and I ſhall probably be accuſed of being in the intereſt of the Bookſeller, and of making an aſſertion merely to catch this ſort of readers, when I ſay that the Engliſh have more need of information on the real character and condition of the United States of America, than any other people of Europe; and eſpecially when I add, that this book is infinitely better calculated to convey that information, than any other, or than all others of the kind that have hitherto appeared.

I do not know how to convince an Engliſh reader of the firſt of theſe remarks; but the latter I am ſure he will find true on peruſing the work.

The fact is, we have always been ſurprizingly ignorant both of the Americans and of their country. Had we known either the one or the other while they were colonies, they would have been ſo at this day, and probably for many days longer; did we know them now, we ſhould endeavour

your to draw that advantage from them
that the natural and adventitious circumftances of the two countries would indi-
cate to reafonable men. There is no fpot
on the globe, out of England, fo interefting for us to ftudy under all its connections and relations, as the territory of the
United States. Could we barter all the
Canadas and Nova-Scotias, with all their
modifications and fubdivifions, for fuch an
amicable intercourfe as might have been
eftablifhed with that people fince the clofe
of the war, we fhould have every reafon
to rejoice in the change.

Minifters, as wicked as they are, do
more mifchief through ignorance, than
from any lefs pardonable caufe. And what
are the fources of information on this fubject, that are generally drawn from in this
kingdom? Thofe Americans, who beft know
their own country, do not write; they
have always been occupied in more important affairs. A few light fuperficial travellers, fome of whom never appear to have
quitted Europe, who have not knowledge
enough

enough even to begin to enquire after knowledge; a few minifterial governors of royal
provinces, whofe bufinefs it always was
to give falfe information: fuch are the men
whofe errors have been uniformly copied
by fucceeding writers, fyftematized by philofophers, and acted out by politicians.

Thefe Blunders affume different fhapes,
and come recommended to us under various
authorities. You fee them muftered and
embodied in a gazetteer or a geographical
grammar *, marching in the fplendid re-
tinue of all the fciences in the Encyclopedia; you find them by regiments preffed
into the fervice of De Paw, tortured into
difcipline and taught to move to the mufic
of Raynal, and then mounted among the
heavy armed cavalry of Robertfon.   Under

* Perhaps no work, that is not fyftematically falfe, contains more errors than the Geographical Grammar publifhed
under the name of William Guthrie ; I fpeak only of that
part which refpects the United States. To thofe who wifh
to be informed on this fubject, I would recommend *Morfe's
American Geography*, publifhed in America, and now reprinted
for Stockdale in London. It contains more information relative to that country, than all the books ever written in Europe.

                                        fuch

such able commanders, who could doubt of their doing execution? Indeed their operations have been too fatal to us. Our false ideas of the Americans have done us more injury, even since the war, than twenty Ruffian or Spanish armaments. But the evil still continues; and every day lessens the opportunity of profiting from their acquaintance.

We have refused, ever since the war, to compliment them with an envoy; we have employed, to take care of our consular interests, and represent the epitomized majesty of the British nation, an American Royalist, who could be recommended to us only for his stupidity, and to them only for his suspected perfidy to their cause.

The book that bears the name of Lord Sheffield on the American trade, has served as the touchstone, the stateman's confession of faith, relative to our political and commercial intercourse with that country. It is said to have been written by an American

can who had left his country in difgrace,
and therefore intended to write againft it.
And the book really has this appearance;
it has paffed for a long time in England as
a moft patriotick and ufeful performance;
it has taught us to defpife the Americans
in peace and commerce, as the works of
other men of this caft had before told us to do
in war and politics. The details in it, furnifhed by the clerks of the cuftom-houfe,
are doubtlefs accurate, though of little confequence; but the reafoning is uniformly
wrong, the predictions are all falfe, and the
conclufions which he draws, and which of
courfe were to ferve as advice to the government, are calculated to flatter our vanity,
to confirm us in our errors, and miflead
us in our conduct. Had the ableft fophift
in Europe been employed to write a book
profeffedly againft Great-Britain and in favour of America, he could not have fucceeded fo well. It perfuaded us to refufe
any kind of commercial treaty with them;
which forced them to learn a leffon, of
which they might otherwife have been
ignorant

ignorant for half a century, That after beating our armies they could rival our manufactories; that they could do without us much better than we could without them.

M. de Warville has taught his countrymen to think very differently of that people. I believe every reader of these travels, who underftands enough of America to enable him to judge, will agree with me in opinion, that his remarks are infinitely more judicious, more candid, and lefs erroneous than thofe of any other of the numerous obfervers that have vifited that country. Moft of them have been uniformly fuperficial, often fcurrilous, blending unmerited cenfure with fulfome praife, and huddling together, to form the whole piece, a parcel of unfinifhed images, that give no more a picture of that people, than of the Arabs or the Chinefe. Their only object, like that of a novel writer, is to make a book that will fell; and yet they preferve not even that confiftency with themfelves, which is indifpenfable in the wildeft romance.

M. de

M. de Warville is a fober, uniform, in-defatigable, and courageous defender of the rights of mankind; he has certainly done much in his own country in bringing forward the prefent Revolution. His great object in thefe travels, feems to have been, to obferve the effects of habitual liberty on man in fociety; and his remarks appear to be thofe of a well-informed reafoner, and an unprejudiced inquirer.

LONDON,
Feb. 1, 1792.

NEW

PREFACE

OF THE

AUTHOR.

THE publication of Voyages and Travels will doubtlefs appear, at firft view, an operation foreign to the prefent circumftances of France. I fhould even myfelf regret the time I have fpent in reducing this Work to order, if I did not think that it might be ufeful and neceffary in fupporting our Revolution. The object of thefe Travels was not to ftudy antiques, or to fearch for unknown plants, but to ftudy men who had juft acquired their liberty. A free people can no longer be ftrangers to the French.

We have now, likewife, acquired our liberty. It is no longer neceffary to learn of the Americans the manner of acquiring it,

but

but we muft be taught by them the fecret of
preferving it. This fecret confifts in the morals of the people; the Americans have it;
and I fee with grief, not only that we do not
yet poffefs it, but that we are not even thoroughly perfuaded of its abfolute neceffity in
the prefervation of liberty. This is an important point; it involves the falvation of
the revolution, and therefore merits a clofe
examination.

What is liberty? It is the moft perfect
ftate of fociety: it is the ftate in which man
depends but upon the laws which he makes;
in which, to make them good, he ought to
perfect the powers of his mind; in which, to
execute them well, he muft employ all his
reafon; for coercive meafures are difgraceful
to freemen—they are almoft ufelefs in a free
State; and when the magiftrate calls them to
his aid, liberty is on the decline, morals are
nothing more than reafon applied to all the
actions of life; in their force confifts the execution of the laws. Reafon or morals are to
the execution of the laws among a free people, what fetters, fcourges, and gibbets are
among flaves. Deftroy morals, or practical
reafon, and you muft fupply their place by
fetters

fetters and fcourges, or elfe fociety will no longer be but a ftate of war, a fcene of deplorable anarchy, to be terminated by its deftruction.

Without morals there can be no liberty. If you have not the former, you cannot love the latter, and you will foon take it away from others; for if you abandon yourfelf to luxury, to oftentation, to exceffive gaming, to enormous expences, you neceffarily open your heart to corruption; you make a traffic of your popularity, and of your talents; you fell the people to that defpotifm which is always endeavouring to replunge them into its chains.

Some men endeavour to diftinguifh public from private morals; it is a falfe and chimerical diftinction, invented by vice, in order to difguife its danger. Doubtlefs a man may poffefs the private virtues without the public; he may be a good father, without being an ardent friend of liberty; but he that has not the private virtues, can never poffefs the public; in this refpect they are infeparable; their bafis is the fame, it is *practical reafon.* What! within the walls of your houfe, you trample

trample reafon under foot; and do you refpect it abroad, in your intercourfe with your
fellow-citizens? He that refpects not reafon
in the lonely prefence of his houfehold gods,
can have no fincere attachment to it at all;
and his apparent veneration to the law is but
the effect of fear, or the grimace of hypocrify. Place him out of danger from the public force, his fears vanifh, and his vice appears. Befides, the hypocrify of public virtue entrains another evil; it fpreads a dangerous fnare to liberty over the abyfs of defpotifm.

What confidence can be placed in thofe
men who, regarding the revolution but as
their road to fortune, affume the appearance
of virtue but to deceive the people; who deceive the people but to pillage and enflave
them; who, in their artful difcourfes, where
eloquence is paid with gold, preach to others
the facrifice of private intereft, while they
themfelves facrifice all that is facred to their
own? men whofe private conduct is the
affaffin of virtue, an opprobrium to liberty,
and gives the lie to the doctrines which they
preach:

Qui Curius fimulant, et baccanalia vivunt.

Happy

Happy the people who defpife this hypocrify, who have the courage to degrade, to
chaftife, to excommunicate thefe double men,
poffeffing the tongue of Cato, and the foul
Tiberius. Happy the people who, well convinced that liberty is not fupported by eloquence, but by the exercife of virtue, efteem
not, but rather defpife, the former, when it is
feparated from the latter. Such a people, by
their fevere opinions, compel men of talents
to acquire morals; they exclude corruption
from their body, and lay the foundation for
liberty and long profperity.

But if this people, improvident and irrefo-
lute, dazzled by the eloquence of an orator
who flatters their paffions, pardon his vices
in favour of his talents; if they feel not an
indignation at feeing an Alcibiades training a
mantle of purple, lavifhing his fumptuous
repafts, lolling on the bofom of his miftrefs,
or ravifhing a wife from her tender hufband;
if the view of his enormous wealth, his exterior graces, the foft found of his fpeech,
and his traits of courage, could reconcile
them to his crimes; if they could render
him the homage which is due only to talents united with virtue; if they could lavifh

upon

upon him praifes, places, and honours; then it is that this people difcover the full meafure of their weaknefs, their irrefolution, and their own proper corruption; they become their own executioners; and the time is not diftant, when they will be ready to be fold, by their own Alcibiades, *to the great king, and to his fatraps.*

Is it an ideal picture which I here trace, or, is it not ours? I tremble at the refemblance! Great God! fhall we have atchieved a revolution the moft inconceivable, the moft unexpected, but for the fake of drawing from nihility a few intriguing, low, ambitious men, to whom nothing is facred, who have not even the mouth of gold to accompany their foul of clay? Infamous wretches! they endeavour to excufe their weaknefs, their venality, their eternal capitulations with defpotifm, by faying, Thefe people are too much corrupted to be trufted with complete liberty. They themfelves give them the example of corruption; they give them new fhackles, as if fhackles could enlighten and ameliorate men.

O Providence! to what deftiny referved thou

thou the people of France? They are good, but they are flexible; they are credulous, they are enthufiaftic, they are eafily deceived. How often, in their infatuation, have they applauded fecret traitors, who have advifed them to the moft perfidious meafures! Infatuation announces either a people whofe aged weaknefs indicates approaching diffolution, or an infant people, or a mechanical people, a people not yet ripe for liberty: for the man of liberty is by nature a man of reafon; he is rational in his applaufes, he is fparing in his admiration, if, indeed, he ever indulges this paffion; he never profanes thefe effufions, by lavifhing them on men who difhonour themfelves. A people degraded to this degree, are ready to carefs the gilded chains that may be offered them. Behold the people of England dragging in the dirt that parliament to whom they owed their liberty, and crowning with laurels the infamous head of Monk, who fold them to a new tyrant.

I have fcrutinized thofe men, by whom the people are fo eafily infatuated. How few patriots was I able to number among them! How few men, who fincerely love the people, who labour for their happinefs and amelioration,

lioration, without regard to their perſonal intereſt! Theſe true friends, theſe real brothers
of the people, are not to be formed in thoſe
infamous gambling houſes, where the repreſentatives ſport with the blood of their fellow
citizens; they are not found among thoſe
vile courtezans who, preſerving their diſpoſi-
tion, have only changed their maſk; they
are not found among thoſe patriots of a day,
who, while they are preaching the Rights of
Man, are gravely occupied with a giided
phaeton, or an embroidered veſt. The man
of this frivolous taſte has never deſcended
into thoſe profound meditations, which make
of humanity, and the exerciſe of reaſon, a
conſtant pleaſure and a daily duty. The ſimplicity of wants and of pleaſures, may be
taken as a ſure ſign of patriotiſm. He that
has few wants, has never that of ſelling himſelf; while the citizen, who has the rage of
oſtentation, the fury of gambling, and of ex-
penſive frivolities, is always to be ſold to the
higheſt bidder; and every thing around him
betrays his corruption!

Would you prove to me your patriotiſm?
Let me penetrate into the interior of your
houſe. What! I ſee your antichamber full
of

of infolent lackies, who regard me with difdain, becaufe I am like Curius, *incomptis ca-
pillis:* they addrefs you with the appellation
of *lordfhip*; they give you ftill thofe vain
titles which liberty treads under foot, and you
fuffer it, and you call yourfelf a patriot!—I
penetrate a little further: your cielings are
gilded; magnificent vafes adorn your chim-
ney pieces; I walk upon the richeft carpets;
the moft coftly wines, the moft exquifite
difhes, cover your table; a crowd of fervants
furround it; you treat them with haughtinefs:—No, you are not a patriot, the moft
confummate pride reigns in your heart, the
pride of birth, of riches, and of talents. With
this triple pride, a man never believes in the
doctrine of equality: you belie your confcience, when you proftitute the word patriot.

But whence comes this difplay of wealth?
you are not rich. Is it from the people?
they are ftill poor. Who will prove to me
that it is not the price of their blood? Who
will affure me that there is not this moment exifting, a fecret contract between you
and the court? Who will affure me that you
have not faid to the court, Truft to me the
power which remains to you, and I will

bring

bring back the people to your feet; I will attach them to your car; I will enchain the tongues and pens of thofe independent men who brave you. A people may fometimes be fubjugated without the aid of baftilles.

I do not know if fo many pictures as every day ftrike our eyes, will convince us of the extreme difficulty of connecting public incorruptibility with corruption of morals; but I am convinced, that if we wifh to preferve our conftitution, it will be eafy, it will be neceffary, to demonftrate this maxim: " Without private virtue, there can be no public " virtue, no public fpirit, no liberty."

But how can we create private virtue among a people who have juft rifen fuddenly from the dregs of fervitude, dregs which have been fettling for twelve centuries on their heads?

Numerous means offer themfelves to our hands; laws, inftruction, good examples, education, encouragement to a rural life, parceling of real property among heirs, refpect to the ufeful arts.

Is it not evident, for inftance, that private
morals

morals affociate naturally with a rural life; that, of confequence, manners would much improve, by inducing men to return from the city to the country, and by difcouraging them from migrating from the country to the city? The reafon why the Americans poffefs fuch pure morals is, becaufe nine-tenths of them live difperfed in the country. I do not fay that we fhould make laws direct to force people to quit the town, or to fix their limits; all prohibition, all reftraint, is unjuft, abfurd, and ineffectual. Do you wifh a perfon to do well? make it for his intereft to do it. Would you re-people the country? make it his intereft to keep his children at home. Wife laws and taxes well diftributed will produce this effect. Laws which tend to an equal diftribution of real property, to diffufe a certain degree of eafe among the people, will contribute much to the refurrection of private and public morals; for mifery can take no intereft in the public good, and want is often the limit of virtue.

Would you extend public fpirit through all France? Into all the departments, all the villages, favour the propagation of knowledge,

the

the low price of books and of newfpapers.
How rapidly would the revolution confoli-
date, if the government had the wifdom to
frank the public papers from the expence of
poftage! It has often been repeated, that
three or four millions of livres expended in
this way, would prevent a great number of
diforders which ignorance may countenance
or commit; and the reparation of which cofts
many more millions. The communication
of knowledge would accelerate a number of
ufeful undertakings, which greatly diffufe
public profperity.

I will ftill propofe another law, which
would infallibly extend public fpirit and
good morals; it is the fhort duration of public functioners in their office, and the impoffibility of re-electing them without an interval. By that the legiflative body would
fend out every two years, into the provinces,
three or four hundred patriots, who, during
their abode at Paris, would have arifen to
the horizon of the revolution, and obtained
inftruction, activity in bufinefs, and a public
fpirit. The commonwealth, better under-
ftood, would become thus fucceffively the
bufinefs of *all;* and it is thus that you would

repair

repair the defect with which reprefentative republics are reproached, that the common-wealth is the bufinefs of but few.

I cannot enlarge upon all the means; but it would be rendering a great fervice to the Revolution, to feek and point out thofe which may give us morals and public fpirit......

Yet I cannot leave this fubject without in-dulging one reflection, which appears to me important; Liberty, either political or indi-vidual, cannot exift a long time without per-fonal independence. There can be no inde-pendence without a property, a profeffion, a trade, or an honeft induftry, which may in-fure againft want and dependence.

I affure you that the Americans are and will be for a long time free; it is becaufe nine tenths of them live by agriculture; and when there fhall be five hundred millions of men in America, all may be proprietors.

We are not in that happy fituation in France: the productive lands in France amount to fifty millions of acres; this, equally divided, would be two acres to a perfon;

thefe

thefe two acres would not be fufficient for his
fubfiftence; the nature of things calls a great
number of the French to live in cities. Commerce, the mechanic arts, and divers kinds
of induftry, procure there fubfiftence to the
inhabitants; for we muft not count much at
prefent on the produce of public offices.
Salaries indemnify, but do not enrich; neither do they infure againft future want. A
man who fhould fpeculate upon falaries for a
living, would only be the flave of the people,
or of foreign powers: every man, therefore,
who wifhes fincerely to be free, ought to exercife fome art or trade. At this word, *trade*,
the patriots ftill fhiver; they begin to pay
fome refpect to commerce; but though they
pretend to cherifh equality, they do not feel
themfelves frankly the equals of a mechanic.
They have not yet abjured the prejudice
which regards the tradefman, as below the
banker or the merchant. This vulgar arifto-
cracy will be the moft difficult to deftroy *.
.....If

---

* It extends even to officers chofen by the people. With
what difdain they regard an artifan from head to foot!
With what feverity many of our national guards treat thofe
wretches who are arrefted by them! With what infolence
they execute their orders:—Obferve the greater part of the
public officers: They are as haughty in the exercife of their
functions,

.....If you wifh to honour the mechanic arts, give inftruction to thofe who exercife them: choofe among them the beft inftructed, and advance them in public employments; and difdain not to confer upon them diftinguifhed places in the affemblies.

I regret that the National Affembly has not yet given this falutary example; that they have not yet crowned the genius of agriculture, by calling to the prefident's chair the good cultivator, Gerard; that the merchants and other members of the Affembly, who exercife mechanic arts, have not enjoyed the fame honour. Why this exclufion? It is very well to infert in the Declaration of Rights, that all men are equal; but we muft practife this equality, engrave it in our hearts, confecrate it in all our actions, and it belongs to the National Affembly to give the great example. It would perhaps force the executive power to refpect it likewife. Has he ever been known to defcend into the clafs of profeffions, there to choofe his minifters, his agents, from men of fimplicity of manners, not rich, but well inftructed, and no courtezans?

functions, as they were grovelling in the Primary Affemblies. A true patriot is equal at all times; equally diftant from bafenefs at elections, and infolence in office.

Our

Our democrats of the court praife indeed,
with a borrowed enthufiafm, a Franklin or
an Adams; they fay, and even with a filly
aftonifhment, that the one was a printer, and
the other a fchoolmafter: But, do they go to
feek in the work-fhops, the men of information? No.——But what fignifies at prefent the
conduct of an adminiftration, whofe deteftable foundation renders them antipopular, and
confequently perverfe? they can never appear
virtuous, but by hypocrify. To endeavour
to convert them, is a folly; to oppofe to them
independent adverfaries, is wifdom: the fecret
of independence is in this maxim, *Have few
wants, and a fteady employment to fatisfy them.*

With thefe ideas man bends not his front
before man. The artizan glories in his trade
that fupports him: he envies not places of
honour; he knows he can attain them, if he
deferves them: he idolizes no man; he refpects himfelf too much to be an idolater:
he efteems not men becaufe they are in place,
but becaufe they deferve well from their country. The leaders of the revolution in Holland, in the fixteenth century, feated on the
grafs at a repaft of herrings and onions, received, with a ftern fimplicity, the deputies

of

of the haughty Spaniard. This is the portrait of men who feel their dignity, and know
the fuperiority of freemen over the flaves of
kings.

Quem neque pauperies, neque mors, neque vincula terrent.

When fhall we have this elevated idea of
ourfelves? When will all the citizens look
with difdain on thofe idols on whom they
formerly proftituted their adoration? Indeed,
when fhall we experience a general diffufion
of public fpirit?

I have no uneafinefs about the rifing generation: the pure fouls of our young men
breathe nothing but liberty; the contagious
breath of perfonal intereft has not yet infected
them. An education truly national, will create men furpaffing the Greeks and Romans;
but people advanced in life, accuftomed to
fervitude, familiarized with the idolatry of
the great—What will reclaim them? What
will ftrip them of the old man? Inftruction;
and the beft means of diffufing it, is to multiply popular clubs, where all thofe citizens
fo unjuftly denominated paffive, come to
gain information on the principles of the
Conftitution, and on the political occurrences
of every day. It is there that may be placed
under

under the eyes of the people, the great examples of virtue furnifhed by ancient and modern hiftory; it is there that detached parts
of the work, which I now publifh, may
ferve to fhew my fellow-citizens the means
of preferving their liberty.

O Frenchmen! who wifh for this valuable inftruction, ftudy the Americans of the
prefent day. Open this book : you will here
fee to what degree of profperity the bleffings
of freedom can elevate the induftry of man ;
how they dignify his nature, and difpofe
him to univerfal fraternity : you will here
learn by what means liberty is preferved ;
that the great fecret of its duration is in good
morals. It is a truth that the obfervation of
the prefent ftate of America demonftrates at
every ftep. Thus you will fee, in thefe Travels, the prodigious effects of liberty on morals, on induftry, and on the amelioration of
men. You will fee thofe ftern prefbyterians,
who, on the firft fettlement of their country,
infected with the gloomy fuperftitions of Europe, could erect gibbets for thofe who
thought differently from themfelves. You
will fee them admitting all fects to equal charity and brotherhood, rejecting thofe fuperftitions

ftitions which, to adore the Supreme Being, make martyrs of part of the human race. Thus you will fee all the Americans, in whofe minds the jealoufy of the mother country had diffeminated the moft abfurd prejudices againft foreign nations, abjure thofe prejudices, reject every idea of war, and open the way to an univerfal confederation of the human race. You will fee independent America contemplating no other limits but thofe of the univerfe, no other reftraint but the laws made by her reprefentatives. You will fee them attempting all forts of fpeculations; opening the fertile bofom of the foil, lately covered by forefts; tracing unknown feas; eftablifhing new communications, new markets; naturalizing, in their country, thofe precious manufactures which England had referved to herfelf; and, by this accumulation of the means of induftry, they change the balance that was formerly againft America, and turn it to their advantage. You will fee them faithful to their engagements, while their enemies are proclaiming their bankruptcy. You will fee them invigorating their minds, and cultivating their virtues; reforming their government, employing only the language of reafon to convince the

refractory;

refractory;   multiplying every-where moral inftitutions and patriotic eftablifhments; and, above all, never feparating the idea of public from private virtues.   Such is the confoling picture, which thefe Travels will offer to the friend of liberty.

The reverfe is not felf-confoling; if liberty is a fure guarantee of profperity; if, in per-fecting the talents of man, it gives him vir-tues, thefe virtues, in their turn, become the fureft fupport of liberty.   A people of uni-verfal good morals would have no need of government; the law would have no need of an executive power.   This is the reafon why liberty in America is fafely carried to fo high a degree that it borders on a ftate of nature, and why the government has fo little force.   This, by ignorant men, is called anarchy: enlightened men, who have exa-mined the effects on the fpot, difcern in it the excellence of the government; becaufe, not-withftanding its weaknefs, fociety is there in a flourifhing ftate. The profperity of a fociety is always in proportion to the extent of liberty; liberty is in the inverfe proportion to the extent of the governing power : the latter cannot in-creafe itfelf, but at the expence of the former.

Can

Can a people without government be happy? Yes; if you can fuppofe a whole people with good morals; and this is not a chimera. Will you fee an example? obferve the Quakers of America. Though numerous, though difperfed over the furface of Pennfylvania, they have paffed more than a century, without municipal government, without police, without coercive meafures, to adminifter the State, or to govern the hofpitals. And why? See the picture of their manners; you will there find the explanation of the phenomenon.

Coercive meafures and liberty never go together: a free people hates the former; but if thefe meafures are not employed, how will you execute the law? By the force of reafon and good morals;—take away thefe, and you muft borrow the arm of violence, or fall into anarchy. If, then, a people wifhes to banifh the difhonourable means of coercion, they muft exercife their reafon, which will fhew them the neceffity of a conftant refpect for the law.

The exercife of this faculty produces among the Americans, a great number of men defignated by the name of *principled men*. This

appellation

appellation indicates the character of a clafs
of men fo little known among us, that they
have not acquired a name. There will be
one formed, I have no doubt; but, in the
mean time, I fee none but vibrating, vacillat-
ing beings, who do good by enthufiafm,
and never by reflection. There can be no
durable revolution, but where reflection
marks the operation, and matures the ideas.
It is amongft thofe men of principle that you
find the true heroes of humanity, the How-
ards, Fothergills, Penns, Franklins, Wafh-
ingtons, Sidneys, and Ludlows.

Shew me a man of this kind, whofe wants
are circumfcribed, who admits no luxury,
who has no fecret paffion, no ambition, but
that of ferving his country—a man who, as
Montaigne fays, *aie des opinions fuperceleftes,
fans avoir des mœurs fouterreines;*—a man
whom reflection guides in every thing; this
is the man of the people.

In a word, my countrymen, would you be
always free, always independent in your elections, and in your opinions? Would you confine the executive power within narrow
limits, and diminifh the number of your
laws?

laws?—have morals!—*in peſſima republica plu-
rimæ leges.* Morals fupply perfectly, the neceſſity of laws; laws fupply but imperfectly,
and in a miferable manner, the place of morals. Would you augment your population,
that chief wealth of nations? Would you
augment the eafe of individuals, induſtry,
agriculture, and every thing that contributes
to general profperity?—*have morals!*

Such is the double effect of morals in the
United States, whofe form of government
ſtill frightens puſillanimous and fuperſtitious
men. The portraits offered to view, in thefe
Travels, will juſtify that republicaniſm which
knaves calumniate with defign, which ignorant men do not underſtand, but which they
will learn to know and refpect. How can
we better judge of a government than by its
effects? Reafoning * may deceive; experience is always right. If liberty produces
good morals, and diffufes information, why
do freemen continue to carp at that kind of
government, which, being founded on the

---

* If you would fee excellent reafoning on this fubject, read
the work juſt publiſhed by the celebrated Paine, intitled, *Rights
of Man*; efpecially the mifcellaneous chapter.

greateſt

greateſt degree of liberty, ſecures the greateſt degree of proſperity ?

I thought it very uſeful and very neceſſary to prove theſe principles from great exam-ples; and this is my reaſon for publiſhing theſe Travels. Examples are more power-ful than precepts. Morality, put in action, carries ſomething of the dramatic, and the French love the drama.

This, then, is my firſt object; it is national, it is univerſal: for, when it is demonſtrated that liberty creates morals, and morals, in their turn, extend and maintain liberty, it is evident, that, to reſtrain the progreſs of liber-ty, is an execrable project; ſince it is to re-ſtrain the happineſs, the proſperity, and the union of the human race.

A ſecond object which guides me in this publication, is likewiſe national. I wiſhed to deſcribe to my countrymen a people with whom we ought, on every account, to con-nect ourſelves in the moſt intimate manner. The moral relations which ought to connect the two nations, are unfolded in the two firſt

volumes;

volumes; the third comprifes particularly the commercial connections. This third volume was publifhed in 1787, by Mr. Claviere and me.

There is ftill wanting, to complete this work, a fourth volume, which ought to treat of the political connections, and of the pre-fent federal government of the United States. I have the materials, but I have not the time to reduce them to order. The comparative view of their conftitution with ours, requires a critical and profound examination. Expe-rience has already determined the qualities of one; the other is ftill in its infancy. Per-haps, indeed, it requires a time of more calm-nefs, lefs ignorance and prejudice in the pub-lic mind, to judge wifely of the American conftitution. We muft prepare the way for this maturity of judgment; and thefe Travels will accelerate it, in fetting forth with truth the advantages of the only government which merits any confidence.

If I had confulted what is called the Love of Glory, and the Spirit of Ancient Literature, I could have fpent feveral years in polifhing this Work; but I believed, that, though ne-cef.fary ceſſary at preſent, it might be too late, and, perhaps, uſeleſs, in a few years. We have arrived at the time when men of letters ought to ſtudy, above all things, to be uſeful; when they ought, for fear of loſing time, to precipitate the propagation of truths, which the people ought to know; when, of conſe-quence, we ought to occupy ourſelves more in things than in words; when the care of ſtyle, and the perfection of taſte, are but ſigns of a trifling vanity, and a literary ariſtocracy. Were Monteſquieu to riſe from the dead, he would ſurely bluſh at having laboured twenty years in making epigrams on laws : he would write for the people; for the revolution can-not be maintained but by the people, and by the people inſtructed : he would write, then, directly and ſimply from his own ſoul, and not torment his ideas to render them bril-liant.

When a man would travel uſefully, he ſhould ſtudy, firſt, *men*; ſecondly, *books*; and, thirdly, *places*. To ſtudy men, he ſhould ſee them of all claſſes, of all parties, of all ages, and in all ſituations.

I read in the Gazettes, that the ambaſſa-dors

dors of Tippo Sultan were feafted by every
body; they were carried to the balls, to the
fpectacles, to the manufactures, to the arfe-
nals, to the palaces, to the camps. After
being thus feafted for fix months, I wonder
if, on returning home, they conceived that
they knew France. If fuch was their opinion,
they were in an error; for they faw only the
the brilliant part, the furface; and it ɩnot
by the furface that one can judge of the force
of a nation. The ambaffador fhould defcend
from his dignity, travel in a common carriage without his attendants, go into the
ftables to fee the horfes, into the barns to
fee the grain and other productions of the
country. It is thus that Mr. Jefferfon travelled in France and Italy; he had but one
fervant with him; he faw every thing with
his own eyes. I believe that few voyages
have been made with fo much judgment
and utility, as thofe of that philofopher. But
his modefty conceals his obfervations from
the public eye.

People difguife every thing, to deceive men
in place. A prince goes to an hofpital; he
taftes the foup and the meat. Does any one
fuppofe that the fuperintendant was fool
enough

enough not to have given orders to the cook
that day ?

True obfervation is that of every day. A
traveller, before fetting out, ought to know
from books and men the country he goes to
vifit.

He will have fome *data;* he will confront
what he fees, with what he has heard.

He ought to have a plan of obfervation ;
if he wifhes that nothing fhould efcape him,
he fhould accuftom himfelf to feize objects
rapidly, and to write, every night, what he
has feen in the day.

The choice of perfons to confult, and to
rely upon, is difficult.

The inhabitants of a country have generally a predilection in favour of it, and
ftrangers have prejudices againft it. In America I found this prejudice in almoft every
ftranger. The American revolution con-
founds them. They cannot familiarize the
idea of a *king-people* and an *elective chief,*
who fhakes hands with a labourer, who has
no

no guards at his gate, who walks on foot, &c. The foreign confuls are thofe who de-cry, with the moft virulence, the American conftitution; and, I fay it with grief, I faw much of this virulence among fome of ours. According to them, the United States, when I landed in America, were juft falling to ruin. They had no government left, the conftitution was deteftable; there was no confidence to be placed in the Americans, the public debt would never be paid; and there was no faith, no juftice among them.

Being a friend of liberty, thefe calumnies againft the American government were re-volting to me: I combated them with rea-foning. My adverfaries, who objedted to me then their long abode there, and the fhort-nefs of mine, ought to be convinced by this time that the telefcope of reafon is rather better than the microfcope of office. They have, in general, fome abilities and fome information; but they have generally been educated in the inferior places in the French adminiftration, and they have well imbibed its prejudices. A republic is a monftrous thing in their fight; a minifter is an idol that they adore; the people, in their view,

is

is a herd that muft be governed with rigour. A man who lives upon the rapines
of defpotifm, is always a bad judge of a free
country ; they feel that they fhould be nothing in fuch a ftate; and a man does not
like to fall into nothing *.

I met in our French travellers, the fame
prejudices as in the confuls. The greater
part of Frenchmen who travel or emigrate,
have little information, and are not prepared
to the art of obfervation. Prefumptuous to
excefs, and admirers of their own cuftoms
and manners, they ridicule thofe of other
nations. Ridicule gives them a double pleafure ; it feeds their own pride, and humbles
others. At Philadelphia, for inftance, the
men are grave, the women ferious, no fini-
cal airs, no libertine wives, no coffee-houfes,

* Judge, by the following inftance, with what infolence the
agents of defpotifm treat the chiefs of refpe&able republics.—
I heard M. de Mouftier boafting, that he told the prefident of
congrefs, at his own houfe, that he was but a *tavern-keeper* ;
and the Americans had the complaifance not to demand his
recall ! What horror muft this man have for our revolution !
He declared himfelf the enemy of it when he was in America, and exprefled himfelf with violence againft its leaders.
Thefe fa&s are public ; I denounced them to M. Montmorin,
who neverthelefs, to recompenfe him for his anti-revolution
manœuvres, has fent him ambaffador to Berlin.

no agreeable walks. My Frenchman finds every thing deteſtable at Philadelphia; be-cauſe he could not ſtrut upon a bonlevard, babble in a coffee-houſe, nor ſeduce a pretty woman by his important airs and his fine curls. He was almoſt offended that they did not admire him; that they did not ſpeak French.

He was greatly troubled that he could ſpeak American with the ſame facility; he loſt ſo much in not being able to ſhow his wit.

If, then, a perſon of this caſt attempts to deſcribe the Americans, he ſhows his own character, but not theirs. A people grave, ſerious, and reflecting, cannot be judged of and appreciated, but by a perſon of a like character.

It is to be hoped that the revolution will change the character of the French. If they ameliorate their morals, and augment their information, they will go far; for it is the property of reaſon and enlightened liberty to perfect themſelves without ceaſing, to ſub-ſtitute truth to error, and principle to preju-dice. They will then inſenſibly lay aſide their political prejudices, which tarniſh ſtill

the

the glorious conftitution which they have founded. They will imitate the Americans as far as local and phyfical circumftances will permit;—they will imitate them, and they will be the happier for it; for general happinefs does not confift with abfurdities and contradictions; it cannot arife from the complication, nor from the fhock of powers. There is but one real power in government, and it is in referring it back to its fource as often as poffible, that it is to be rendered beneficent; it becomes dangerous in proportion as it is diftant from its fource: in one word, *the lefs active and powerful the government, the more active, powerful, and happy is the fociety.* This is the phenomenon demonftrated in the prefent Hiftory of the United States.

Thefe Travels give the proof of the fecond part of this political axiom; they prove the activity, the power, the happinefs of the Americans; that they are deftined to be the firft people on earth, without being the terror of others.

To what great chain are attached thefe glorious deftinies? To three principles: 1. All
power

power is elective in America. 2. The legiflative is frequently changed. 3. The executive has, moreover, but little force *.

It

---

* This laft point merits fome attention, in the prefent circumftances of France. The prefident of the United States is
elected like all other prefidents and governors of States. A
man cannot conceive, in that country, *that wifdom and capacity
are hereditary*. The Americans, (who fhake their heads at this
European folly), from fixteen years experience, have found
none of thofe troubles, at the time of electing a prefident, as
were apprehended by ignorant people in Europe. The fame
tranquillity reigns in this election, as in that of the fimple reprefentatives. Men who cannot anfwer to arguments, raife
phantoms, in order to have fomething to combat ; they attend
not to the effects of the progrefs of reafon, and the *inflinct of
analogy* which the people poffefs. The moment they are accuftomed to the election of the reprefentative body, all other
elections are eafy to them. It is the fame reafon among men
inftructed, and the fame inftinct of analogy among thofe not
inftructed, which infpires an eternal diftruft of the executive
power, in countries where the chiefs are hereditary, and not
elective. The moment that we decreed the monarchy hereditary, we decreed an eternal diftruft in the people, of the executive power. It would be, indeed, againft nature, that they
fhould have confidence in individuals, who pretend to a fuper-
natural fuperiority, and who really have one in fact, being independent of the people. There cannot exift an open confidence, but in governments where the executive power is
elective, becaufe the governing is dependent on the governed.

Now, as confidence is impoffible under an hereditary monarchy, as it refults neceffarily from a government elective in
all its members, we may explain,—whence the eternal quarrels between the people and the government, in the firft cafe,
—whence

It will be eafy for me one day to deduce from thefe three principles, all the happy effects which I have obferved in America. At prefent I content myfelf with defcribing their effects, becaufe I wifh to leave to my Readers the pleafure of recurring to the caufes, and then of defcending from thofe caufes, and making the application to France. I have not even told all the facts; I had fo little time both to detail the facts, and draw the confequences. I am aftonifhed to have been able to finifh a work fo voluminous, in the midft of fo many various occupations which

—whence the frequent recurrence to force,—whence treafons and minifterial delinquencies go unpunifhed,—whence liberty is violated,—and whence nations, thus governed, enjoy but a fictitious and partial profperity, often ftained with blood; while, in the other cafe, where the people, by elections, hold in check the members of the government, there exifts an unity of interefts, which produces a profperity, real, general, and pacific.

The prefident of the United States can make no treaty, fend no ambaffador, nominate to no place, without the advice of the fenate. This fenate is elective; the prefident is refponfible; he may be accufed, profecuted, fufpended, condemned; the public good fuffers nothing from this refponfibility; the places of prefident and minifters are not vacant on that account; but they are filled by men of acknowledged merit; for the people, who elect, do not, like chance, take fools for governors; nor do they, like kings, make minifters of knaves and petty tyrants.

continually

continually furround me ; charged *alone* with compiling and publifhing a daily paper, undertaken with the fole defire of eftablifhing, in the public opinion, this powerful inftrument of revolutions; a paper in which the defence of good principles, the watching over a thoufand enemies, and repulfing perpetual attacks, occupy my attention without ceafing. Much of my time is likewife taken up by my political and civil funĉtions; by many particular pamphlets ; by the neceffity of affifting at clubs, where truths are prepared for the public eye; by the duty which I have prefcribed to myfelf, to defend the men of colour and the blacks.

I mention thefe faĉts to my Readers, to prove to them that I have ftill fome right to their indulgence. I merit it, likewife, for the motive which direĉts me. *Confilium futuri ex præterito venit :* Great profpeĉts are opening before us. Let us haften, then, to make known, that people whofe happy experience ought to be our guide.

Paris, April 21. 1791.

NEW TRAVELS

IN THE

UNITED STATES OF AMERICA.

LETTER I.

From M. CLAVIERE to M. BRISSOT DE WARVILLE.

PLAN OF OBSERVATIONS

On the Political, Civil, and Military State of the Free Americans; their Legiflation, &c.

May 18, 1788.

THE voyage that you are going to undertake, my dear friend, will doubtlefs form the moft interefting period of your contemplative life. You are going to tranfport yourfelf into a part of the globe, where a perfon may, with the leaft obftruction, bring into view the moft ftriking and interefting fcenes that belong to humanity. It is with a little

courage,

courage, much patience, a continual diffidence of his own habits of mind and manners, a total oblivion of his moſt cheriſhed
opinions, and of himſelf, and with a determination to be cautious and flow in judging,
that he may conclude, what is the ſituation
where man, the child of the earth, may aſſemble the greateſt ſum, and the longeſt duration of public and private happineſs.

In a few years, and without great dangers,
you may contemplate the moſt varied ſcenes;
you may paſs in America, from a ſoil the
beſt cultivated, and grown old with an active
population, into the deſerts, where the hand
of man has modified nothing, where time,
vegetation, and the dead maſs of matter, ſeem
to have furniſhed the expence of the theatre.

Between theſe extremes, you will find in-
termediate ſtages of improvement; and it is,
doubtleſs, in contemplating theſe, that reaſon
and ſenſibility will find the happieſt ſituation
in life.

The preſent ſtate of independent America,
will, perhaps, give us a glance at the higheſt
perfection of human life that we are permitted to hope for; but who, in judging of
it,

it, can feparate himfelf from his age, from
his temperament, from his education, from
the impreffion of certain circumftances? Who
can filence his imagination, and govern the
fenfations which excite it? I hope, my friend,
that you may have this power; and you
ought to negled nothing to acquire it, if you
wifh to anfwer the end of your travels. You
wifh to enlighten mankind, to fmoothe
the way to their happinefs; for this reafon,
you ought to be more on your guard than
any one, not to deceive yourfelf by appearances.

When, therefore, you fhall form your opinion on the fpot of thofe celebrated American conftitutions, do not exaggerate too much
either the vices of Europe, to which you
compare them, or the virtues of America,
which you bring into the contraft. Make it
a principal objed to determine whether it
may not be faid, *in reality things are here as
they are with us; the difference is fo fmall,
that it is not worth the change.* This is a
proper method to guard againft error. It is
well, at the fame time, to form a juft idea of
the difficulty of change; this fhould be always prefent to the mind. Voltaire fays,

La patrie eft aux lieux où l'ame eft enchaînée.

You

You wifh to contemplate the effects of liberty on the progrefs of men, of fociety, and
of government.   May you, in this examination, never lofe fight of impartiality and cool
circumfpection, that your friends may not be
expofed either to incredulity, or to decep-
tion.

I do not imagine that you can find in
America, new motives to engage every reafonable European to the love of liberty.
What they will moft thank you for is, to
defcribe to us what America in fact is, and
what, in opinion, fhe may be, in a given
time, making a reafonable allowance for thofe
accidents which trouble the repofe of life.

Men always difpute ; they are every where
formed of the fame materials, and fubject to
the fame paffions ; but the matters on which
they difpute, are, in a given country, more
or lefs fitted to difturb the general harmony
and individual happinefs.   Thus a ftate of
univerfal toleration renders harmlefs the di-
verfity of opinion in religious matters.

In proportion as political inftitutions fubmit the ruling power to well-defined forms,
at the fame time that they have the public
opinion

opinion in their favour, political diffentions are lefs dangerous. This, my friend, is the point of view under which the political ftate of America ought to be known to us. Let us know, above all, what we have to expect, for the prefent and future, from that variety which diftinguifhes fo confiderably fome ftates from others, and whether fome great inconvenience will not refult from it; whether the federal tranquillity will ever be fhaken by it; whether this variety will corrupt the juftice of fome ftates towards others in their ordinary commerce, and in thofe cafes where the confederation is the judge; whether fome ftates will not give themfelves commotions and agitations, for the fake of forming their governments, fimilar, or diffimilar, to that of fome others; whether ftate jealoufies do not already exift, occafioned by thefe varieties. Such jealoufies greatly injure the Swifs cantons; they have ruined Holland, and will prevent its reftoration. If thefe jealoufies are unknown to the Americans, and will never arife there, explain to us this phenomenon, why it exifts, and why it will continue; for you know, that from what you may obferve to us on this fingle point, your friends may be induced either to ftay where
they

they are, or to give the preference to one
ſtate in the union over another.

There is one advantage in America which
Europe does not offer; a man may ſettle himſelf in the deſert, and be ſafe from political
commotions. But is there no danger in this?
Endeavour to explain to us the ſtate of the
ſavages on that great continent, the moſt
certain account of their numbers, their manners, the cauſes, more or leſs, inevitable, of
wars with them. This part of your accounts
will not be the leaſt intereſting. Forget not
to give us, as far as you have opportunity,
all that can be known relative to the ancient
ſtate of America.

Obſerve what are the remains of the military ſpirit among the Americans; what are
their prejudices in this reſpect; are there
men among them who wiſh to ſee themſelves at the head of armies? Do they enliſt
any ſoldiers? Can you perceive any germe,
which, united to the ſpirit of idleneſs, would
make the profeſſion of a ſoldier preferable to
that of a cultivator, or an artizan? for it is
this wretched ſituation of things in other
countries, which furniſhes the means of great
armies.

armies. Inform us about thofe *cincinnati*, a body truly diftreffing to the political philofopher.

Solomon fays, there is nothing new under the fun. This may be true; but are we yet acquainted with all political revolutions, in order to make the circle complete? Hiftory furnifhes the picture of no revolution like that of the United States, nor any arrangements fimilar to theirs. Thus you may look into futurity, and fee what perfeverances or changes may contradict the philofophy of hiftory.

You ought, likewife, to forefee whether foreign wars are to be expected; whether the Europeans are right in faying, that the United States will one day wifh to be conquerors. I do not believe it; I believe rather that their revolution will be contagious, efpecially if their federal fyftem fhall maintain union and peace in all parts of the confederation. This is the mafter-point of the revolution; it ought to engage the whole force of your meditations.

Tell

Tell us, finally, if the rage of law-making
has paffed the feas with the colonifts of the
United States. You will doubtlefs find there,
many minds ftruck with the diforders refulting from war and independence; others, who
preferve a lively image of the great liberty
which each individual ought to enjoy; the
firft will be frightened at the leaft difturb-
ance, and wifh to fee a law or a ftatute applied to every trivial thing; the others think
that laws can never be too few. What is
the prevailing opinion there on this fubject?
When we confider what charms and what
utility muft be found in the private occupations of men in that country, we fhould think
that the commonwealth would remain a long
time without intermingling with them. But
we are affured that lawyers abound there,
and enjoy a dangerous influence; that the
civil legiflation is there, as in England, an
abundant fource of law-fuits and of diftrefs.
Enlighten us on this fubject. We have often
obferved, that civil legiflation has corrupted
the beft political inftitutions; it is often a
crime againft fociety.

Internal police, every where in Europe, is
founded

founded on the opinion, that man is de-
praved, turbulent, and wicked ; and the timi-
dity that wealth infpires, difpofes the rich to
regard the poor as capable only of being reftrained by fetters. Is this European truth
a truth in America ?

LETTER

LETTER II.

On the Soil, Productions, Cultivation, &c.

May 20, 1788.

AFTER having inftructed us on all political fubjects, and principally thofe on
which depend internal and external peace,
and the fecurity of individuals, you will have
to contemplate the foil of America as relative
to human induftry, which, in its turn, influences prodigioufly the different modes of
living.

It feems, in this refpect, that all the great
divifions of the earth fhould refemble each
other. It is poffible, however, that America
offers, in the fame fpace, more aliments to
induftry, more *data*, than can be found in
Europe. Fix our ideas upon thofe invitations that nature has traced on the foil of
America, in addreffing herfelf to the human
underftanding. To particularize minutely
what the maps only give us in grofs, will be
more worthy of your attention, than the details

tails which intereft the painter, the poet, or
the lover of an Englifh garden.

We have undertaken to advife the Americans to be cultivators, and to leave to the Europeans thofe manufactures which agree not
with a country life. You will be curious to
difcover their difpofition in this refpect. It
ought to depend much on the facility of
communication; and if, as it appears, independent America, in a little time, and with
fmall expence, may be interfected by canals
in all directions; if this advantage is fo generally felt, that they will apply themfelves to
it at an early period, there is no doubt but
in America human activity will be occupied
principally in the production of fubfiftence,
and of raw materials.

It is the opinion in Europe, that confumption caufes production, and that the failure
of confumption difcourages labour; for this
reafon they require cities and manufactures.
But there is, in all thefe opinions, a great
confufion of ideas, which the fpectacle of nations, rifing under the protection of liberty,
will aid you in clearing up. You will fee,
perhaps, with evidence, that a man ceafes to
fear the fuperfluity of fubfiftences, when he

is

is no longer under the neceſſity of exchanging them for money, to pay his taxes and his
rents. Should this be his fear, and he has
near him the means of a cheap tranſport, if
he may himſelf load his boat and carry his
proviſions to market, and make his traffic
without quitting his boat, man is too fond of
activity to ſuffer ſuperfluity to impede his induſtry. Thus, to engage him to open the
boſom of the earth, there is no need that he
ſhould be aſſured beforehand what he ſhall
do with his grain. Expences are the im-
pediments of induſtry ; and you will ſee,
without doubt, in America, a new order of
things, where theſe expences are not embar-
raſſing ; the theory of conſumption, and production, is doubtleſs very different from what
is ſuppoſed in Europe. Endeavour, my
friend, to call to mind, that in this we have
need of more details, compariſons, calculations, facts, and proofs, than travellers generally bring together; and that this part of
political œconomy is ſtill entirely new, on
account of the embarraſſments, abſtractions,
difficulties, and diſguſts which attend them
in Europe.

It is on the accounts that you will give us
in this reſpect, that the opinions of your
friends

friends will be formed. So many misadventures and misinformations have hitherto accompanied emigrants, though virtuous, and otherwise well-informed, that people are intimidated from the attempt, though ill-situated in Europe. You know what the Genevians have suffered, rather than to go to Ireland.

Thus, my friend, if you wish to instruct those who would fly from the tyranny of Europe, and who would find a situation of honest industry for their children, study the history of emigrants. Study the causes of the disasters of travellers; judge of their illusions; go to the places of debarkation, and learn the precautions necessary to be taken to render easy and agreeable their first arrival.

Begin with such as you know to be in easy circumstances, and descending, by degrees, to the honest individual, who, full of health and vigour, his coat on his back, and his staff in his hand, carries with him all he possesses; inform each one what he ought to expect, if, after conquering all his aversions, and taking all his precautions, he determines to quit Europe, to go to the land of liberty.

Finally,

Finally, my friend, in all that concerns private life, as in political relations, in the means of acquiring fortune ; as in the honeſt ambition of ſerving the public, let your obſervations atteſt that you have neglected no means of comparing the enjoyments of Europe, with what may be expected among the free Americans.

LETTER

LETTER III.

Plan of a Colony to be eſtabliſhed in America.

May 21, 1788.

WHEN we contemplate the American Revolution, the circumſtances which have oppoſed its perfection, the knowledge we are able to collect for the inſtitution of republics on a more perfect plan, the lands deſtined by Congreſs for new States, and the multitude of happy circumſtances which may facilitate their preparatives, and protect their infancy, we are hurried inſenſibly into projects chimerical at the firſt ſight, which become attracting by reflection, and which we abandon, but with regret, on account of the difficulty of finding a ſufficient number of perſons for their execution.

When a tract of land is offered for ſale, and its limits aſcertained, why cannot it be prepared, in all circumſtances, for a republic, in the ſame manner as you prepare a houſe for your friends?

Penn

Penn had already feen the neceffity of re-
gulating beforehand, the conduct of a colony
on the foil which they were going to inhabit.
We have at prefent many more advantages
than he had, to ordain and execute the fame
thing with more fuccefs ; and, inftead of favages, who gave him trouble, we fhould at
prefent be fuftained and protected by the
States, with which we fhould be connected.

I have no doubt, that, having acquired the
foil, we might eftablifh a republic, better calculated for peace and happinefs, than any
now exifting, or that ever did exift. Hitherto
they have formed from chance and involuntary combinations ; it has been neceffary in
them all, that national innovations fhould be
reconciled with abfurdities, knowledge with
ignorance, good fenfe with prejudices, and
wife inftitutions with barbarifms. Hence
that chaos, that eternal fource of diftreffes,
difputes, and diforders.

If men of wifdom and information fhould
organize the plan of a fociety before it exifted,
and extend their forefight to every circumftance of preparing proper inftitutions for the
forming of the morals public and private,
and the encouragement of induftry, ought
they

they to be condemned as having formed an Eutopia? I do not believe it; it is my opinion, even that the love of gain, the love of novelty, and the spirit of philosophy, would lend a hand to an enterprise, which, before the American Revolution, might have been judged impracticable.

Profit, therefore, of your travels in America, to inform yourself, if, among the lands to be sold by Congress, there exists not a situation of easy access, where the nature of the soil is favourable to industry, and its other circumstances inviting to the first settlers. It should be furnished with easy communications by land and water.

For this purpose, there should be a topographical map and description, sufficiently minute and extended, to enable us to trace upon it the smaller divisions. There ought to be found levels, relative to a certain point, in order to know beforehand the possibility of canals. All other objects of consequence ought to be noted at the same time: such as the nature of the soil in every part, the kinds of timber, the quarries of stone, &c. This will doubtless be an expensive operation; but any expences may be undertaken by great associations, affociations, and here are motives fufficient to encourage and reward a very expenfive one.

It will be neceffary to know, on what conditions the Congrefs would treat for the ceffion of fuch a tract, and whether they would agree to take the principal part of the payment, only as faft as the fettlers fhould come to take poffeffion of their lands.

It would be defirable that the territory chofen fhould be fuch that, at the place of the firft fettlement, it would be eafy to eftablifh conveniences for the reception of the fettlers, to provide them fuch neceffaries as will pre-ferve them from thofe embarraffments and calamities which fometimes throw infant fet-tlements into trouble, mifery, and defpair.

After having acquired an exact idea of what may be expected from the nature of the foil, and its connection with neighbouring places, we might then undertake the work of forming a political and civil legiflation, fuited to the new republic, and its local circumftan-ces. Such fhould be the tafk to be accom-plifhed before the people departed from hence; that every fettler might know before-hand what laws he is to live under, fo that

he

he will confent to them beforehand by choice.

The previous regulations ought to be carried fo far, that every perfon fhould forefee where he was going, and what he was to do in order to fulfil his engagements; whether he was a purchafer of lands, or had inrolled himfelf as a labourer.

The lands fhould not be fold out to individuals by chance, and according to the caprice of each purchafer; but a plan fhould be purfued in the population, that the people might aid each other in their labours, and be a mutual folace and protection by their neighbourhood.

The public expences, thofe of religion and education, fhould be furnifhed by the produce of a portion of land referved in each diftrict for that purpofe. Thefe lands could be the public domain; they ought to be put in cultivation the firft. There ought perhaps to be a regulation for a regular fupply of workmen on the public lands, roads, and other public works. By this we fhould always have employment for new comers, and might receive all men capable of labour, provided

vided their manners and character were such
as to entitle them to be members of the new
republic.

These details will be sufficient to recall to
your mind, our frequent conversations on a
plan of this kind. If you can acquire from
Congress the certainty of being able to realize
it, so far as it depends on them, and we have
only to find the company here to undertake
it; I believe it may be easily done in Europe.

The company will have lands to sell;
their price will augment in proportion as they
come in vogue; the company will endeavour
to render it an object of general attention, by
the preparations made for the reception of the
first settlers, in order to avoid the difficulties
incident to the beginning of an establishment.
I doubt not, therefore, that this project will
offer a sufficient prospect of gain, to engage
people to adventure in it many millions of
livres.

The better to determine them to it, the
interest should be divided into small shares,
and proper measures taken to assure the hold-
ers of shares of an administration worthy of
confidence, to prevent the abuses of trust,
and

and watch over the execution of their refolves, both refpecting their intereft, and that of the fettlers.

A profpectus, fufficiently detailed, fhould inform the public of the nature of the enterprife, the principal object of which fhould be to realize a republic, founded on the leffons of experience and good fenfe, on the principles of fraternity and equality, which ought to unite mankind.

The principal means of its execution will be, to have purchafed the lands fo as to be able to refell them at a price fufficiently low, to encourage their cultivation, and at the fame time with fufficient profit to the company. For it is natural to obferve, that the difference between the original value of lands in their wild ftate, and their value when an active fettlement is begun upon them, will affure to the firft purchafers a prodigious profit from their firft advances.

This, however, fuppofes, as I have already mentioned, that, receiving a fmall proportion of the purchafe-money when the purchafe is made, the Congrefs will confent to receive the principal payments only in proportion as
the

the lands may be re-fold to individuals; without this condition, the enterprife would require fuch great advances as to difcourage the undertaking.

Thus, the funds of the company fhould be compofed, 1. of the firft payments to be made to Congrefs; 2. the expences neceffary in acquiring a topographical knowledge of the territory, and in making its divifions; 3. the funds neceffary for public works, and the eftablifhment for the reception of thofe who arrive, to enfure them againft want and difcouragement.

Thefe three objects will doubtlefs require a confiderable fund; but the rifing value of the lands to be fold, and to be paid for only as faft as they are fold, will greatly indemnify the undertakers. Thefe are the folid arguments to be offered to the lovers of gain. Many other confiderations might be detailed in the profpectus, to determine philofophers and friends of humanity to become fharers.

This is enough, my friend, to recall to your mind more ideas than I can give you on the fubject. Study it; and if at the firft view it looks romantic, find the means of
faving

faving it from that objection ; converfe upon
it with intelligent perfons; find fuch as are
fufficiently attached to great objects, to be
willing to concur in them with zeal, when
they are defigned for the aid and confolation
of humanity.

Age will prevent me from undertaking in
this great work. It feems to me, that there
is nothing like it in times paft, that it would
be greatly ufeful to the future, and would
mark the American revolution with one of
the happieft effects which it can produce. Is
not this enough to animate the generous ambition of thofe who have youth, health, and
courage, fo as not to be frightened at difficulties, or difheartened by delays ?

LETTER

LETTER IV.

May 21, 1788.

THE Utopia will be but a dream; and you will find, without doubt, the new American fettlements invincibly deftined to a fcattering herd of people, who will form infenfibly, by the addition of new families and individuals; without following any plan, without providing fuch laws as would be fuitable to them, when their herds fhall become fufficiently numerous to be reprefented as a republic in the federal union. It is thus that all political fyftems feem condemned to refemble what has already taken place in fuch and fuch a ftate, according as the multitude, or fome bold leader, fhall decide.

We muft, then, abandon this project; and then, where will you place thofe friends whom we wifh to eftablifh in America? You will inform yourfelf, for them, of the progrefs of population and civilization in Kentucky, of which they tell fo many wonders. But reflect on two things: firft, That our fettlement will be very uncertain, if we muft go ourfelves to

prepare

prepare it, build houſes, &c. Some perſons
muſt, therefore, go before the others; and
when ſhall. they rejoin? How many accidents may intervene! When the emigrant
ſociety ſhall be formed in Europe, the members ought all to go at once; but in that caſe
they ſhould make choice of a certain tract in
the neighbourhood of a town, where the people could be lodged, till they could build their
houſes. This precaution ſeems to exclude
Kentucky; for no good town is ſufficiently
near it. You will ſee, then, my friend, how
it will be poſſible to reconcile every thing, and
find a poſition where the pain and vexation
will not ſurpaſs the ſatisfaction. Your taſk
is not a trifling one in making this examination; for you muſt not forget, that, to ſatisfy
the perſons whom we wiſh not to leave behind, we muſt have a ſituation where we can
unite the advantages of commerce with thoſe
of agriculture; we muſt be near a navigable
river, communicating with the ſea; we muſt
have a town, where we can find ſailors, veſſels, &c.: in a word, thoſe among us who
ſhall have been accuſtomed to the affairs of
commerce and of manufactures, muſt not be
placed in a poſition which ſhall force them
abſolutely to renounce their habits, and ex-
poſe themſelves to regrets; for you know
that

that one is never weary in walking, as long
as a horfe or a carriage marches by his fide,
which he may ufe whenever he pleafes.

It is a pity that Pittfburg is not more
populous, or that Virginia is feparated by
deferts from the new ftates.

It is ufelefs to enter into more particular
details on this matter; you know us : I fhall
only recommend to you an attention to the
climate. A fine fky, temperature of Paris,
no mufketoes, agreeable fituation, and good
foil, are things indifpenfable.

The numerous obfervations which you
propofe to collect for the inftruction of the
public, will inform us of many other things,
which I fhould mention here, if they did not
enter into your general plan. In obferving
cuftoms and taftes, forget not the article of
mufic, confidered in its effects on the powers
of the mind. The tafte for mufic is general
in Europe; we make of it one of the principal objects of education. Is it fo in America?

Finally, As we are not needy adventurers,
think what anfwers you muft give, when our
wives, our children, and even ourfelves, fhall
afk

aſk you what is to be done on our arrival in conſiderable numbers in any town in America; for, as we cannot ſend forward a meſſenger, we ought to provide for our debarkation in an unknown country.

LETTER

LETTER V.

May 22, 1788.

AFTER having given you my thoughts on general fubjects, it is unneceffary to be more particular on thofe which promife a more certain and palpable advantage to your travels. I mean the purchafe of lands or public funds, according as circumftances may invite.

Three claffes of perfons may wifh to purchafe lands in the United States: thofe who mean to employ others to cultivate them, thofe who will cultivate for themfelves, and thofe who wifh to place their money in them, with the profpect that thefe lands will increafe in value, in proportion to the population.

Let us leave the two firft claffes to make their own choice. Your general obfervations, to be publifhed on your return, will inftruct fuch as wifh to remove to America, how to go and choofe for themfelves.

The

The cafe of the fimple fpeculators is different. Some wifh to purchafe, to fell again to a profit as foon as poffible; others extend their views farther, and, calculating the viciffitudes of Europe, find it very prudent to place a dead fund in lands, which, by the effect of neighbouring population, will acquire a great value in the courfe of years.

Many heads of families, provident for their defcendants, place dead funds in a bank, to accumulate, in favour of their children. A greater number would do the fame thing, if there were a fatisfactory folution of all queftions in the Chapter of Accidents. Now, nothing appears to me better to anfwer this wife precaution, than to place fuch money on the cultivated foil of the United States.

The information that you will be able to give on this fubject, will be very ufeful. There are lands which, from their pofition, muft remain uncleared for a longer or fhorter period; others rendered valuable by the neighbourhood of rivers and other important communications; others on account of their timber, &c. &c.

But, can lands be purchafed with full furety?

ty? Are there any fure methods eftablifhed, to recognife territorial property, that may reft for fome time without vifible marks or bounds? Is there no rifk of finding one's property in the poffeffion of another, or of having pur-chafed that of another?

The prefent is the epoch that will decide the Europeans, as to their confidence in the United States. I doubt not but the States in general will fanction the conftitution; and from that time every eye ought to look upon America as being in the road of unfailing profperity. Then, without doubt, many Eu-ropeans will think of purchafing lands there. I know of no period when the fpirit of fpe-culation has been fo general as at prefent; no period which prefents a revolution like that of independent America; and no foun-dation fo folid as that which they are about to eftablifh. Thus, paft events prove nothing againft what I prefume of the difpofitions of mens minds relative to this bufinefs.

I fhould not be aftonifhed, then, if he who applies himfelf to the knowledge of lands in this point of view, and gives folutions to all queftions of caution and diffidence, fhould en-gage the Europeans to very great purchafes.

LETTER

LETTER VI.

Method of Observations for my Travels in America *.

May 1788.

MY principal object is *to examine the effects of liberty on the character of man, of society, and of government.* This being the grand point of all my observations, in order to arrive at it, I must write every evening, in a journal, what has principally struck me in the day. As my observations will refer to five or six grand divisions, I shall make a tablet for each division. The following are the divisions:

Federal Government.

To collect all those points in which the ancient system resembles the new:—to obtain all that has been written on the subject; among other things, the Letters of *Publius:* —to remark the inconveniences of the old

---

* I thought proper to publish this method; it may be useful to other travellers. The method is mine; the observations are from M. Claviere.

system,

fyftem, the advantages of the new, the objections made againft it, the general opinions on the new government.

Obfervations of my Friend Claviere.

A number of little ftates, whofe extent is not fo great as to render the operations of their individual government too complicated, may be united under one general government, charged with maintaining internal peace, and rendering their union refpectable abroad. Such, without doubt, is the political affociation which is attended with the greateft advantages. You muft then endeavour principally to find what we have a right to expect from the prefent federal form of the United States.

Government of each State.

To confider the compofition of the legiflative body, the fenate, and executive power; elections; any abufes that may be in them. Compare the effects of each legiflature, to judge which is the beft.

Obfervations.—What are we to expect from their diffimilarities? In what do they confift

principally

principally? They all acknowledge the fu-
premacy of the people; but it is not preferved to them in an equal manner in all;
and where they cannot refume it without a
fedition, there can be little certainty of peace.
Peace is very doubtful, likewife, where the
will of the people is fubject to the flow forms
of inftruction. The different ftates fhould be
examined after this principle.

Legiflation, Civil, Criminal; Police.

In examining thefe objects, facts only are
to be attended to. Their comparifon with
thofe of other countries can be made afterwards.

State of the Commerce between each State, and the Savages, the Canadians, Nova Scotia, the Englifh Iflands, France, Spain, Holland, Northern States of Europe, Mexico, China, India, Africa.

To remark the principal articles of exportation and importation; the number of
veffels employed; the ftate of money ufed in
commerce.

Obfervations.—Forget not to fix well the
matters

matters of exchange, efpecially with the Spanifh poffeffions; for it is principally thence
that their gold and filver muft come. Do
they go by land to the weftern coaft of America? Do the free Americans travel among
their neighbours the Spaniards?

Is their money-fyftem a fimple one? Has
it a ftandard conftant and eafy to conceive?
Is it of a permanent nature; fo that, in a
courfe of time, one may always judge of the
price of things, in bringing them to a term
of comparifon not liable to change? This
can only be done by having one integral
metal, to which others relate, either as merchandize, or as a bill of credit referring to
money, with regard to which it expreffes a
right, but not an intrinfic value. A piece of
coined copper, for inftance, is a bill of credit,
on a portion of that metal which is adopted
as the ftandard of value; for coined copper
has by no means the intrinfic value of that
portion of money which it reprefents.

Banks.

Obfervations.—Banks are an important article in the commonwealth; the proportion
which they obferve between the money they
contain

contain, and the bills they circulate, is their great fecret, the criterion of their folidity. Thofe which have little or no money, and which circulate many bills, are in a precarious and dangerous condition. Read with attention in Smith, the Hiftory of Banks in Scotland. It is very natural to be led aftray on this fubject, which cannot be too much fimplified, if you wifh to examine it thoroughly.

Federal Revenue of each State—Taxes which they impofe—Manner of collecting them— Effect of thefe Taxes.

Obfervations.—What is the prevailing fyftem of taxation? Is land confidered as the bafis of taxes? In that cafe, is it known that it is dangerous to difcourage the farmer? Why have they not referved a domain to the States?

The Federal Debt of every State—Thofe of Individuals—Federal Expences of each State— Their Accountability.

Obfervations.—The debt has been reduced; and they juftify this reduction by the enormous

mous prices of provisions and stores which have formed the debt. Read again the Memoirs of Mr. S. you will see that there was a moment when the scale of depreciation was unjust.

There are curious enquiries to be made on this subject. Why did they gain so much before they allowed a depreciation? Because they ran a risk of another kind; they doubted of the possibility of payment, because they were not sure of the success of the revolution. In this point of view, how do they justify the scale of depreciation, especially towards those who had no interest in the revolution?

Money was very scarce; this was a great cause of discredit. It must have been distressing to those who were reduced to the necessity of borrowing: hence great augmentations in the prices of articles. In some instances, was not the reduction unjust? This, taken from first to last, must be a very curious history. It will, perhaps, teach us, that they have made a fraudulent bankruptcy. But, in this case, there is nothing to fear from this conclusion; besides, supposing extortion on the part of the creditors, it does not justify a
reduction

reduction on the part of the debtor: nothing but neceffity can juftify this. The new Encyclopedia fays, that the diforders which occafioned the depreciation, exifted before the war.

But if paper-money exifted then, that of every ftate was not in difcredit; and yet the depreciation has ftruck at all paper-money without exception.

It is faid in the Encyclopedia, that the depreciation has not injured ftrangers. Is this a fact?

It is very important to obtain a juft idea of the public expences neceffary to the Americans in future; and to penetrate, as much as poffible, the public opinion on this fubject. What do they think of loans? They are fometimes a benefit; but the wifeft governments are the moft careful to avoid this refource. When they once begin, they know not where they can ftop.

Public loans are always fo much taken from induftry; and the theory of reftoring to it what is thus taken, is always deceitful.

The

The Americans ought to hold them in
averfion, from the evils which they now
experience from them; at leaft, unlefs they
owe their liberty to them.

State of the Country near the great Towns—
Interior Parts—Frontiers—Cultivation; its
Expences and Produce; clearing new Lands;
what encourages or hinders it—Money cir-
culating in the Country—Country Manufac-
tures.

Obfervations.—It is faid, that the lands are
uncultivated near New-York; that this town
is furrounded with forefts, and that though
fire-wood is cheap, they prefer coals, even at
a high price.

It fhould feem, that commerce was in fuch
a ftate at New-York, that agriculture is defpifed there, or that they purchafe provifions at a lower price than they can raife
them.   If this be true, there are fingularities
to be explained, which we know nothing of
in Europe.

Confider the ftate of commerce and of agriculture in America, under fuch a point of
view

view as to determine why they incline to the one rather than to the other.

You will find, perhaps, that the origin of new comers determines their vocation. The Englifh arrive with their heads filled with commerce, becaufe they have fome property; the Scotch, Irifh, Germans, and others, who arrive poor, turn to agriculture, and are, befides, for the greater part, peafants. In clearing up thefe facts, you will tell us what a little property, the love of labour, united to fimplicity of manners, and turned to agriculture, will produce.

What is the true reafon of the low price of cultivated farms and houfes? Doubtlefs there is a great excefs of productions, compared with the confumptions; in that cafe, farming renders little profit.

They fpeak much of the advantages of rearing cattle. Nations have prejudices, taftes, whims, like individuals. What do they think of manufactures in the United States? What is the prevailing mode of agriculture in America? Do they fpeak of the great and the little culture?

Private

Private Morals in the Towns and in the Country.

Obfervations.—Do you find manners truly American? or do not you rather, at every inftant, find Europe at your heels? Speak to us of education public and private. Do they, as in Europe, facrifice the time of the youth in ufelefs and infignificant ftudies? Make acquaintance, as far as poffible, with the minifters of religion. Is paternal authority more refpected there, than in Europe? Does the mild education of Rouffeau prevail among the free Americans?

Inequalities of Fortune.

Forget not, under this head, the fubject of marriages, dowers, and teftaments. Ufages, in thefe refpects, prevent or accelerate inequality.

LETTER

LETTER I.

From M. DE WARVILLE.

Havre de Grace, June 3. 1788.

I AM at laft, my friend, arrived near the ocean, and in fight of the fhip that is to carry me from my country. I quit it without regret; fince the minifterial defpotifm which overwhelms it, leaves nothing to expect for a long time, but frightful ftorms, flavery, or war. May the woes which threaten this fine country, fpare what I leave in it, the moft dear to my heart!

I fhall not defcribe the cities and countries which I have paffed on my way hither. My imagination was too full of the diftreffing fpectacle I was leaving behind ; my mind was thronged with too many cares and fears, to be able to make obfervations. Infenfible to all the fcenes which prefented themfelves to me, I was with difficulty drawn from this intellectual paralyfis, at the view of fome parts of Normandy, which brought England to my mind.

The

The fields of Normandy, efpecially the canton of Caux, difplay a great variety of culture. The houfes of the peafants, better built, and better lighted than thofe of Picardy and Beauce, announce the eafe which generally reigns in this province. The peafants are well clad. You know the odd head-drefs of the women of Caux ; the cap in the form of a pyramid, the hair turned back, conftrained, plaiftered with powder and greafe, and the tinfil which always disfigures fimple nature. But we excufe this little luxury, in confidering that, if their hufbands were as miferable as the peafants of other provinces, they would not have the means of paying the expence. The Norman peafants have that air of contentment and independence which is obfervable in thofe of the Auftrian Flanders ; that calm and open countenance, an infallible fign of the happy mediocrity, the moral goodnefs, and the dignity of man. If ever France fhall be governed by a free conftitution, no province is better fituated, or enjoys more means to arrive at a high degree of profperity.

Bolbec and Bottes, near Havre, contain fome fituations quite picturefque and delicious for the hermitage of a philofopher, or the
manfion

manfion of a family who feek their happinefs within themfelves.

I fled from Rouen as from all great towns.
Mifery dwells there at the fide of opulence.
You there meet a numerous train of wretches
covered with rags, with fallow complexions,
and deformed bodies.   Every thing announces that there are manufactories in that town ;
that is to fay, a crowd of miferable beings,
who perifh with hunger, to enable others to
fwim in opulence.

The merchants at Havre complain much
of the treaty of commerce between France
and England ; they think it at leaft prema-
ture, confidering our want of a conftitution,
and the fuperiority of the Englifh induftry.
They complain likewife that the merchant
was not confulted in forming it.   I endeavoured to confole them, by faying, that the
confequences of this treaty, joined with other
circumftances, would doubtlefs lead to a free
conftitution ; which, by knocking off the
fhackles from the French induftry and commerce, would enable us to repair our loffes ;
and that fome bankruptcies would be but a
fmall price for liberty.   With regard to the
indifference of the miniftry in confulting the
merchants,

merchants, I convinced them, that it was
as much the refult of fervile fear, and want
of public fpirit in the merchants, as of the
principles of an unlimited monarchy.   It admits to the adminiftration none but fhort-
fighted intriguers, and prefumptuous knaves ;
and this kind of minifters love not confult-
ations.

Havre is, next to Nantz and Bordeaux,
the moft confiderable place for the flave trade.
Many rich houfes in this city, owe their
fortunes to this infamous traffic, which increafes, inftead of diminifhing.   There is, at
prefent, a great demand for flaves in the colonies, occafioned by the augmentation of the
demand for fugar, coffee, and cotton in Europe.   Is it true then that wealth increafes ?
You may believe it, perhaps, if you look into
England ; but the interior parts of France
give no fuch idea.

Our negro traders believe, that were it not
for the confiderable premiums given by the
government, this trade could not fubfift ;
becaufe the Englifh fell their flaves at a much
lower price than the French. I have many of
thefe details from an American captain, who
is well acquainted with the Indies, and with
Africa.

Africa. He affures me, that the negroes are, in general, treated much better on board the French than the Englifh fhips. And, perhaps, this is the reafon why the French cannot fupport a concurrence with the Englifh, who nourifh them worfe, and expend lefs.

I fpoke with fome of thefe merchants of the focieties formed in America, England, and France, for the abolition of this horrid commerce. They did not know of their exiftence, and they confidered their efforts as the movements of a blind and dangerous enthufiafm. Filled with old prejudices, and not having read any of the profound difcuffions which this philofophical and political infurrection has excited in England, they ceafed not to repeat to me, that the culture of fugar could not be carried on, but by the blacks, and by black flaves. The whites, they fay, cannot undertake it, on account of the extreme heat; and no work can be drawn out of the blacks, but by the force of the whip.

To this objection, as to twenty others which I have heard a hundred times repeated, I oppofed the victorious anfwers which you know *; but I converted nobody. In-

* See Clarkfon, Froffard, &c.

tereft

tereft ftill fpeaks too high ; and it is not
enough inftructed.

Thefe French merchants have confirmed
to me a fact, which the fociety in London
has announced to us ; it is, that the Englifh
carry on this trade under the name of French
houfes, and thus obtain the premiums which
the French government gives to this commerce. Thefe premiums amount to one
half of the original price of the flaves.

I mentioned to them an eftablifhment formed at Sierra Leona, to cultivate fugar by free
hands, and extend their culture and civilization in Africa. They anfwered me, that this
fettlement would not long fubfift ; that the
French and Englifh merchants viewed it with
an evil eye, and would employ force to deftroy their rifing colony *.

Thefe merchants appeared to me to have
more prejudice than inhumanity ; and that
if they could be told of a new commerce
more advantageous, it would not be difficult

* This infernal project has fucceeded, but the triumph will
not be long ; for two focieties are formed in London, to colo-
nize in Africa, and civilize the blacks. See, on this fubject,
an excellent pamphlet, intitled, *L'Amiral refuté par lui même.*

to induce them to abandon the fale of the wretched Africans. Write then, print, and be not weary in giving information.

I fee in this port, one of thofe packets deftined for the correfpondence between France and the United States, and afterwards employed in the very ufelefs and expenfive royal correfpondence with our Iflands ;—a fyftem adopted only to favour, at the public expence, fome of the creatures of the miniftry. This fhip, called *Marechal de Caftries*, was built in America, and is an excellent failer. This is the beft anfwer to all the fables uttered at the Office of Marine at Verfailles, againft the American timber, and the American conftruction.

Adieu, my friend! the wind is fair, and we are on the point of embarking. I am impatient; for every thing here afflicts me; even the accents of patriotifm are alarming and fufpicious. Such is the fatal influence of arbitrary governments: they fever all connections, they cramp confidence, induce fufpicion, and, of confequence, force men of liberty and fenfibility to fequefter themfelves, to be wretched, or to live in eternal fear. I

paint

paint to you, here, the martyrdom which I have endured for fix months ; I have not feen a new face, that has not given me fufpicion. This fituation is too violent for me— in a few hours my breaft will be at eafe, my foul will be quiet. What happinefs I am going to enjoy in breathing a free air !

LETTER

LETTER II.

Boſton, July 30, 1788.

WITH what joy, my good friend, did I leap to this ſhore of liberty! I was weary of the ſea; and the ſight of trees, of towns, and even of men, gives a delicious refreſhment to eyes fatigued with the deſert of the ocean. I flew from deſpotiſm, and came at laſt to enjoy the ſpectacle of liberty, among a people, where nature, education, and habit had engraved the equality of rights, which every where elſe is treated as a chimera. With what pleaſure did I contemplate this town, which firſt ſhook off the Engliſh yoke! which, for a long time, reſiſted all the ſeductions, all the menaces, all the horrors of a civil war! How I delighted to wander up and down that long ſtreet, whoſe ſimple houſes of wood border the magnificent channel of Boſton, and whoſe full ſtores offer me all the productions of the continent which I had quitted! How I enjoyed the activity of the merchants, the artizans, and the ſailors! It was not the noiſy vortex of Paris; it was not the unquiet, eager mien of

my

my countrymen; it was the fimple, dignified
air of men, who are confcious of liberty, and
who fee in all men their brothers and their
equals. Every thing in this ftreet bears the
marks of a town ftill in its infancy, but
which, even in its infancy, enjoys a great
profperity. I thought myfelf in that Salentum, of which the lively pencil of Fenelon
has left us fo charming an image. But the
profperity of this new Salentum was not the
work of one man, of a king, or a minifter;
it is the fruit of liberty, that mother of induftry. Every thing is rapid, every thing
great, every thing durable with her. A royal
or minifterial profperity, like a king or a
minifter, has only the duration of a moment.
Bofton is juft rifing from the devaftations of
war, and its commerce is flourifhing; its
manufactures, productions, arts, and fciences,
offer a number of curious and interefting
obfervations.

The manners of the people are not exactly
the fame as defcribed by M. de Crevecœur.
You no longer meet here that Prefbyterian
aufterity, which interdicted all pleafures, even
that of walking; which forbade travelling on
Sunday, which perfecuted men whofe opinions were different from their own. The
Boftonians

Boſtonians unite ſimplicity of morals with
that French politeneſs and delicacy of manners which render virtue more amiable.
They are hoſpitable to ſtrangers, and obliging to friends; they are tender huſbands,
fond and almoſt idolatrous parents, and
kind maſters. Muſic, which their teachers
formerly proſcribed as a diabolic art, begins
to make part of their education. In ſome
houſes you hear the forte-piano. This art,
it is true, is ſtill in its infancy; but the
young novices who exerciſe it, are ſo gentle,
ſo complaiſant, and ſo modeſt, that the proud
perfection of art gives no pleaſure equal to
what they afford. God grant that the Boſtonian women may never, like thoſe of
France, acquire the malady of perfection in
this art! It is never attained, but at the expence of the domeſtic virtues.

The young women here, enjoy the liberty
they do in England, that they did in Geneva
when morals were there, and the republic
exiſted; and they do not abuſe it. Their
frank and tender hearts have nothing to fear
from the perfidy of men. Examples of this
perfidy are rare; the vows of love are believed; and love always reſpects them, or
ſhame follows the guilty.

The

The Boſtonian mothers are reſerved; their
air is however frank, good, and communi-
cative.   Entirely devoted to their families,
they are occupied in rendering their huſbands
happy, and in training their children to virtue.

The law denounces heavy penalties againſt
adultery; ſuch as the pillory, and impriſonment.   This law has ſcarcely ever been called
into execution.   It is becauſe families are
happy; and they are pure, becauſe they are
happy.

Neatneſs without luxury, is a charac-
teriſtic feature of this purity of manners;
and this neatneſs is ſeen every where at Boſton, in their dreſs, in their houſes, and in
their churches.   Nothing is more charming
than an inſide view of a church on Sunday.
The good cloth coat covers the man; callicoes and chintzes dreſs the women and children, without being ſpoiled by thoſe gewgaws which whim and caprice have added
to them among our women.   Powder and
pomatum never fully the heads of infants
and children: I ſee them with pain, however, on the heads of men: they invoke the
art of the hair-dreſſer; for, unhappily, this
art has already croſſed the ſeas.

I ſhall

I fhall never call to mind, without emotion, the pleafure I had one day in hearing the refpectable Mr. Clarke, fucceffor to the learned Doctor Chauncey, the friend of mankind. His church is in clofe union with that of Doctor Cooper, to whom every good Frenchman, and every friend of liberty, owes a tribute of gratitude, for the love he bore the French, and the zeal with which he defended and preached the American independence. I remarked in this auditory, the exterior of that eafe and contentment of which I have fpoken; that collected calmnefs, refulting from the habit of gravity, and the confcious prefence of the Almighty; that religious decency, which is equally diftant from grovelling idolatry, and from the light and wanton airs of thofe Europeans who go to a church as to a theatre.

Spectatum veniant, veniant fpectentur ut ipfæ.

But, to crown my happinefs, I faw none of thofe livid wretches, covered with rags, who in Europe, foliciting our compaffion at the foot of the altar, feem to bear teftimony againft Providence, our humanity, and the order of fociety. The difcourfe, the prayer, the worfhip, every thing, bore the fame fimplicity.

plicity. The fermon breathed the beft morality, and it was heard with attention.

The excellence of this morality characterizes almoft all the fermons of all the fects
through the Continent. The minifters rarely
fpeak dogmas: univerfal tolerance, the child
of American independence, has banifhed the
preaching of dogmas, which always leads
to difcuffion and quarrels. All the fects
admit nothing but morality, which is the
fame in all, and the only preaching proper
for a great fociety of brothers.

This tolerance is unlimited at Bofton; a
town formerly witnefs of bloody perfecutions,
efpecially againft the Quakers; where many
of this fect paid, with their life, for their
perfeverance in their religious opinions. Juft
Heaven! how is it poffible there can exift
men believing fincerely in God, and yet
barbarous enough to inflict death on a
woman, the intrepid Dyer *, becaufe fhe
thee'd

---

* M. de Warville appears to have been mifinformed with
refpect to the feverity of the perfecutions againft the Quakers
in Maffachufetts; and particularly the circumftances relating
to Mrs. Dyer. This woman, I believe, is the only perfon ever
put to death in that colony for any thing connected with religious

thee'd and *thou'd* men, becaufe fhe did not
believe in the divine miffion of priefts, becaufe
fhe would follow the Gofpel literally ? But
let us draw the curtain over thefe fcenes of
horror ; they will never again fully this new
continent, deftined by Heaven to be the
afylum of liberty and humanity. Every one

gious principles. The higheft penalties inflicted by law againft
the Quakers, or any other fect, on account of its religion, was
banifhment. The Quakers then formed a fettlement at Rhode-
Ifland ; but feveral of them returned frequently to Maffachufetts, with fuch a zeal for making profelytes, as to difturb the
order of fociety. The difobedience of returning from banifhment was then interdicted by the penalty of whipping ; this
not anfwering the purpofe, the terrors of death were added.
This unhappy woman, infpired, it feems, with the frenzy of
martyrdom, came to provoke the pains of this fevere law. She
raved in the ftreets, againft the magiftrates and the church ;
went into religious affemblies, raifed loud cries to drown the
voice of the preachers, called them the worfhippers of Baal ;
defied the judges, and faid fhe would leave them no peace till
they fhould incur the vengeance of Heaven, and the down-
fall of their own fect, by putting her to death !

The caufes on both parties, which led to this event, were
doubtlefs culpable; but, to compare the demerit of each, would
require a refearch equally difficult and ufelefs at the prefent
day. Perfecution and contumacy are reciprocal caufes and
effects of the fame evils in fociety ; and perhaps thefe particular perfecuted Quakers were as different in their character
from the prefent refpectable order of *Friends* in America, as
the firft Puritans of Bofton were from its prefent inhabitants.

The delirium about witchcraft in Maffachufetts, is fometimes ignorantly confounded with the perfecution of the
Quakers.

TRANSLATOR.

at

at prefent worfhips God in his own way, at
Bofton. Anabaptifts, Methodifts, Quakers,
and Catholics, profefs openly their opinions:
and all offices of government, places and
emoluments, are equally open to all fects.
Virtue and talents, and not religious opinions,
are the tefts of public confidence.

The minifters of different fects live in
fuch harmony, that they fupply each other's
places when any one is detained from his
pulpit.

On feeing men think fo differently on
matters of religion, and yet poffefs fuch virtues, it may be concluded, that one may be
very honeft, and believe, or not believe, in
tranfubftantiation, and the word. They have
concluded that it is beft to tolerate each other,
and that this is the worfhip moft agreeable
to God.

Before this opinion was fo general among
them, they had eftablifhed another: it was
the neceffity of reducing divine worfhip to
the greateft fimplicity, to difconnect it from
all its fuperftitious ceremonies, which gave
it the appearance of idolatry; and particularly, not to give their priefts enormous falaries,

ries, to enable them to live in luxury and idlenefs; in a word, to reftore the evangelical fimplicity. They have fucceeded. In the country, the church has a glebe; in town, the minifters live on collections made each Sunday in the church, and the rents of pews. It is an excellent practice to induce the minifters to be diligent in their ftudies, and faithful in their duty; for the preference is given to him whofe difcourfes pleafe the moft *, and his falary is the moft confiderable : while, among us, the ignorant and the learned, the debauchee and the man of virtue, are always fure of their livings. It refults, likewife, from this, that a mode of worfhip will not be impofed on thofe who do not believe in it. Is it not a tyranny to force men to pay for the fupport of a fyftem which they abhor?

* The truth of this remark ftruck me at Bofton and elfewhere in the United States. Almoft all the minifters are men of talents, or at leaft, men of learning. With thefe precarious falaries, the minifters of Bofton not only live well, but they marry, and rear large families of children. This fact confirms the judicious remarks of M. Claviere on the advantages of the priefts marrying, even when their falary is fmall. Their alliance would be fought after, by fathers who would wifh to give their daughters hufbands well inftructed, and of good morals. The fame thing will happen in France when the priefts fhall be allowed to marry. They ought not then to dread marriage, though their falaries fhould be fmall.

The

The Boftonians are become fo philofophical on the fubject of religion, that they have
lately ordained a man who was refufed by
the bifhop. The fect to which he belongs
have inftalled him in their church, and given
him the power to preach and to teach; and
he preaches, and he teaches, and difcovers
good abilities; for the people really deceive
themfelves in their choice.—This economical inftitution, which has no example but in
the primltive church, has been cenfured by
thofe who believe ftill in the tradition of orders by the direct defcendants of the Apoftles.
But the Boftonians are fo near believing that
every man may be his own preacher, that
the apoftolic doctrine has not found very
warm advocates. They will foon be, in
America, in the fituation where M. d'Alembert
has placed the minifters of Geneva.

Since the ancient puritan aufterity has
difappeared, you are no longer furprifed to
fee a game of cards introduced among thefe
good Prefbyterians. When the mind is tranquil, in the enjoyment of competence and
peace, it is natural to occupy it in this way,
efpecially in a country where there is no
theatre, where men make it not a bufinefs to
pay court to the women, where they read
few

few books, and cultivate ftill lefs the fciences.
This tafte for cards is certainly unhappy in a
republican ftate. The habit of them contracts
the mind, prevents the acquifition of ufeful
knowledge, leads to idlenefs and diffipation,
and gives birth to every malignant paffion.
Happily it is not very confiderable in Bofton : you fee here no fathers of families
rifking their whole fortunes in it.

There are many clubs at Bofton. M.
Chaftellux fpeaks of a particular club held
once a week. I was at it feveral times, and
was much pleafed with their politenefs to
ftrangers, and the knowledge difplayed in
their converfation. There is no coffee-houfe
at Bofton, New-York, or Philadelphia. One
houfe in each town, that they call by that
name, ferves as an exchange.

One of the principal pleafures of the inhabitants of thefe towns, confifts in little parties
for the country, among families and friends.
The principal expence of the parties, efpecially after dinner, is tea. In this, as in
their whole manner of living, the Americans
in general refemble the Englifh. Punch,
warm and cold, before dinner; excellent beef,
and Spanifh and Bordeaux wines, cover their
tables,

tables, always folidly and abundantly ferved. Spruce beer, excellent cyder, and Philadelphia porter, precede the wines. This porter is equal to the Englifh : the manufacture of it faves a vaft tribute formerly paid to the Englifh induftry. The fame may foon be faid with refpect to cheefe. I have often found American cheefe equal to the beft Chefhire of England, or the Rocfort of France. This may with truth be faid of that made on a farm on Elizabeth Ifland, belonging to the refpectable Governor Bowdoin.

After forcing the Englifh to give up their domination, the Americans determined to rival them in every thing ufeful. This fpirit of emulation fhews itfelf every where : it has erected at Bofton an extenfive glafs manufactory, belonging to M. Breek and others.

This fpirit of emulation has opened to the Boftonians, fo many channels of commerce, which lead them to all parts of the globe.

> Nil mortalibus arduum eft ;
> Audax Japeti genus.

If thefe lines could ever apply to any people, it is to the free Americans. No danger, no diftance, no obftable impedes them. What
have

have they to fear? All mankind are their brethren : they wifh peace with all.

It is this fpirit of emulation, which multiplies and brings to perfection fo many manufactories of cordage in this town; which has erected filatures of hemp and flax, proper to occupy young people, without fubjecting them to be crouded together in fuch numbers as to ruin their health and their morals; proper, likewife, to occupy that clafs of women, whom the long voyages of their feafaring hufbands and other accidents reduce to inoccupation.

To this fpirit of emulation are owing the manufactories of falt, nails, paper and paper-hangings, which are multiplied in this ftate. The rum diftilleries are on the decline, fince the fuppreffion of the flave trade, in which this liquor was employed, and fince the diminution of the ufe of ftrong fpirits by the country people.

This is fortunate for the human race; and the American induftry will foon repair the fmall lofs it fuftains from the decline of this fabrication of poifons.

Maffa-

Maffachufetts wifhes to rival, in manufactures, Connecticut and Pennfylvania; fhe has,
like the laft, a fociety formed for the encouragement of manufactures and induftry.

The greateft monuments of the induftry
of this ftate, are the three bridges of Charles,
Malden, and Effex.

Bofton has the glory of having given the
firft college or univerfity to the new world.
It is placed on an extenfive plain, four miles
from Bofton, at a place called Cambridge;
the origin of this ufeful inftitution was in
1636. The imagination could not fix on a
place that could better unite all the conditions effential to a feat of education; fufficiently near to Bofton, to enjoy all the advantages of a communication with Europe
and the reft of the world; and fufficiently
diftant, not to expofe the ftudents to the contagion of licentious manners, common in
commercial towns.

The air of Cambridge is pure, and the environs charming, offering a vaft fpace for
the exercife of the youth.

The buildings are large, numerous, and
well

well diftributed. But, as the number of the ftudents augments every day, it will be neceffary foon to augment the buildings. The library, and the cabinet of philofophy, do honour to the inftitution. The firft contains 13,000 volumes. The heart of a Frenchman palpitates on finding the works of Racine, of Montefquieu, and the Encyclopædia, where, 150 years ago, arofe the fmoke of the favage calumet.

The regulation of the courfe of ftudies here, is nearly the fame as that at the univerfity of Oxford. I think it impoffible but that the laft revolution muft introduce a great reform. Free men ought to ftrip themfelves of their prejudices, and to perceive, that, above all, it is neceffary to be a man and a citizen; and that the ftudy of the dead languages, of a faftidious philofophy and theology, ought to occupy few of the moments of a life, which might be ufefully employed in ftudies more advantageous to the great family of the human race.

Such a change in the ftudies is more probable, as an academy is formed at Bofton, compofed of refpectable men, who cultivate all the fciences; and who, difengaged from

religious

religious prejudices, will doubtlefs very foon point out a courfe of education more fhort, and more fure in forming good citizens and philofophers.

Mr. Bowdoin, prefident of this academy, is a man of univerfal talents. He unites with his profound erudition, the virtues of a magif-trate, and the principles of a republican poli-tician. His conduct has never difappointed the confidence of his fellow-citizens; though his fon-in-law, Mr. Temple, has incurred their univerfal deteftation, for the verfatility of his conduct during the war, and his open attachment to the Britifh fince the peace. To recompenfe him for this, the Englifh have given him the confulate-general of America.

But, to return to the univerfity of Cam-bridge — Superintended by the refpectable prefident Willard. Among the affociates in the direction of the ftudies, are diftinguifhed, Dr. Wigglefworth and Dr, Dexter. The latter is profeffor of natural philofophy, che-miftry and medicine; a man of extenfive knowledge, and great modefty. He told me, to my great fatisfaction, that he gave lectures on the experiments of our fchool of chemif-try. The excellent work of my refpectable mafter,

mafter, Dr. Fourcroy, was in his hands, which taught him the rapid ftrides that this fcience has lately made in Europe.

In a free country, every thing ought to bear the ftamp of patriotifm. This patriotifm, fo happily difplayed in the foundation, endowment, and encouragement of his univerfity, appears every year in a folemn feaft celebrated at Cambridge in honour of the Sciences. This feaft, which takes place once a year in all the colleges of America, is called the *commencement :* it refembles the exercifes and diftribution of prizes in our colleges. It is a day of joy for Bofton ; almoft all its inhabitants affemble in Cambridge. The moft diftinguifhed of the ftudents difplay their talents in prefence of the public ; and thefe exercifes, which are generally on patriotic fubjects, are terminated by a feaft, where reign the freeft gaiety, and the moft cordial fraternity.

It is remarked, that, in countries chiefly devoted to commerce, the fciences are not carried to any high degree. This remark applies to Bofton. The univerfity certainly contains men of worth and learning ; but fcience is not diffufed among the inhabitants of
the

the town. Commerce occupies all their ideas, turns all their heads, and abforbs all their fpeculations. Thus you find few eftimable works, and few authors. The expence of the firft volume of the Memoirs of the Academy of this town, is not yet covered; it is two years fince it appeared. Some time fince was publifhed, the hiftory of the late troubles in Maffachufets; it is very well written. The author has found much difficulty to indemnify himfelf for the expence of printing it. Never has the whole of the precious hiftory of New Hampfhire, by Belnap, appeared, for want of encouragement,

Poets, for the fame reafon, muft be more rare than other writers. They fpeak, however, of an original, but lazy poet, by the name of *Allen.* His verfes are faid to be full of warmth and force. They mention particularly, a manufcript poem of his, on the famous battle of Bunker-Hill; but he will not print it. He has for his reputation and his money the careleffnefs of *La Fontaine.*

They publifh a Magazine here, though the number of Gazettes is very confiderable. The multiplicity of Gazettes proves the activity of commerce, and the tafte for politics and news,

news; the merits and multiplicity of Literary
and Political Magazines are figns of the culture of the fciences.

You may judge from thefe details, that the
arts, except thofe that refpect navigation, do
not receive much encouragement here.   The
hiftory of the Planetarium of Mr. Pope is a
proof of it.   Mr. Pope is a very ingenious
artift, occupied in clock-making.   The machine which he has conftructed, to explain
the movement of the heavenly bodies, would
aftonifh you, efpecially when you confider
that he has received no fuccour from Europe,
and very little from books.   He owes the
whole to himfelf; he is, like the painter
Trumbull, the child of nature.   Ten years
of his life have been occupied in perfecting
this Planetarium.   He had opened a fubfcription to recompenfe his trouble ; but the fubfcription was never full.

This difcouraged artift told me one day,
that he was going to Europe to fell this machine, and to conftruct others.   This country, faid he, is too poor to encourage the
arts.   Thefe words, *this country is too poor*,
ftruck me.   I reflected, that if they were pronounced

nounced in Europe, they might lead to wrong
ideas of America; for the idea of poverty
carries that of rags, of hunger; and no country is more diftant from that fad condition.
When riches are centred in a few hands, thefe
have a great fuperfluity; and this fuperfluity
may be applied to their pleafures, and to favour the agreeable and frivolous arts. When
riches are equally divided in fociety, there is
very little fuperfluity, and confequently little
means of encouraging the agreeable arts. But
which of thefe two countries is the rich, and
which is the poor? According to the European ideas, and in the fenfe of Mr. Pope, it
is the firft that is rich; but, to the eye of reafon, it is not; for the other is the happieft.
Hence it refults, that the ability of giving encouragement to the agreeable arts, is a fymp-
tom of national calamity.

Let us not blame the Boftonians; they
think of the ufeful, before procuring to themfelves the agreeable. They have no brilliant
monuments; but they have neat and commodious churches, but they have good houfes, but they have fuperb bridges, and excellent fhips. Their ftreets are well illuminated
at night; while many ancient cities of Europe,
containing

containing proud monuments of art, have never yet thought of preventing the fatal effects of nocturnal darknefs.

Befides the focieties for the encouragement of agriculture and manufactures, they have another, known by the name of the Humane Society. Their object is to recover drowned perfons. It is formed after the model of the one at London, as that is copied from the one at Paris. They follow the fame methods as in Europe, and have rendered important fuccours.

The Medical Society is not lefs ufeful, than the one laft mentioned. It holds a correfpondence with all the country towns; to know the fymptoms of local difeafes, propofe the proper remedies, and give inftruction thereupon to their fellow-citizens.

Another eftablifhment is the alms-houfe. It is deftined to the poor, who, by age and infirmity, are unable to gain their living. It contains at prefent about 150 perfons.

Another, called the work-houfe, or houfe of correction, is not fo much peopled as you might imagine. In a rifing country, in an active

active port, where provisions are cheap, good morals predominate, and the number of thieves and vagabonds is small. These are vermin attached to misery; and there is no misery here.

The state of exports and imports of this industrious people, to prove to you how many new branches of commerce they have opened since the peace, I refer to the general table of the commerce of the United States, which I propose to lay before you.

An employment which is, unhappily, one of the most lucrative in this state, is the profession of the Law. They preserve still the expensive forms of the English practice, which good sense, and the love of order, ought to teach them to suppress; they render advocates necessary; they have likewise borrowed from their fathers, the English, the habit of demanding exorbitant fees. But, notwithstanding the abuses of law proceedings, they complain very little of the Lawyers. Those with whom I have been acquainted, appear to enjoy a great reputation for integrity; such as Sumner, Wendell, Lowell, Sullivan.

They did themselves honour in the affair of

of the Tender Act, by endeavouring to prevent it from being enacted, and afterwards to diminish as much as possible its unjust effects.

It is in part to their enlightened philanthropy, that is to be attributed the Law of the 26th of March 1788, which condemns to heavy penalties, all persons who shall import or export slaves, or be concerned in this infamous traffic.

Finally, they have had a great part in the Revolution, by their writings, by their discourses, by taking the lead in the affairs of Congress, and in foreign negociations.

To recall this memorable period, ·is to bring to mind one of the greatest ornaments of the American bar, the celebrated Adams; who, from the humble station of a schoolmaster, has raised himself to the first dignities; whose name is as much respected in Europe, as in his own country, for the difficult embassies with which he has been charged. He has, finally, returned to his retreat, in the midst of the applauses of his fellow-citizens, occupied in the cultivation of his farm, and forgetting what he was when he trampled on the pride of his king, who had put a

price

price upon his head, and who was forced to receive him as the ambaffador of a free country. Such were the generals and ambaffadors of the beft ages of Rome and Greece; fuch were Epaminondas, Cincinnatus, and Fabius.

It is not poffible to fee Mr. Adams, who knows fo well the American conftitutions, without fpeaking to him of that which appears to be taking place in France. I don't know whether he has an ill opinion of our character, of our conftancy, or of our underftanding; but he does not believe that we can eftablifh a liberty, even equal to what the Englifh enjoy *; he does not believe, even that we have the right, like the ancient States-General, to require that no tax fhould be impofed without the confent of the people. I had no difficulty in combating him, even by authorities, independent of the focial compact, againft which no time, no conceffions can prefcribe.

Mr. Adams is not the only man diftinguifhed in this great revolution, who have retired to the obfcure labours of a country

---

* The event has proved how much he was deceived.

life.

life. General Heath is one of thofe worthy imitators of the Roman Cincinnatus; for he likes not the American *Cincinnati:* their eagle appears to him a gewgaw, proper only for children. On fhewing me a letter from the immortal Wafhington, whom he loves as a father, and reveres as an angel— this letter, fays he, is a jewel which, in my eyes, furpaffes all the eagles and all the ribbons in the world. It was a letter in which that General had felicitated him for his good conduct on a certain occafion. With what joy did this refpectable man fhew me all parts of his farm! What happinefs he enjoys on it! He is a true farmer. A glafs of cyder, which he prefented to me with franknefs and good humour painted on his countenance, appeared to me fuperior to the moft exquifite wines. With this fimplicity, men are worthy of liberty, and they are fure of enjoying it for a long time.

This fimplicity characterifes almoft all the men of this ftate, who have acted diftinguifhed parts in the revolution: fuch, among others, as Samuel Adams, and Mr. Hancock the prefent governor. If ever a man was fincerely an idolater of republicanifm, it is Samuel Adams; and never a man united more

virtues

virtues to give refpect to his opinions.   He
has the excefs of republican virtues, untaint-
ed probity, fimplicity, modefty *, and, above
all, firmnefs: he will have no capitulation
with abufes ; he fears as much the defpotifm
of virtue and talents, as the defpotifm of vice.
Cherifhing the greateft love and refpect for
Wafhington, he voted to take from him the
command at the end of a certain term ; he
recollected, that Cæfar could not have fucceeded in overturning the republic, but
by prolonging the command of the army.
The event has proved that the application
was falfe ; but it was by a miracle, and the
fafety of a country fhould never be rifked on
the faith of a miracle.

Samuel Adams is the beft fupporter of the
party of Governor Hancock.   You know
the great facrifices which the latter made
in the revolution, and the boldnefs with
which he declared himfelf at the beginning
of the infurrection.   The fame fpirit of patriotifm animates him ftill.   A great genero-

* When I compare our legiflators, with their airs of im-
portance, always fearing they fhall not make noife enough, that
they fhall not be fufficiently praifed ; when I compare them to
thefe modern republicans, I fear for the fuccefs of the revolution.   The vain man can never be far from flavery.

fity,

fity, united to a vaſt ambition, forms his character : he has the virtues and the addreſs of
populariſm; that is to ſay, that, without effort,
he ſhews himſelf the equal, and the friend of
all. I ſupped at his houſe with a hatter, who
appeared to be in great familiarity with him.
Mr. Hancock is amiable and polite, when he
wiſhes to be; but they ſay he does not
always chuſe it. He has a marvellous gout,
which diſpenſes him from all attentions, and
forbids the acceſs to his houſe. Mr. Hancock has not the learning of his rival, Mr.
Bowdoin; he ſeems even to diſdain the ſciences. The latter is more eſteemed by enlightened men; the former more beloved
by the people. Among the partizans of the
governor, I diſtinguiſhed two brothers, by
the name of Jarvis; one is comptroller general of the ſtate ; the other, a phyſician, and
member of the legiſlature. The firſt has as
much calmneſs of examination and profundity of thought, as the latter has of rapidity
in his penetration, agility in his ideas, and
vivacity in his expreſſion. They reſemble
each other in one point, that is, in ſimplicity—the firſt of republican virtues; a virtue
born with the Americans, and only acquired
with us. If I were to paint to you all the
eſtimable characters which I found in this
charming town, my portraits would never be
finiſhed.

finifhed. I found every where, that hofpitality,
that affability, that friendfhip for the French
which M. Caftellux has fo much exalted.
I found them efpecially with Meffrs. Breck,
Ruffel, Gore, Barrett, &c.

The parts adjacent to Bofton, are charming
and well cultivated, adorned with elegant
houfes and agreeable fituations.   Among the
furrounding eminences you diftinguifh Bunker-hill.   This name will recal to your mind
the famous Warren; one of the firft martyrs
of American liberty.   I owed an homage to
his generous manes; and I was eager to pay
it.   You arrive at Bunker-hill by the fuperb
bridge at Charlefton, of which I have fpoken.
This town was entirely burnt by the Englifh,
in their attack of Bunker-hill.   It is at prefent
rebuilt with elegant houfes of wood.   You
fee here the ftore of Mr. Gorham, formerly
prefident of Congrefs.   This hill offers one of
the moft aftonifhing monuments of American
valor; it is impoffible to conceive how feven
or eight hundred men, badly armed, and fatigued, having juft conftructed, in hafte, a few
miferable intrenchments, and who knew nothing, or very little, of the ufe of arms, could
refift, for fo long a time, the attack of thoufands of the Englifh troops, frefh, well difci-
plined, fucceeding each other in the attack.
But

But fuch was the vigorous refiftance of the
Americans, that the Englifh loft 1200 men,
killed and wounded, before they became
mafter of the place. Obferve that they had
two frigates, which, croffing their fire on
Charlefton, prevented the arrival of fuccour
to the Americans. Yet it is very probable that
the Englifh would have been forced to retire,
had not the Americans failed in ammunition.

While the friend of liberty is contemplating this fcene, and dropping a tear to the
memory of Warren, his emotions of enthufiafm are renewed on viewing the expreffive
picture of the death of that warrior, painted
by Mr. Trumbull, whofe talents may equal,
one day, thofe of the moft famous mafters.

I muft finifh this long, and too long, letter.
Many objects remain ftill to entertain you
with in this ftate, fuch as the conftitution,
debts, taxes; but I refer them to the general
table which I fhall make of them for the
United States. The taxable heads of this
ftate are upwards of 100,000, acres of arable
land 200,000, pafturage 340,000, uncultivated 2,000,000, tons of fhipping at Bofton
60,000.

LETTER

LETTER III.

Journey from Boston to New-York, by land.

9th Aug. 1788.

THE distance of these towns is about two hundred and fifty miles. Many persons have united in establishing a kind of diligence, or public stage, which passes regularly for the convenience of travellers. In the summer season, the journey is performed in four days.

We set out from Boston at four o'clock in the morning, and passed through the handsome town of Cambridge. The country appears well cultivated as far as Weston, where we breakfasted; thence we passed to Worcester to dinner, forty-eight miles from Boston. This town is elegant, and well peopled : the printer, Isaiah Thomas, has rendered it famous through all the Continent. He prints most of the works which appear; and it must be granted that his editions are correct. Thomas

Thomas is the *Didot* of the United States. The tavern, where we had a good American dinner *, is a charming houfe of wood, well ornamented; it is kept by Mr. Peafe, one of the proprietors of the Bofton ftage.   He has much merit for his activity and induftry; but it is to be hoped he will change the pre- fent plan, fo far as it refpects his horfes : they are over-done with the length and dif- ficulty of the courfes, which ruins them in a fhort time, befides retarding very much the progrefs.

We flept the firft night at Spenfer, a new village in the midft of the woods.   The houfe of the tavern was but half built; but the part that was finifhed, had an air of cleanlinefs which pleafes, becaufe it announces that de- gree of competence, thofe moral and delicate habits, which are never feen in our villages. The chambers were neat, the beds good,   the fheets clean, fupper paffable; cyder, tea, punch, and all for fourteen pence a-head.   There were four of us.   Now, compare, my friend, this order of things with what you have a

---

* If I fometimes :ite dinners and fuppers, it is not in me- mory of eating and drinking, but it is to fhow the manner of living of the country, and likewife to fpeak of the prices of provifions, fo much exaggerated by Chaftellux.

thoufand

thoufand times feen in our French taverns—
chambers dirty and hideous, beds infected
with bugs, thofe infects which Sterne calls
the rightful inhabitants of taverns, if indeed
long poffeffion gives a right ; fheets ill-
wafhed, and exhaling a fetid odour ; bad
covering, wine adulterated, and every thing
at its weight in gold ; greedy fervants, who
are complaifant only in proportion to your
equipage ; grovelling towards a rich traveller, and infolent towards him whom they
fufpect of mediocrity.   Such are the eternal
torments of travellers in France : add to this,
the fear of being robbed, the precautions
neceffary to be taken every night to prevent
it ; while, in the United States, you travel
without fear, as without arms*; and you
fleep quietly among the woods, in an open
chamber of a houfe whofe doors fhut without locks.   And now judge which country
merits the name of civilized, and which bears
the afpect of the greateft general happinefs.

We left Spenfer at four o'clock in the

---

* I travelled with a Frenchman, who, thinking he had
much to fear in a favage country, had furnifhed himfelf with
piftols. The good American fmiled at his precautions, and
advifed him to put his piftols in his trunk : he had wit enough
to believe him.

morning.

morning. New carriage, new proprietor. It was a carriage without fprings, a kind of waggon. A Frenchman, who was with me, began, at the firft jolt, to curfe the carriage, the driver, and the country. Let us wait, faid I, a little, before we form a judgment: every cuftom has its caufe ; there is doubtlefs fome reafon why this kind of carriage is preferred to one hung with fprings. In fact, by the time we had run thirty miles among the rocks, we were convinced that a carriage with fprings would very foon have been overfet and broke.

The traveller is well recompenfed for the fatigue of this route, by the variety of romantic fituations, by the beauty of the profpects which it offers at each ftep, by the perpetual contraft of favage nature and the efforts of art. Thofe vaft ponds of water, which lofe themfelves in the woods ; thofe rivulets, that wafh the meadow, newly fnatched from uncultivated nature ; thofe neat houfes, fcattered among the forefts, and containing fwarms of children, joyous and healthy, and well clad ; thofe fields, covered with trunks of trees, whofe deftruction is committed to the hand of time, and which are covered under the leaves of Indian corn ; thofe oaks, which

which preferve ftill the image of their ancient
vigor, but which, girdled at the bottom,
raife no longer to heaven but dry and naked
branches, which the firft ftroke of wind muft
bring to the earth :—all thefe objeðs, fo new
to an European, arreft him, abforb him, and
plunge him into an agreeable reverie. The
depths of the forefts, the prodigious fize
and height of the trees, call to his mind the
time when the favages were the only inhabitants of this country. This ancient tree has
beheld them ; they filled thefe forefts : they
have now given place to another generation.
The cultivator fears no more their vengeance;
his mufket, formerly his neceffary companion
at the plough, now refts fufpended in his
houfe. Alone, with his wife and children,
in the midft of the forefts, he fleeps quietly,
he labours in peace, and he is happy. Such
were the ideas which occupied me the greater
part of my journey : they fometimes gave
place to others, arifing from the view of the
country houfes, which are feen at fmall diftances through all the forefts of Maffachufetts. Neatnefs embellifhes them all. They
have frequently but one ftory and a garret ;
their walls are papered : tea and coffee appear on their tables ; their daughters, clothed
in callicoes, difplay the traits of civility, frank--
nefs,

nefs, and decency; virtues which always
follow contentment and eafe. Almoft all
thefe houfes are inhabited by men who are
both cultivators and artizans; one is a tan-
ner, another a fhoemaker, another fells
goods; but all are farmers. The country
ftores are well afforted; you find in the fame
fhop, hats, nails, liquors. This order of
things is neceffary in a new fettlement : it is
to be hoped that it will continue; for this
general retail occupies lefs hands, and de-
taches fewer from the great object of agriculture. It is not fuppofed that one third of
the land of Maffachufetts is under cultivation : it is difficult to fay when it will all
be fo, confidering the invitations of the weftern country and the province of Maine.
But the uncleared lands are all located, and
the proprietors have inclofed them with
fences of different forts. Thefe feveral kinds
of fences are compofed of different materials,
which announce the different degrees of culture in the country. Some are compofed
of the light branches of trees; others, of the
trunks of trees laid one upon the other; a
third fort is made of long pieces of wood,
fupporting each other by making angles at
the end; a fourth kind is made of long pieces
of hewn timber, fupported at the ends by
paffing into holes made in an upright poft;
a fifth

a fifth is like the garden fences in England;
the laft kind is made of ftones thrown together to the height of three feet. This
laft is moft durable, and is common in Maffachufetts. From Spenfer to Brookfield is
fifteen miles. The road is good as far as this
laft town. A town you know in the interior
of America, defignates an extent of eight or
ten miles, where are fcattered a hundred or
two hundred houfes. This divifion into
towns, is neceffary for affembling the inhabitants for elections and other purpofes.
Without this divifion, the inhabitants might
go fometimes to one affembly, and fometimes
to another, which would lead to confufion.
Befides, it would render it impoffible to
know the population of any particular canton; this ferves for the bafis of many regulations. No people carry their attention in
this particular, fo far as the Americans.

The fituation of Brookfield is picturefque.
While breakfaft was preparing, I read the
gazettes and journals, which are diftributed
through all the country. Our breakfaft confifted of coffee, tea, boiled and roafted meat;
the whole for ten-pence, New England cur-
rency, for each traveller. From this place to
Wilbraham the road is covered with rocks,
and bordered with woods. At this place,

a new

a new proprietor, and a new carriage. A fmall light carriage, well fufpended, and drawn by two horfes, took place of our heavy waggon. We could not conceive how five of us could fit in this little parifian chariot, and demanded another. The conductor faid he had no other; that there were fo few travellers in this part of the road, that he could not afford to run with more than two horfes; that moft of the travellers from New-York ftopped in Connecticut, and moft of thofe from Bof-ton at Worcefter. We were obliged to fubmit. We ftarted like lightning; and arrived, in an hour and a quarter, at Springfield, ten miles. This road appeared really enchanting: I feemed the whole way to be travelling in one of the alleys of the palais-royal. This man was one of the moft lively and induftrious, at the fame time the moft patient, I ever met with. In my two journies through this place, I have heard many travellers treat him with very harfh language: he either anfwers not at all, or anfwers by giving good reafons. The greater part of men of this profeffion, in this country, obferve the fame conduct in fuch cafes; while the leaft of thefe injuries in Europe would have occafioned bloody quarrels. This fact proves to me, that, in a free country, reafon extends her empire over all claffes of men.

Spring-

Springfield, where we dined, refembles
an European town ; that is, the houfes are
placed near together.   On a hill that overlooks this town, is a magazine of ammunition
and arms belonging to the ftate of Maffachufetts.   This is the magazine that the rebel
Shays endeavoured to take, and was fo happily defended by General Shepard.   We fet
out from Springfield, after dinner, for Hartford.   We paffed in a ferry-boat, the river
that wafhes the environs of Springfield.

I have paffed twice through Hartford, and
both times in the night ; fo that I cannot
give an exact defcription of it.   It is a confiderable rural town ; the greater part of the
inhabitants live by agriculture ; fo that eafe
and abundance univerfally reign in it,   It is
confidered as one of the moft agreeable in
Connecticut, on account of its fociety.   It
is the refidence of one of the moft refpectable
men in the United States, Colonel Wadfworth.   He enjoys a confiderable fortune,
which he owes entirely to his own labour
and induftry.   Perfectly verfed in agriculture
and commerce; univerfally known for the
fervice he rendered to the American and
French armies during the war ; generally
efteemed and beloved for his great virtues ;
he

he crowns all his qualities by an amiable and
fingular modefty. His addrefs is frank, his
countenance open, and his difcourfe fimple.
Thus you cannot fail to love him as foon
as you fee him; efpecially as foon as you
know him. I here defcribe the impreffion
he made on me.

M. de Chaftellux, in making the eulogium
of this refpectable American, has fallen into
an error which I ought to rectify. He fays,
that he has made many voyages to the coaft
of Guinea. It is incredible that this writer
fhould perfift in printing this as a fact, after
Colonel Wadfworth begged him to fupprefs
it. " To advance," faid he, " that I have
" carried on the Guinea trade, is to give the
" idea that I have carried on the flave trade;
" whereas I always had the greateft abhor-
" rence for this infamous traffic. I prayed
" M. de Chaftellux, that in the edition he
" was about to publifh in France, he would
" fupprefs this, as well as many other ftriking
" errors which appeared in the American
" edition of his work; and I cannot conceive
" why he has rectified nothing."

The environs of Hartford difplay a charming cultivated country; neat elegant houfes,

vaft

vaft meadows covered with herds of cattle
of an enormous fize, which furnifh the market of New-York, and even Philadelphia.
You there fee fheep refembling ours; but not,
like ours, watched by fhepherds, and tormented by dogs : hogs of a prodigious fize,
furrounded with numerous families of pigs,
wearing on the neck a triangular piece of
wood, invented to hinder them from paffing
the barriers which inclofe the cultivated
fields ; geefe and turkeys in abundance, as
well as potatoes and all other vegetables.
Productions of every kind are excellent and
cheap : the fruits, however, do not partake
of this excellent quality, becaufe they are lefs
attended to. Apples ferve for making cyder ;
and great quantities of them are likewife
exported.

To defcribe the neighbourhood of Hartford, is to defcribe Connecticut; it is to
defcribe the neighbourhood of Middleton,
of Newhaven, &c. Nature and Art have here
difplayed all their treafures ; it is really the
Paradife of the United States. M. de Crevecœur, who has been fo much reproached with
exaggeration, is even below the truth in his
defcription of this part of the country. Read
again his charming picture, and this reading
will

will fupply the place of what it would be
ufelefs here to repeat.

This ftate owes all its advantages to its
fituation. It is a fertile plain, inclofed between two mountains, which render difficult
its communications by land with the other
ftates. It is wafhed by the fuperb river Connecticut, which falls into the fea, and furnifhes
a fafe and eafy navigation. Agriculture being the bafis of the riches of this ftate, they
are here more equally divided. There is
here more equality, lefs mifery, more fimplicity, more virtue, more of every thing which
conftitutes republicanifm.

Connecticut appears like one continued
town. On quitting Hartford, you enter
Wethersfield, a town not lefs elegant, very
long, confifting of houfes well built. They
tell me it gave birth to the famous Silas
Deane, one of the firft promoters of the
American revolution ; from a fchoolmafter
in this town, elevated to the rank of an Envoy
from Congrefs to Europe : he has fince been
accufed of betraying this glorious caufe. Is
the accufation true, or falfe ? It is difficult
to decide. But he has been for a long time
miferable in London : and it is in favour

of

of the goodnefs of heart of the Americans, to
recount, that his beft friends and benefactors
are ftill among the ancient American Whigs.

Wethersfield is remarkable for its vaft fields
uniformly covered with onions ; of which
great quantities are exported to the Weft-
Indies.   It is likewife remarkable for its elegant meeting-houfe, or church.   On Sunday
it is faid to offer an enchanting fpectacle,
by the number of young handfome perfons,
who affemble there, and by the agreeable
mufic with which they intermingle the divine
fervice.

Newhaven yields not to Wethersfield for
the beauty of the fair fex.   At their balls
during the winter, it is not rare to fee an
hundred charming girls, adorned with thofe
brilliant complexions feldom met with in
journeying to the South, and dreffed in elegant fimplicity.   The beauty of complexion
is as ftriking in Connecticut, as its numerous
population.   You will not go into a tavern
without meeting with neatnefs, decency, and
dignity.   The tables are ferved by a young
girl, decent and pretty; by an amiable mother,
whofe age has not effaced the agreeablenefs of
her features; by men who have that air of dignity

nity which the idea of equality infpires; and who are not ignoble and bafe, like the greateft part of our tavern-keepers. On the road you often meet thofe fair Connecticut girls, either driving a carriage, or alone on horfe-back, galloping boldly; with an elegant hat on the head, a white apron, and a calico gown;—ufages which prove at once the early cultivation of their reafon, fince they are trufted fo young to themfelves, the fafety of the road, and the general innocence of manners. You will fee them hazarding themfelves alone, without protectors, in the public ftages—I am wrong to fay *hazarding;* who can offend them? They are here under the protection of public morals, and of their own innocence: it is the confcioufnefs of this innocence, which renders them fo complaifant, and fo good; for a ftranger takes them by the hand, and laughs with them, and they are not offended at it.

Other proofs of the profperity of Connecticut, are the number of new houfes everywhere to be feen, and the number of rural manufactories arifing on every fide, of which I fhall fpeak hereafter. But even in this ftate there are many lands to fell. A principal caufe of this is the tafte for emigration to the

weftern

weftern country.   The defire of finding better, embitters the enjoyments even of the inhabitants of Connecticut.   Perhaps this tafte
arifes from the hope of efcaping taxes, which,
though fmall, and almoft nothing in comparifon with thofe of Europe, appear very
heavy.   In a country like the United States,
every thing favours the forming of new fettlements.   The new comers are fure, every-
where, of finding friends and brothers, who
fpeak their own language, and admire their
courage.   Provifions are cheap the whole
way ; they have nothing to fear from the
fearch of cuftom-houfe clerks, on entering
from one province to another, nor river-tolls,
nor impofts, nor vexations ;—man is free as
the air he breathes.   The tafte for emigration
is every day augmenting, by the accounts
in the public papers of the arrival of different
families.   Man is like fheep every-where :
he fays, *Such an one has fucceeded, why fhall
not I fucceed ? I am nothing here, I fhall be
fomething on the Ohio ; I work hard here, I
fhall not work fo hard there.*

Before arriving at Middleton, where we
were to breakfaft, we ftopped on the hill
which overlooks that town and the immenfe
valley on which it is built.   It is one of the
fineft

fineft and richeft profpects that I have feen in America. I could not fatiate myfelf with the variety of the fcenes which this landfcape laid before me.

Middleton is built like Hartford: broad ftreets, trees on the fides, and handfome houfes. We changed horfes and carriages at Durham; and after admiring a number of picturefque fituations on the road, we arrived at Newhaven, where we dined. The univer-fity here enjoys a great reputation through the continent; the port is much frequented; the fociety is faid to be very agreeable. New-haven has produced the celebrated poet, Trumbull *, author of the immortal poem M'Fingal, which rivals, if not furpaffes, in keen pleafantry, the famous Hudibras. Colonel Humphreys *, whofe poem, much efteemed in America, is tranflated by M. de Chaftellux, is likewife a native of this town. The uni-verfity is prefided by a refpectable and learn-ed man, Mr. Stiles. We were obliged to quit this charming town, to arrive in the evening at Fairfield. We paffed the incon-venient ferry at Stratford; afterwards, affailed by a violent ftorm, we were well enough

* M. de Warville is here mifinformed. Mr. Trumbull is a native of Waterbury, and Mr. Humphreys of Derby.

defended

defended from it by a double curtain of leather which covered the carriage. The driver, though pierced through with the rain,
continued his route through the obscurity of
a very dark night. Heaven preserved us
from accident, at which I was much astonished. We passed the night at Fairfield, a town
unhappily celebrated in the last war. It experienced all the rage of the English, who
burnt it. You perceive still the vestiges of
this infernal fury. Most of the houses are
rebuilt; but those who have seen this town
before the war, regret its ancient state, and
the air of ease, and even opulence, that then
distinguished it. They shewed me the house
of the richest inhabitant, where all travellers of distinction met an hospitable reception;
and where was often feasted, the infamous
Tryon, who commanded this expedition of
cannibals. Forgetting all sentiments of gratitude and humanity, he treated with the
last extremity of rigour the mistress of this
house, who had received him as a friend;
and after having given her his word for the
safety of her house, he ordered it to be set on
fire. At Fairfield finished the agreeable part of
our journey. From this town to Rye, thirty-
three miles, we had to struggle against rocks
and precipices. I knew not which to admire
most

moſt in the driver, his intrepidity or dexterity. I cannot conceive how he avoided
twenty times daſhing the carriage in pieces,
and how his horſes could retain themſelves in
deſcending the ſtair-caſes of rocks. One of
theſe is called Horſeneck; a chain of rocks
ſo ſteep, that if a horſe ſhould ſlip, the carriage muſt be thrown into a valley two or
three hundred feet.

From Horſeneck we paſſed to New Rochelle, a colony founded the laſt century by
ſome French emigrants, which appears not
to have proſpered. Perhaps this appearance
reſults from the laſt war; for this place ſuffered much from the neighbourhood of the
Engliſh, whoſe head-quarters were at New-
York. This place, however, will always be
celebrated for having given birth to one of
the moſt diſtinguiſhed men of the laſt revolution—a republican remarkable for his firmneſs and his coolneſs, a writer eminent for
his nervous ſtyle, and his cloſe logic, Mr.
Jay, at preſent miniſter of foreign affairs.

The following anecdote will give an idea
of the firmneſs of this republican: at the
time of laying the foundation of the peace in
1783, M. de Vergennes, actuated by ſecret
motives,

motives, wifhed to engage the ambaffadors of Congrefs to confine their demands to the fifheries, and to renounce the weftern territory; that is, the vaft and fertile country beyond the Alleganey mountains. This Minifter required particularly, that the independence of America fhould not be confidered as the bafis of the peace; but, fimply, that it fhould be conditional. To fucceed in this projeft, it was neceffary to gain over Jay and Adams. Mr. Jay declared to M. de Vergennes, that he would fooner lofe his life than fign fuch a treaty; that the Americans fought for independence; that they would never lay down their arms, till it fhould be fully confecrated; that the Court of France had recognifed it, and that there would be a contradiction in her conduct, if fhe fhould deviate from that point. It was not difficult for Mr. Jay to bring Mr. Adams to this determination; and M. de Vergennes could never fhake his firmnefs *.

Confider here the ftrange concurrence of

* The talents of Mr. Jay fhone with diftinguifhed luftre in the convention of the State of New-York for examining the new federal Conftitution. Mr. Clinton, the Governor, at the head of the Antifederialifts, had at firft a great majority; but he could not refift the logic of Mr. Jay, and the eloquence of Mr. Hamilton.

events.

events. The American, who forced the Court of France, and gave laws to the English minister, was the grandson of a French refugee of the last century, who fled to New Rochelle. Thus the descendant of a man, whom Louis XIV. had persecuted with a foolish rage, imposed his decisions on the descendent of that sovereign, in his own palace, a hundred years after the banishment of the ancestor.

Mr. Jay, was equally immoveable by all efforts of the English minister, whom M. de Vergennes had gained to his party. He proved to him, that it was the interest of the English themselves, that the Americans should be independent, and not in a situation which should render them dependent on their ally. He converted him to this sentiment; for his reasoning determined the court of St. James's. When Mr. Jay passed through England to return to America, Lord Shelbourne desired to see him. Accused by the nation of having granted too much to the Americans, he desired to know, in case he had persisted not to accord to the Americans the werstern territory, if they would have continued the war? Mr. Jay answered, that he

he believed it, and that he fhould have advifed it.

It is thirty-one miles from Rye to New-
York.   The road is good, even, and gravelly.
We ftopped at one of the beft taverns I have
feen in America.   It is kept by Mrs. Havi-
land.   We had an excellent dinner, and
cheap.   To other circumftances very agreeable, which gave us good cheer at this houfe,
the air of the miftrefs was infinitely graceful
and obliging; and fhe had a charming daughter, genteel and well educated, who played
very well the forte-piano.   Before arriving
at New-York, we paffed by thofe places
which the Englifh had fo well fortified while
the were mafters of them.   You ftill fee their
different redoubts and fortifications, which
atteft to the eye of the obferver the folly of
this fratricidious war.

LETTER

L E T T E R IV.

Journey from Boston to New-York, by Providence *.

ON the 12th of October, we set out from Boston at half past seven in the morning, and arrived by six in the evening at Providence. It is forty-nine miles; the road good, the soil stoney, gravelly and sandy, and, as usual for such a soil, covered with pines. The country bordering the road, appears neither fertile, nor well peopled : you may here see houses in decay, and children covered with rags. They had, however, good health, and good complexions. The silence which reigns in the other American towns on Sunday, reigns at Providence even on Monday. Every thing here announces the decline of business. Few vessels are to be seen in the port. They were building, however, two distilleries; as if the manufactories of this

---

* Though this journey was made after the date of several of the succeeding letters, it was thought best to insert it here, as an appendage to the other journey by land.

poison

poifon were not already fufficiently numerous in the United States. Whether it be from prejudice or reality, I feemed to perceive everywhere the filence of death, the effect of paper-money. I feemed to fee, in every face, the air of a Jew; the refult of a traffic founded on fraud and fineffe. I feemed to fee, likewife, in every countenance, the effects of the contempt which the other States bear to this, and the confcioufnefs of meriting that contempt. The paper-money at this time was at a difcount of ten for one.

I went from Providence to Newport in a packet-boat. This journey might be made by land ; but I preferred the water. We arrived in feven hours and an half; and during two hours we had contrary wind. This diftance is thirty miles. We never loft fight of land; but it offers nothing picturefque or curious. A few houfes, fome trees, and a fandy foil, are all that appears to the eye.

The port of Newport is confidered as one of the beft in the United States. The bottom is good, the harbour capable of receiving the largeft fhips, and feems deftined by nature to be of great confequence. This place was

one

one of the principal fcenes of the laft war. The fucceffive arrival of the American, Englifh, and French armies, left here a confiderable quantity of money*.

Since the peace, every thing is changed †. The reign of folitude is only interrupted by groups of idle men, ftanding with folded arms at the corners of the ftreets; houfes falling to ruin; miferable fhops, which prefent nothing but a few coarfe ftuffs, or bafkets of apples, and other articles of little value; grafs growing in the public fquare, in front of the court of juftice; rags ftuffed in the windows, or hung upon hideous women and lean unquiet children.

Every thing announces mifery, the triumph of ill faith, and the influence of a bad government. You will have a perfect idea of it, by calling to mind the impreffion once made upon us on entering the city of Liege. Recollect the crowd of mendicants befieging us at every ftep, to implore charity; that irregular mafs of Gothic houfes falling to

* The Englifh deftroyed all the fine trees of ornament and fruit: they took a pleafure in devaftation.

† This town owed a part of its profperity to the flave trade, which is at prefent fuppreffed.

ruin,

ruin, windows without glafs, roofs half un-
covered; recall to your mind the figures of
men fcarcely bearing the print of humanity,
children in tatters, and houfes hung with rags;
in fhort, reprefent to yourfelf the afylum of
famine, the rafcallity and the impudence that
general mifery infpires, and you will recollect
Liege, and have an image of Newport.

Thefe two places are neverthelefs well fituated for commerce, and furrounded by lands
by no means unfruitful; but at Liege, the productions of the country ferve to fatten about
fifiy idle ecclefiaftics, who, by the aid of ancient
religious prejudices, riot in pleafure, in the
midft of thoufands of unhappy wretches who
are dying with hunger*. At Newport, the
people, deceived by two or three knaves,
have brought on their own mifery, and
deftroyed the bleffings which Nature had
lavifhed upon them. They have themfelves
fanctified fraud; and this act has rendered
them odious to their neighbours, driven commerce from their doors, and labour from
their fields.

* When I wrote thefe lines, I was far from forefeeing the
revolutions of Liege. Liberty difplays her banners there. God
grant that fhe may triumph, and atchieve her work !

Read

Read again, my friend, the charming defcription given of this town and this State, by M. de Crevecœur. It is not exaggerated. Every American whom I have queftioned on this fubject, has defcribed to me its ancient fplendor, and its natural advantages, whether for commerce, agriculture, or the enjoyments of life.

The State of Rhode-Ifland will never again fee thofe happy days, till they take from circulation their paper-money, and reform their government. The magiftrates fhould be lefs dependent on the people than they are at prefent, and the members of the legifla-ture fhould not be fo often elected. It is inconceivable that fo many honeft people fhould groan under the prefent anarchy; that fo many Quakers, who compofe the bafis of the population of this State, fhould not com-bine together to introduce this reform *.— If this reform is not fpeedily executed, I doubt not but the State will be unpeopled.

---

* The author is happy to find, that before the publication of this letter, this State has acceded to the new federal govern-ment. This fact proves, that good principles will predominate at laft, and particular abufes will difappear.

A great

A great part of the emigration for the fettlement at Mufkingum on the Ohio, is from
this State.   General Varnum is at their head.
A number of families are preparing to join
them.   Nearly all the honeft people of Newport would quit the place, if they could fell
their effects.   I doubt not, likewife, but the
example of Rhode-Ifland will be a proof,
in the eyes of many people, that republican
government is difaftrous.   This would be a
wrong conclufion:—this example only proves,
that there fhould not be a too frequent rota-
tion in the legiflative power, and that there
ought to be a ftability in the executive; that
there is as much danger in placing the magiftrates in a ftate of too great dependence on
the people, as there is in making them too
independent.   It argues, in fact, againft a
pure democracy, but not againft a *reprefentative democracy*; for a reprefentation of fix
months, is but a government by the people
themfelves.   Reprefentation, in this cafe, is
but a fhadow, which paffes too fuddenly to
be perceived, or to feel its own exiftence.
Of confequence, this example proves nothing
againft the wife fyftem of reprefentation, more
durable, more independent, and which conftitutes the true republican government, fuch as
that

that of the other United States. But in the
midſt of theſe diſorders, you hear nothing of
robberies, of murders, or of mendicity; for
the American poor does not degrade himſelf
ſo far as to abjure all ideas of equity, and all
ſhame. And this is a trait which ſtill marks
a difference between Newport and Liege;
the Rhode-Iſlander does not beg, and he
does not ſteal—the ancient American blood
ſtill runs in his veins.

I was detained at Newport by the ſouth-
weſt winds, till the 13th, when we ſet
ſail at midnight; the Captain not wiſh-
ing to ſail ſooner, for fear of touching
before day on Block-Iſland. The wind
and tide carried us at the rate of nine
or ten miles an hour; and we ſhould have
arrived at New-York the next evening, but
we were detained at Hell-Gate, a kind of
gulph, eight miles from New-York. This is
a narrow paſſage, formed by the approach of
Long-Iſland to York-Iſland, and rendered
horrible by rocks, concealed at high water.
The whirlpool of this gulph is little perceived
at low water; but it is not ſurpriſing that
veſſels which know it not, ſhould be daſhed
in pieces. They ſpeak of an Engliſh frigate
loſt

loft there the laft war. This Hell-Gate is
an obftacle to the navigation of this ftrait;
but it is not rare in fummer to run from
Newport to New-York, two hundred miles,
in twenty hours. As you approach this city,
the coafts of thefe two iflands prefent the
moft agreeable fpectacle. They are adorned
with elegant country-houfes. Long-Ifland
is celebrated for its high ftate of cultivation.
The price of paffage and your table from
Providence to New-York is fix dollars.

I ought to fay one word of the packet-
boats of this part of America, and of the
facilities which they offer. Though, in my
opinion, it is more advantageous, and often
lefs expenfive, to go by land; yet I owe
fome praifes to the cleanlinefs and good order
obfervable in thefe boats. The one which I
was in contained fourteen beds, ranged in
two rows, one above the other; every one
had its little window. The chamber was
well aired; fo that you do not breathe that
naufeous air which infects the packets of the
Englifh channel. It was well varnifhed;
and two clofe corners were made in the poop.
which ferve as private places, The provifions were good. There is not a little town
on

on all this coaſt, but what has this kind of packets going to New-York; ſuch as, New-haven, New-London, &c. They have all the ſame neatneſs, the ſame embelliſhment, the ſame convenience for travellers. You may be aſſured, that there is nothing like it on the old continent.

LETTER

LETTER V.

On NEW-YORK.

Auguſt 1788.

I HAVE read again, my dear friend, the deſcription given by Mr. Crevecœur, of this part of the United States; and after having compared all the articles of it with what I have ſeen, I muſt declare, that all the traits of his picture are juſt.

Nothing is more magnificent than the ſituation of this town—between two majeſtic rivers, the north and the eaſt. The former ſeparates it from New Jerſey: it is ſo profound, that ſhips of the line anchor in it. I have at this moment under my eyes, a French ſhip of 1200 tons, deſtined to the Eaſt-India trade, which has come into it to refit. Two inconveniences are, however, experienced in this river; the deſcent of ice in the winter, and the force of the north-weſt wind. Ships mount this commodious river as far as Albany, a town ſituated an hundred and ſeventy miles from New-York.

Albany

Albany will yield very foon, in profperity, to a town called Hudfon, built on a fpot where, four years ago, there was only a fimple farm-houfe. At prefent, it contains an hundred good dwelling-houfes, a court-houfe, public fountains, &c. More than fifty fhips are owned there, which export the American productions to the Iflands and to Europe. Two whaleing fhips are of the number. Their veffels do not winter idly, like thofe of Albany, in the port. They trade in the Weft Indies during this feafon. Poughkeepfie, on the fame river, has doubled its population and its commerce fince the war. The inattention of the people of Albany to foreign commerce, may be attributed to the fertility of their lands. Agriculture abounds there, and they like not to hazard themfelves to the dangers of the fea, for a fortune which they can draw from the bounty of the foil which furrounds them. The fertility of the uncultivated lands, and the advantages which they offer, attract fettlers to this quarter. New fettlements are forming here; but flowly, becaufe other ftates furnifh lands, if not as fertile, at leaft attended with more advantages for agriculture, as they are lefs expofed to the exceffive rigours of fo long a winter.

When

When this part of America fhall be well
peopled, the north river will offer one of the
fineft channels for the exportation of its productions. Navigable for more than two hundred miles from the ocean, it communicates
with the river Mohawk, with the lakes
Oneida, Ontario, Erie, and all that part of
Canada. The falls which are found in this
route may be eafily vanquifhed by canals, fo
eafy to conftruct in a country abounding
with men and money. This river communicates with Canada in another quarter, by
the lakes George and Champlaine. It is this
fituation which will render New-York the
channel of the fur-trade, at leaft during the
exiftence of this kind of commerce, which
fuppofes the exiftence of favages, and great
quantities of uncultivated lands.

By the Eaft River, New-York communicates with Long-Ifland, and with all the
Eaftern States. Ships of the line anchor
likewife in this river, and near the quay,
where they are fheltered from the ftorms
which fometimes ravage thefe coafts. This
happy fituation of New-York will explain to
you the caufes why the Englifh give it the
preference over the other parts of America.
Being the great market for Connecticut and

New-

New-Jerfey, it pours in upon thofe States the productions of the Eaft Indies, and of Europe. It is difficult to obtain an account of the exportations and importations of this State. Colonel Lamb, who is at the head of the cuftom-houfe, invelopes all his operations in the moft profound myftery; it is an effect of the Dutch fpirit, which ftill governs this city. The Dutchman conceals his gains and his commerce; he lives but for himfelf. I have been able, however, to procure fome details, which you will find in the general table, of the commerce of the United States. The Englifh have a great predilection for this city, and for its productions; thus its port is always covered with Englifh fhips. They prefer even its wheat; fo that the American merchants bring wheat from Virginia, and fell it for that of New-York.

The prefence of Congrefs with the diplomatic body and the concourfe of ftrangers, contributes much to extend here the ravages of luxury. The inhabitants are far from complaining at it; they prefer the fplendour of wealth, and the fhow of enjoyment, to the fimplicity of manners, and the pure pleafures refulting from it. The ufage of fmoking has not difappeared in this town, with

with the other cuftoms of their fathers, the
Dutch. They fmoke cigars, which come
from the Spanifh iflands. They are leaves
of tobacco, rolled in form of a tube, of fix
inches long, which are fmoked without the
aid of any inftrument. This ufage is re-
volting to the French. It may appear dif-
agreeable to the women, by deftroying the
purity of the breath. The philofopher condemns it, as it is a fuperfluous want.

It has, however, one advantage ; it accuftoms to meditation, and prevents loquacity.
The fmoker afks a queftion ; the anfwer
comes two minutes after, and it is well-
founded. The cigar renders to a man the
fervice that the philofopher drew from the
glafs of water, which he drank when he
was in anger.

The great commerce of this city, and the
facility of living here, augments the population of the State with great rapidity. In 1773,
they reckoned 148,124 whites ; in 1786,
the number was 219,996.

If there is a town on the American continent where the Englifh luxury difplays its
follies, it is New-York. You will find here
the

the Englifh fafhions. In the drefs of the women, you will fee the moft brilliant filks,
gauzes, hats, and borrowed hair. Equipages
are rare ; but they are elegant. The men
have more fimplicity in their drefs ; they difdain gewgaws, but they take their revenge
in the luxury of the table.

Luxury forms already, in this town, a clafs
of men very dangerous in fociety—I mean
bachelors. The expence of women caufes
matrimony to be dreaded by men.

Tea forms, as in England, the bafis of the
principal parties of pleafure. Fruits, though
more attended to in this State, are far from
poffeffing the beauty and goodnefs of thofe
of Europe. I have feen trees, in September,
loaded at once with apples and with flowers.

M. de Crevecœur is right in his defcription of the abundance and good quality of
provifions at New-York, in vegetables, flefh,
and efpecially in fifh. It is difficult to unite
fo many advantages in one place. Provifions
are dearer at New-York, than in any other of
the northern or middle States. Many things,
efpecially thofe of luxury, are dearer here
than in France. A hair-dreffer afks twenty
                                    fhillings

shillings per month; washing costs four shillings for a dozen pieces.

Strangers, who, having lived a long time in America, tax the Americans with cheating, have declared to me, that this accusation must be confined to the towns, and that in the country you will find them honest. The French are the most forward in making these complaints; and they believe that the Americans are more trickish with them than with the English. If this were a fact, I should not be astonished at it. The French, whom I have seen, are eternally crying up the services which their nation has rendered to the Americans, and opposing their manners and customs, decrying their government, exalting the favours rendered by the French government towards the Americans, and diminishing those of Congress to the French.

One of the greatest errors of travellers is to calculate prices of provisions in a country, by the prices in taverns and boarding-houses. It is a false basis; we should take, for the town, the price at the market, and this is about half the price that one pays at the tavern. This basis would be still false, if it were applied to the country. There are many articles

ticles which are abundant in the country, and are scarcely worth the trouble of collecting and bringing to market. These reflections appear to me necessary to put one on his guard against believing too readily in the prices estimated by hasty travellers. Other circumstances likewise influence the price; such, for example, as war, which Mr. Chastellux takes no notice of in his exaggerated account of American prices.

These prices were about double in New-York during the war, to what they are now. Boarding and lodging by the week, is from four to six dollars. The fees of lawyers are out of all proportion ; they are, as in England, excessive. Physicians have not the same advantage in this respect as lawyers : the good health generally enjoyed here, renders them little necessary ; yet they are sufficiently numerous.

I conversed with some of them, and asked what were the diseases most common ? They told me, bilious fevers ; and that the greatest part of diseases among them, were occasioned by excessive cold, and the want of care ; but there are few diseases here, added they. The air is pure ; the inhabitants are
tolerably

tolerably temperate; the people in good circumftances, are not fufficiently rich to give
themfelves up to thofe debaucheries which
kill fo many in Europe; and there are no
poor, provifions being fo cheap.

Let thofe men who doubt the prodigious
effects that liberty produces on man, and on
his induftry, tranfport themfelves to America.
What miracles will they here behold! Whilft
every-where in Europe the villages and towns
are falling to ruin, rather than augmenting,
new edifices are here rifing on all fides. New-
York was in great part confumed by fire in
the time of the war. The veftiges of this
terrible conflagration difappear; the activity
which reigns every-where, announces a rifing
pofterity; they enlarge in every quarter, and
extend their ftreets. Elegant buildings, in
the Englifh ftyle, take place of thofe fharp-
roofed floping houfes of the Dutch. You
find fome ftill ftanding in the Dutch ftyle;
they afford fome pleafure to the European
obferver; they trace to him the origin of
this colony, and the manners of thofe who
inhabit it, whilft they call to his mind the
ancient Belgic State.

I walk out by the fide of the North River;
what

what a rapid change in the fpace of fix
weeks! The river is forced back 200 feet,
and, by a fimple mechanifm, they have conftructed a kind of encafement, compofed of
large trunks of trees croffing each other at
convenient diftances, and faftened together
by ftrong beams. They conduct this floating
dyke to the place where it is to be fixed, and
where there is often forty feet of water. Arrived at its deftination, it is funk with an
enormous weight of ftones. On a l fides,
houfes are rifing, and ftreets extending: I
fee nothing but bufy workmen building and
repairing.

At the fame time they are erecting a building for Congrefs. They are likewife repairing the hofpital: this building is in a bad
condition; not a fick perfon could be lodged
in it at the end of the war; it was a building almoft abandoned : they have reftored the
adminiftration of it to the Quakers, from
whom it had been taken away during the
war; they have ordered it to be repaired, and
the reparations are executing with the greateft vigor. This building is vaft; it is of brick,
and perfectly well-fituated on the bank of the
North River. It enjoys every advantage : air
the moft falubrious, that may be renewed at
pleafure;

pleafure ; water in abundance ; pleafant and extenfive walks for the fick ; magnificent and agreeable profpects ; out of the town, and yet fufficiently near it.

It is likewife to the Quakers, to thefe men fo much calumniated, of whom I fhall fpeak more fully hereafter, that is owing the order obfervable in the work-houfe, of which they have the fuperintendance.

It is to their zeal that is to be attributed the formation of the fociety for the abolition of flavery. As I fhall confecrate to this import-ant article a particular chapter, I fhall not fpeak of it here.

A fociety of a more pompous title, but whofe fervices are lefs real, has been lately formed. Its object is the general promotion of fcience and ufeful knowledge. They affemble rarely, and they do nothing. They have, however, eight hundred pounds in the bank, which remain idle. Their prefident is Governor Clinton ; and he is any other thing rather than a man of learning.

This fociety will have little fuccefs here— the Dutch are no lovers of letters.

But

But though men of learning do not abound in this city, the prefence of Congrefs attracts, from time to time, at leaft from all parts of America, the moft celebrated men. I have feen particularly, Meffrs. Jay, Maddifon, Hamilton, King, and Thornton. I have already fpoke to you of the firft.

The name of Maddifon, celebrated in America, is well known in Europe, by the merited elogium made of him by his countryman and friend, Mr. Jefferfon.

Though ftill young, he has rendered the greateft fervices to Virginia, to the American confederation, and to liberty and humanity in general. He contributed much, with Mr. White, in reforming the civil and criminal codes of his country. He diftinguifhed himfelf particularly, in the conventions for the acceptation of the new federal fyftem. Virginia balanced a long time in adhering to it. Mr. Maddifon determined to it the members of the convention, by his eloquence and his logic. This republican appears to be but about thirty-three years of age. He had, when I faw him, an air of fatigue; perhaps it was the effect of the immenfe labours to which he has devoted himfelf for fome time paft.

paft. His look announces a cenfor; his converfation difcovers the man of learning; and
his referve was that of a man confcious of
his talents and of his duties.

During the dinner, to which he invited
me, they fpoke of the refufal of North Carolina to accede to the new conftitution. The
majority againft it was one hundred. Mr.
Maddifon believed that this refufal would
have no weight on the minds of the Americans, and that it would not impede the operations of Congrefs. I told him, that though
this refufal might be regarded as a trifle in
America, it would have great weight in Europe; that they would never enquire there
into the motives which dictated it, nor confider the fmall confequence of this State in
the confederation; that it would be regarded as a germe of divifion, calculated to retard
the operations of Congrefs; and that certainly this idea would prevent the refurrection of
the American credit.

Mr. Maddifon attributed this refufal to the
attachment of a great part of the inhabitants
of that State to their paper-money, and their
tender-act. He was much inclined to believe, that this difpofition would not remain
a long time.

Mr.

Mr. Hamilton is the worthy fellow-labourer of Mr. Maddifon : his figure announces a man of thirty-eight or forty years; he is not tall; his countenance is decided; his air is open and martial : he was aid-de-camp to General Wafhington, who had great confidence in him ; and he well merited it. Since the peace, he has taken the profeffion of the law, and devoted himfelf principally to public affairs. He has diftinguifhed himfelf in Congrefs, by his eloquence, and the folidity of his reafoning. Among the works which have come from his pen, the moft diftinguifhed are, a number of letters inferted in the Federalift, of which I fhall have occafion to fpeak hereafter ; and the letters of Phocion, in favour of the royalifts. Mr. Hamilton had fought them with fuccefs during the war. At the eftablifhment of peace, he was of opinion, that it was not beft to drive them to defpair by a rigorous perfecution. And he had the happinefs to gain over to thefe mild fentiments, thofe of his compatriots, whofe refentment had been juftly excited againft thefe people, for the woes they had brought on their country.

This young orator triumphed again in the convention of the State of New-York, where

the

the antifederal party was numerous.   When
the convention was formed at Poughkeepfie,
three quarters of the members were oppofed
to the new fyftem.   Mr. Hamilton, joining
his efforts to thofe of the celebrated Jay, fucceeded in convincing the moft obftinate, that
the refufal of New-York would entrain the
greateft misfortunes to that State, and to the
Confederation.   The conftitution was adopted ; the feaft which followed the ratification
in New-York, was magnificent ; the fhip Federalift, which was drawn in proceffion, was
named Hamilton, in honour of this eloquent
fpeaker.

He has married the daughter of General
Schuyler, a charming woman, who joins to
the graces all the candour and fimplicity of
an American wife.   At dinner, at his houfe,
I found General Miflin, who diftinguifhed
himfelf for his activity in the laft war.   To
the vivacity of a Frenchman, he appears to
unite every obliging characteriftic.

Mr. King, whom I faw at this dinner,
paffes for the moft eloquent man of the
United States.   What ftruck me moft in him,
was his modefty.   He appears ignorant of
his own worth.   Mr. Hamilton has the de-
terminéd

termined air of a republican. Mr. Maddifon, the meditative air of a profound politician.

At this dinner, as at moft others which I made in America, they drank the health of M. de la Fayette. The Americans confider him as one of the heroes of their liberty. He merits their love and efteem ; they have not a better friend in France. His generofity to them has been manifefted on all public occafions, and ftill more in private circum-ftances, where benefits remain unknown. It is not, perhaps, to the honour of France, or the Frenchmen who have been in America, to recount the fact, That he is the only one who has fuccoured the unhappy fufferers in the fire at Bofton *, and the only one whofe doors are open to the Americans.

Doctor Thornton, intimately connected with the Americans whom I have mention-ed, runs a different career, that of humanity. Though, by his appearance, he does not be-long to the Society of Friends, he has their principles, and practifes their morals with regard to the blacks. He told me the ef-forts which he has made for the execution of a vaft project conceived by him for their

* He gave £. 300 fterling.

benefit.

benefit. Perfuaded that there never can exift a fincere union between the whites and the blacks, even on admitting the latter to the rights of freemen, he propofes to fend them back, and eftablifh them in Africa. This plan is frightful at the firft afpect; but, on examination, it appears to be neceffary and advantageous. I fhall not enter upon it here, but referve it for my letter on the ftate of the blacks in this country.—Mr. Thornton, who appears, by his vivacity and his agreeable manners, to belong to the French nation, is born at Antigua: his mother has a plantation there. It is there that, inftead of hardening his heart to the fate of the negroes, as moft of the planters do, he has acquired that humanity, that compaffion for them, with which he is fo much tormented. He told me, he fhould have fet his flaves at liberty, if it had been in his power; but not being able to do this, he treats them like men.

I cannot finifh this letter without fpeaking of another American, whofe talents in finance are well known here; it is Colonel Duer, fecretary to the board of treafury. It is difficult to unite to a great facility in calculation, more extenfive views and a quicker penetration

tion into the moſt complicated projeꞓts. To
theſe qualities he joins goodneſs of heart;
and it is to his obliging charaꞓter, and his
zeal, that I owe much valuable information
on the finances of this country, which I ſhall
communicate hereafter.

I ſhould ſtill be wanting in gratitude, ſhould
I negleꞓt to mention the politeneſs and attention ſhewed me by the Preſident of Congreſs, Mr. Griffin. He is a Virginian, of
very good abilities, of an agreeable figure,
affable, and polite. I ſaw at his houſe, at
dinner, ſeven or eight women, all dreſſed in
great hats, plumes, &c. It was with pain
that I remarked much of pretenſion in ſome
of theſe women; one aꞓted the giddy, viva-
cious; another, the woman of ſentiment. This
laſt had many pruderies and grimaces. Two
among them had their boſoms very naked.
I was ſcandalized at this indecency among
republicans.

A Preſident of Congreſs is far from being
ſurrounded with the ſplendour of European
monarchs; and ſo much the better. He is
not durable in his ſtation; and ſo much the
better. He never forgets that he is a ſimple
citizen, and will ſoon return to the ſtation of
one.

one. He does not give pompous dinners; and fo much the better. He has fewer parafites, and lefs means of corruption.

I remarked, that his table was freed from many ufages obferved elfewhere ;—no fatiguing prefentations, no toafts, fo defpairing in a numerous fociety. Little wine was drank after the women had retired. Thefe traits will give you an idea of the temperance of this country ; temperance, the leading virtue of republicans.

I ought to add one word on the finances of this State. The facility of raifing an impoft on foreign commerce, puts them in a fituation to pay, with punctuality, the expences of the Government, the intereft of their State debt, and their part of the civil lift of Congrefs. Their revenues are faid to amount to £. 80,000, money of New-York. The expences of the city and county of New-York amounted, in 1787, to one-eighth of of this fum, that is, to £. 10,110. I will add here a ftate of thefe expences:

Salaries - - - - - - £.	37	10 —
Elections - - - - - -	62	12 —
Carried over — £. 100	2	—

		£	s	d
Brought over —		100	2	—
Pumps and wells - - - -		204	8	4
Roads and ftreets - - - -		734	2	1
Poor houfes - - - - -		3,791	14	4
Bridewell, or houfe of correction		899	11	4
Lamps - - - - - -		1,439	19	—
Night watch - - - - -		1,931	2	—
Prifoners - - - - - -		372	18	10
Repairs of public buildings -		342	15	11
Quays - - - - - - -		25	—	—
City of New-York - - -		137	19	—
County of New-York - -		130	9	—
	£	10,110	1	10

The bank of New-York enjoys a good reputation; it is well adminiftered. Its cafhier is Mr. William Seton, to whom Mr. de Crevecœur has addreffed his letters; and what will give you a good idea of his integrity, is, that he was chofen to this important place notwithftanding his known attachment to the Englifh caufe. This bank receives and pays, without reward, for merchants and others, who choofe to open an accompt with it.

L E T-

LETTER VI.

Journey from New-York to Philadelphia.

I WENT from New-York the 25th of Auguſt, at ſix o'clock in the morning; and had the north river to paſs before arriving to the ſtage. We paſſed the ferry in an open boat, and landed at Paulus Hook : they reckon two miles for this ferry, for which we pay ſixpence, money of New-York.

The carriage is a kind of open waggon, hung with double curtains of leather and woollen, which you raiſe or let fall at pleaſure : it is not well ſuſpended. But the road was ſo fine, being ſand and gravel, that we felt no inconvenience from that circumſtance. The horſes are good, and go with rapidity. Theſe carriages have four benches, and may contain twelve perſons. The light baggage is put under the benches, and the trunks fixed on behind. A traveller who does not chooſe to take the ſtage, has a one-horſe carriage by himſelf.

Let

Let the Frenchmen who have travelled in thefe carriages, compare them to thofe ufed in France; to thofe heavy diligences, where eight or ten perfons are ftuffed in together; to thofe cabriolets in the environs of Paris, where two perfons are clofely confined, and deprived of air, by a dirty driver, who torments his miferable jades: and thofe carriages have to run over the fineft roads, and yet make but one league an hour. If the Americans had fuch roads, with what rapidity would they travel? fince, notwithftanding the inconvenience of the roads, they now run ninety-fix miles in a day. Thus, with only a century and a half of exiftence, and oppofed by a thoufand obftacles, they are already fuperior to people who have been undifturbed in their progrefs of fifteen centuries.

You find in thefe ftages, men of all profeffions. They fucceed each other with rapidity. One who goes but twenty miles, yields his place to one who goes farther. The mother and daughter mount the ftage to go ten miles to dine; another ftage brings them back. At every inftant, then, you are making new acquaintances. The frequency
of

of thefe carriages, the facility of finding
places in them, and the low and fixed price,
invite the Americans to travel. Thefe carriages have another advantage, they keep up
the idea of equality. The member of Congrefs is placed by the fide of the fhoemaker
who elected him: they fraternize together,
and converfe with familiarity. You fee no
perfon here taking upon himfelf thofe important airs, which you too often meet with
in France. In that country, a man of condition would blufh to travel in a diligence: it
is an ignoble carriage; one knows not with
whom he may find himfelf. Befides, it is in
ftyle *to run poft;* this ftyle ferves to humiliate
thofe who are condemned to a fad mediocrity.
From this inequality refult envy, the tafte for
luxury, oftentation, an avidity for gain, the
habit of mean and guilty meafures to acquire
wealth. It is then fortunate for America,
that the nature of things prevents this diftinction in the mode of travelling.

The artizan, or the labourer, who finds
himfelf in one of thefe ftages with a man in
place, compofes himfelf, is filent; or if he
endeavours to rife to the level of others by
taking part in the converfation, he at leaft
gains

gains inftruction. The man in place has lefs
haughtinefs, and is facilitated in gaining a
knowledge of the people.

The fon of Governor Livingfton was in
the ftage with me; I fhould not have found
him out, fo civil and eafy was his air, had
not the tavern-keepers from time to time addreffed him with refpectful familiarity. I am
told that the governor himfelf often ufes
thofe ftages. You may have an idea of this
refpectable man, who is at once a writer, a
governor, and a plowman, on learning that
he takes a pride in calling himfelf a New Jerfey farmer.

The American ftages, then, are the true
political carriages. I know that the *petits
maitres* of France would prefer a gay well-
fufpended chariot; but thefe carriages roll
in countries of Baftilles, in countries afflicted
with great inequality, and confequently with
great mifery.

The road from New-York to Newark
is in part over a marfh: I found it really
aftonifhing; it recals to mind the indefatigable induftry of the ancient Dutch fettlers,
mentioned by Mr. de Crevecœur. Built
wholly

wholly of wood, with much labour and perfeverance in the midft of water, on a foil
that trembles under your feet, it proves to
what point may be carried the patience of
man, who is determined to conquer nature.

But though much of thefe marfhes are
drained, there remains a large extent of them
covered with ftagnant waters, which infect
the air, and give birth to thofe mufquitoes
with which you are cruelly tormented, and
to an epidemical fever which makes great
ravages in fummer; a fever known likewife
in Virginia and in the Southern States, in
parts adjacent to the fea. I am affured that
the upper parts of New-Jerfey are exempt
from this fever, and from mufquitoes; but
this State is ravaged by a political fcourge,
more terrible than either; it is paper money.
This paper is ftill, in New-Jerfey, what the
people call a legal tender; that is, you are
obliged to receive it at its nominal value, as a
legal payment.

I faw, in this journey, many inconveniences
refulting from this fictitious money. It gives
birth to an infamous kind of traffic, that of
buying and felling it, by deceiving the ignorant; a commerce which difcourages induftry,

try, corrupts the morals, and is a great detri-
ment to the public. This kind of ftock-job-
ber is the enemy to his fellow-citizens. He
makes a fcience of deceiving; and this fcience is extremely contagious. It introduces
a general diftruft. A perfon can neither fell
his land, nor borrow money upon it; for
fellers and lenders may be paid in a medium
which may ftill depreciate, they know not to
what degree it may depreciate. A friend
dares not truft his friend. Inflances of perfidy of this kind have been known, that are
horrible. Patriotifm is confequently at an
end, cultivation languifhes, and commerce
declines. How is it poffible, faid I to Mr.
Livingfton, that a country, fo rich, can have
recourfe to paper-money? New-Jerfey furnifhes productions in abundance to New-
York and Philadelphia. She draws money,
then, conftantly from thofe places; fhe is
their creditor. And fhall a creditor make ufe
of a refource which can be proper only for a
miferable debtor? How is it that the members of your legiflature have not made thefe
reflections? The reafon of it is very fimple,
replied he: At the clofe of the ruinous war,
that we have experienced, the greater part of
our citizens were burdened with debts. They
faw, in this paper-money, the means of ex-
tricating

tricating themfelves; and they had influence
enough with their reprefentatives to force
them to create it.—But the evil falls at length
on the authors of it, faid I; they muft be
paid themfelves, as well as pay others, in this
fame paper; and why do they not fee that it
difhonours their country, that it ruins all
kinds of honeft induftry, and corrupts the
morals of the people? Why do they not re-
peal this *legal tender?* A ftrong intereft op-
pofes it, replied he, of ftock-jobbers and fpeculators. They wifh to prolong this miferable game, in which they are fure to be the
winners, though the ruin of their country
fhould be the confequence. We expect relief only from the new conftitution, which
takes away from the States the power of
making paper-money. All honeft people wifh
the extinction of it, when filver and gold
would re-appear; and our national induftry
would foon repair the ravages of the war.

From Newark we went to dine at New-
Brunfwick, and to fleep at Trenton. The
road is bad between the two laft places, efpecially after a rain; it is a road difficult to be
kept in repair. We paffed by Prince-Town;
this part of New-Jerfey is very well cultivated. Mr. de Crevecœur has not exaggerated

rated in his defcription of it. All the towns
are well built, whether in wood, ftone, or
brick. Thefe places are too well known in
the military annals of this country, to require
that I fhould fpeak of them. The taverns
are much dearer on this road, than in Maffachufetts and Connecticut: I paid at Trenton, for a dinner, three fhillings and fixpence,
money of Pennfylvania.

We paffed the ferry from Trenton at feven
in the morning. The Delaware, which feparates Pennfylvania from New-Jerfey, is a fuperb river, navigable for the largeft fhips. Its
navigation is intercepted by the ice during
two months in the year. Veffels are not attacked here by thofe worms, which are fo
deftructive to them in rivers farther fouth.

The profpect from the middle of the river
is charming: on the right, you fee mills and
manufactories; on the left, two charming
little towns, which overlook the water.
The borders of this river are ftill in their
wild ftate. In the forefts, which cover
them, are fome enormous trees. There are
likewife fome houfes; but they are not equal,
in point of fimple elegance, to thofe of Maffachufetts.

We

We breakfafted at Briftol, a town oppofite to Burlington. It was here that the famous Penn firft planted his tabernacles. But it was reprefented to him, that the river here did not furnifh anchoring ground fo good and fo fafe as the place already inhabited by the Swedes, where Philadelphia has fince been built. He refolved, then, to purchafe this place of them, give them other lands in exchange, and to leave Briftol.

Paffing the river Shammony, on a new bridge, and then the village of Frankford, we arrived at Philadelphia, by a fine road bordered with the beft cultivated fields, and elegant houfes, which announce the neighbourhood of a great town.

LETTER

LETTER VII.

Journey to Burlington.

Aug. 27. 1788.

I HAD paffed but few hours at Philadelphia, when a particular bufinefs called me to Burlington, on the borders of the Delaware. It is an elegant little town, more ancient than Philadelphia. Many of the inhabitants are Friends, or Quakers: this was formerly their place of general rendezvous.

From thence I went to the country-houfe of Mr. Temple Franklin. He is the grand-fon of the celebrated Franklin; and as well known in France for his amiable qualities, as for his general information. His houfe is five miles from Burlington, on a fandy foil, covered with a foreft of pines. His houfe is fimple, his garden is well kept, he has a good library, and his fituation feems deftined for the retreat of a philofopher.

I dined here with five or fix Frenchmen, who began their converfation with invectives

againft

againſt America and the Americans, againſt
their want of laws, their paper-money, and
their ill faith.   I defended the Americans, or
rather I deſired to be inſtructed by facts; for
I was determined no more to believe in the
opinions of individuals.

You wiſh for facts, ſaid one of them, who
had exiſted in this country for three years:
I will give you ſome.—I ſay that the country
is a miſerable one.   In New-Jerſey, where
we now are, there is no money, there is
nothing but paper.   The money is locked up,
ſaid Mr. Franklin.   Would you have a man
be fool enough to exchange it for depreciated
rags?   Wait till the law ſhall take the paper
from circulation.—But you cannot borrow
money on the beſt ſecurity.   I believe it,
ſaid Mr. Franklin; the lender fears to be
paid in paper.—Theſe facts prove not the
ſcarcity of money, but the prudence of thoſe
who hold it, and the influence that debtors
have in the legiſlature.

They paſſed to another point.   Your laws
are arbitrary, and often unjuſt: for inſtance,
there is a law laying a tax of a dollar on the
ſecond dog; and this tax augments in proportion to the number that a man keeps.
Thus

Thus a labourer has need of dogs; but he is deprived of their fuccour. He has no need of them, faid Mr. Franklin, he keeps them but for his pleafure; and if any thing ought to be taxed, it is pleafure. The dogs are injurious to the fheep; inftead of defending them, they often kill them. I was one of the firft to folicit this law, becaufe we are infefted with dogs from this quarter. To get rid of them, we have put a tax on them, and it has produced falutary effects. The money arifing from this tax, is deftined to indemnify thofe whofe fheep are deftroyed by thefe animals.

My Frenchman returned to the charge :— But your taxes are extremely heavy. You fhall judge of that, fays Mr. Franklin : I have an eftate here of five or fix hundred acres; my taxes laft year amounted to eight pounds, in paper money; this reduced to hard money, is fix pounds.

Nothing can be more conclufive than thofe replies. I am fure, however, that this Frenchman has forgot them all; and that he will go and declare in France, that the taxes in New-Jerfey are diftreffingly heavy, and that the impofition on dogs is abominable.

                                        Burlington

Burlington is feparated from Briftol only by the river.   Here is fome commerce, and fome men of confiderable capital.' The children here have that air of health and decency, which characterifes the fect of the Quakers.

LETTER

LETTER VIII.

Aug. 28; 1788;

ON returning from Burlington, I went with Mr. Shoemaker to the houfe of his father-in-law, Mr. Richardfon, a farmer, who lives near Middleton, twenty-two miles from Philadelphia.

Mr. Shoemaker is thirty years of age; he was not educated in the fect of Friends: he declared to me that, in his youth, he was far from their principles; that he had lived in pleafure; that growing weary of them, he reflected on his conduct, and refolved to change it; that he ftudied the principles of the Quakers, and foon became a member of their fociety, notwithftanding the railleries of his friends. He had married the daughter of this quaker, to whofe houfe we were going. I wifhed to fee a true American farmer.

I was really charmed with the order and neatnefs of this houfe, and of its inhabitants. They have three fons and feven daughters.

One

One of the latter only is married; three others are marriageable. They are beautiful, eafy in their manners, and decent in their deportment. Their drefs is fimple; they wear fine cotton on Sunday, and that which is not fo fine on other days. Thefe daughters aid their mother in the management of the family. The mother has much activity; fhe held in her arms a little grand-daughter, which was careffed by all the children. It is truly a patriarchal family. The father is occupied conftantly in the fields. We converfed much on the Society of Friends, the Society in France for the abolition of flavery, the growing of wheat, &c.

No, never was I fo much edified as in this houfe; it is the afylum of union, friendfhip, and hofpitality. The beds were neat, the linen white, the covering elegant; the cabinets, defks, chairs, and tables, were of black walnut, well polifhed, and fhining. The garden furnifhed vegetables of all kinds, and fruits. There were ten horfes in the ftable; the Indian corn of the laft year, ftill on the cob, lay in large quantities in a cabin, of which the narrow planks, placed at fmall diftances from each other, leave openings for the circulation of the air.

The

The barn was full of wheat, oats, &c.; their cows furnifh delicious milk for the family, of which they make excellent cheefes; their fheep give them the wool of which the cloth is made, which covers the father and the children. This cloth is fpun in the houfe, wove and fulled in the neighbourhood. All the linen is made in the houfe.

Mr. Shoemaker fhowed me the place where this worthy cultivator was going to build a houfe for his eldeft fon. You fee, fays he to me, the wealth of this good farmer. His father was a poor Scotchman; he came to America, and applied himfelf to agriculture, and by his induftry and economy amaffed a large fortune. This fon of his is likewife rich: he fells his grain to a miller in the neighbourhood; his vegetables, butter, and cheefe, are fent once a week to town.

I went to fee this miller. I recollected what Mr. de Crevecœur had faid in praife of the American mills. This one merited it for its neatnefs, and for the intelligence with which the different operations were diftributed. There were three fets of ftones deftined to the making of flour of different degrees of finenefs. They employ only the
ftones

ftones of France for the firft quality of flour.
They are exported from Bourdeaux and
Rouen. In thefe mills they have multiplied
the machinery, to fpare hand-labour in all
the operations; fuch as, hoifting the wheat,
cleanfing it, raifing the flour to the place
where it is to be fpread, colleding it again
into the chamber, where it is to be put in
barrels.

Thefe barrels are marked at the mill with
the name of the miller; and this mark indicates the quality of the flour. That which
is defigned for exportation, is again infpeded
at the port; and, if not merchantable, it is
condemned.

The millers here are flour-merchants; mills
are a kind of property which enfures a conftant income.

LETTER

LETTER IX.

Vifit from the good Warner Miflin.

Aug. 30. 1788.

I WAS fick, and Warner Miflin came to fee me. You know Warner Miflin; you have read the eulogium made of him by M. de Crevecœur. It is he that firft freed all his flaves; it is he who, without a paffport, traverfed the Britifh army, and fpoke to General Howe with fo much firmnefs and dignity; it is he who, fearing not the effects of the general hatred againft the Quakers, went, at the rifk of being treated as a fpy, to prefent himfelf to General Wafhington, to juftify to him the conduct of the Quakers; it is he, that in the midft of the furies of war, equally a friend to the French, the Englifh, and the Americans, carried generous fuccours to thofe among them who were fuffering. Well, this angel of peace came to fee me. I am Warner Miflin, fays he; I have read the book wherein thou defendeft the caufe of the Friends, wherein thou preacheft

preacheſt the principles of univerſal benevolence; I knew that thou waſt here, and I
have came to ſee thee; beſides, I love thy
nation. I was, I confeſs, much prejudiced
againſt the French; I even hated them, having been, in this reſpect, educated in the
Engliſh principles. But when I came to ſee
them, a ſecret voice ſaid to me, that I ought
to drive from my heart that prejudice; that
I ought to know them, and love them. I
have then ſought for them. I have known
them; and it is with pleaſure I have found
them poſſeſs a ſpirit of mildneſs and general
benevolence, which I had never found among
the Engliſh.

I cannot report to you all the converſation
of this worthy Quaker; it made a deep impreſſion on my heart. What humanity! and
what charity! It ſeems, that to love mankind, and to ſearch to do them good, conſti-
tutes his only pleaſure, his only exiſtence;
his conſtant occupation is to find the means
of making all men but one family; and
he does not deſpair of it. He ſpoke to
me of the Society of Quakers at Niſmes, and
of ſome friends in America and England,
who have been to viſit them. He regarded
them as inſtruments deſtined to propagate
the

the principles of the fociety through the world. I mentioned to him fome obftacles; fuch as the corruption of our morals, and the power of the clergy. Oh! my friend, faid he, is not the arm of the Almighty ftronger than the arm of man? What were we, when the fociety took its birth in England? What was America thirteen years ago, when Benezet raifed his voice againft the flavery of the blacks? Let us always endeavour to do good; fear no obftacles, and the good will be done.

All this was faid without the leaft oftentation. He faid what he felt, what he had thought a thoufand times; he fpoke from the heart, and not from the head. He realized what he had told me of that fecret voice, that internal fpirit, of which the Quakers fpeak fo much; he was animated by it. Ah! who can fee, who can hear a man, fo much exalted above human nature, without reflecting on himfelf, without endeavouring to imitate him, without blufhing at his own weaknefs? What are the fineft writings, in comparifon with a life fo pure, a conduct fo conftantly devoted to the good of humanity? How fmall I appeared in contemplating him! And fhall we calumniate a fect to which a man fo venerable belongs? Shall we paint it

as

as the center of hypocrify and deceit? We
muft then fuppofe that Miflin counterfeits humanity ; that he is in concert with hypocrites, or that he is blind to their true character. To counterfeit humanity, to confent
to facrifice one's interefts, to be fcoffed and
ridiculed, to impart his goods to the poor, to
affranchife his negroes, and all this by hypocrify, would be a very bad fpeculation ; hypocrify makes better calculations. But, if you
fuppofe this man to be true and honeft as
to himfelf, can you imagine him to be in
concert with knaves? This would be an abfurd contradiction. Finally, on hearing this
man, full of good fenfe, and endowed with a
folid judgment, reafoning with fo much force,
can you believe that he has been, for all his
life, the dupe of a band of fharpers, when he
is at the fame time in all their moft fecret
counfels, and one of their chiefs? Yes, my
friend, I repeat it, the attachment of an angel
like Warner Miflin to the fect of Quakers, is
the faireft apology for that fociety.

He took me one day to fee his intended
wife, Mifs Ameland, whom he was to marry
in a few days. She is a worthy companion
of this reputable quaker. What mildnefs!
what modefty ! and, at the fame time, what
entertaiment

entertainment in her converſation! Miſs Ameland once loved the world. She made verſes and muſic, and was fond of dancing. Though young ſtill, ſhe has renounced all theſe amuſements, to embrace the life of an anchorite. In the midſt of the world, ſhe has perſiſted in her deſign, notwithſtanding the pleaſantries of her acquaintance.

LETTER

L E T T E R   X.

The Funeral of a Quaker—A Quaker Meeting.

I WAS prefent at the funeral of Thomas Holwell, one of the elders of the Society of Friends. James Pemberton conducted me to it. I found a number of Friends affembled about the houfe of the deceafed, and waiting in filence for the body to appear. It appeared, and was in a coffin of black walnut, without any covering or ornament, borne by four Friends; fome women followed, who, I was told, were the neareft relatives and grand-children of the deceafed*. All his friends followed in filence, two by two. I was of the number. There were no places defignated; young and old mingled together; but all bore the fame air of gravity and attention. The burying ground is in the town; but it is not furrounded with houfes. I faw near fome of the graves, fome pieces of black ftones, on which the names only of the

---

* None of them were dreft in black. The Quakers regard this teftimony of grief as childifh.

dead

dead were engraved. The greateſt part of the Quakers diſlike even this; they ſay, that a man ought to live in the memory of his friends, not by vain inſcriptions, but by good actions. The grave was ſix or ſeven feet deep; they placed the body by the ſide of it. On the oppoſite ſide were ſeated, on wooden chairs, the four women, who appeared to be the moſt affected. The people gathered round, and remained for five minutes in profound meditation. All their countenances marked a gravity ſuitable to the occaſion, but nothing of grief. This interval being elapſed, they let down the body, and covered it with earth; when a man advanced near the grave planted his cane in the ground, fixed his hat upon it, and began a diſcourſe relative to this ſad ceremony. He trembled in all his body, and his eyes were ſtaring and wild. His diſcourſe turned upon the tribulations of this life, the neceſſity of recurring to God, &c. When he had finiſhed, a woman threw herſelf on her knees, made a very ſhort prayer, the men took off their hats, and all retired.

I was at firſt ſurpriſed, I confeſs, at this trembling of the preacher. We are ſo accuſtomed, by our European philoſophy, to conſider

thoſe

thcfe appearances as the effect of hypocrify,
and to annex to them the idea of ridicule,
that it was difficult to prevent myfelf from
being feized with a like impreffion: but I recollected that fomething fimilar had happened to me a hundred times; when I had been
warmed with a fubject, and drawn into an
interefting difcuffion, I have been tranfported
out of myfelf to fuch a degree, that I could
neither fee nor hear, but experienced a confiderable trembling. Hence I concluded, that
it might be natural, efpecially to a man continually occupied in meditation on the Almighty, on death, and a future ftate. I went
from thence with thefe Friends to their meeting. The moft profound filence reigned for
near an hour; when one of their minifters,
or elders, who fat on the front bench, rofe,
pronounced four words—then was filent for
a minute, then fpoke four words more; and
his whole difcourfe was pronounced in this
manner. This method is generally followed
by their preachers; for, another who fpoke
after him, obferved the fame intervals.

Whether I judged from habit or reafon, I
know not; but this manner of fpeaking appeared to me not calculated to produce a
great effect: for the fenfe of the phrafe is
perpetually

perpetually interrupted; and the hearer is obliged to guefs at the meaning, or be in fufpenfe; either of which is fatiguing. But before forming a decifive opinion, we ought to enquire into the reafons which have led the Quakers to adopt this method. Certainly the manner of the ancient orators and modern preachers, is better imagined for producing the great effect of eloquence. They fpeak by turns, to the imagination, to the paffions, and to the reafon; they pleafe in order to move; they pleafe in order to convince; and it is by pleafure that they draw you after them. This is the eloquence neceffary for men enervated and enfeebled, who wifh to fpare themfelves the trouble of thinking. The Quakers are of a different character; they early habituate themfelves to meditation; they are men of much reflection, and of few words. They have no need, then, of preachers with founding phrafes and long fermons. They difdain elegance as an ufelefs amufement; and long fermons appear difproportioned to the force of the human mind, and improper for the divine fervice. The mind fhould not be loaded with too many truths at once, if you wifh they fhould make a lafting impreffion. The object of preaching being to convert, it

ought

ought rather to lead to reflection, than to dazzle and amufe.

I obferved, in the countenances of all this congregation, an air of gravity mixed with fadnefs. Perhaps I am prejudiced; but I fhould like better, while people are adoring their God, to fee them have an air which would difpofe perfons to love each other, and to be fond of the worfhip. Such an air would be attracting to young people, whom too much feverity difgufts. Befides, why fhould a perfon with a good confcience, pray to God with a fad countenance?

The prayer which terminated this meeting was fervent; it was pronounced by a mini-fter, who fell on his knees. The men took off their hats; and each retired, after having fhaken hands with his neighbour.

What a difference between the fimplicity of this, and the pomp of the catholic worfhip! Reformation, in all ftages, has diminifhed the formalities: you will find this regular dimi-nution in defcending from the Catholic to the Lutheran, from the Lutheran to the Prefby-terian, and from thence to Quakers and Methodifts.

Methodifts. It is thus that human reafon progreffes towards perfection.

In confidering the fimplicity of the Quaker's worfhip, and the air of fadnefs that in the eyes of ftrangers appears to accompany it, an air which one would think difgufting to young people, even of their own fect, I have been furprifed that the Society fhould maintain a concurrence with more brilliant fects, and even increafe by making profelytes from them. This effect is principally to be attributed to the fingular image of domeftic happinefs which the Quakers enjoy. Renouncing all external pleafures, mufic, theatres, and fhows, they are devoted to their duties as citizens, to their families, and to their bufinefs; thus they are beloved by their wives, cherifhed by their children, and efteemed by their neighbours. Such is the fpectacle which has often drawn to this Society, men who have ridiculed it in their youth.

The hiftory of the Quakers will prove the falfity of a principle often advanced in politics. It is this: that, to maintain order in fociety, it is neceffary to have a mode of worfhip ftriking to the fenfes; and that the more fhow and pomp are introduced into it, the

the better. This is what has given birth to, and ftill juftifies, our full *chants*, our *fpiritual concerts*, our *proceffions*, our *ornaments*, &c. Two or three hundred thoufand Quakers have none of thefe mummeries, and yet they obferve good order.

This fact has led me to another conclufion, the folidity of which has been hitherto difputed. It is, the poffibility of a *nation of Deifts**. A nation of Deifts maintaining good government, would be a miracle in political religion. And why fhould it not exift, when knowledge fhall be more univerfally extended, when it fhall penetrate all ranks of fociety ? What difference would there be between a fociety of Deifts, and one of Quakers, affembling to hear a difcourfe on the immortality of the foul, and to pray God in fimple language !

---

* Neither the Englifh nor Americans attach the fame idea to this word that a Frenchman does. They confider a Deift as a kind of Materialift.—I underftand by a Deift, a man that believes in God, and the immortality of the foul.

LETTER

L E T T E R XI.

Visit to a Bettering-House, or House of Correction *.

Sept. 1. 1788.

THIS hospital is situated in the open country, in one of those parts of the original plan of Philadelphia not yet covered with houses. It is already divided into regular streets; and, God grant that these projected streets may never be any thing more than imaginary! If they should one day be adorned with houses, it would be a misfortune to the hospitals, to Pennsylvania, and to all America.

This hospital is constructed of bricks, and composed of two large buildings; one for men, and the other for women. There is a separation in the court, which is common to them. This institution has several ob-

---

* This house is properly named; because, contrary to the ordinary effect of hospitals, it renders the prisoners better.

jects :

jects: they receive into it, the poor, the fick, orphans, women in travail, and perfons attacked with venereal difeafes. They likewife confine here, vagabonds, diforderly perfons, and girls of fcandalous lives.

There exifts then, you will fay, even in Philadelphia, that difgufting commerce of difeafes, rather than of pleafures, which for fo long a time has empoifoned our continent. Yes, my friend, two or three of the moft confiderable maritime towns of the new continent are afflicted by this leprofy. It was almoft unknown before the revolution; but the abode of foreign armies has naturalized it, and it is one of thofe fcourges for which the free Americans are indebted to us. But this traffic is not carried on fo fcandaloufly as at Paris or London. It is reftrained, it is held in contempt, and almoft imperceptible. I ought to fay, to the honour of the Americans, that it is nourifhed only by emigrants and European travellers; for the fanctity of marriage is ftill univerfally refpected in America. Young people marrying early, and without obftacles, are not tempted to go and difhonour, and empoifon themfelves in places of proftitution.

But,

But, to finifh my account of this hofpital,
there are particular halls appropriated to each
clafs of poor, and to each fpecies of ficknefs ;
and each hall has its fuperintendant.   This
inftitution was rich, and well adminiftered before the war.   The greater part of the adminiftrators were Quakers.   The war and paper-money introduced a different order of
things.   The legiflature refolved not to admit
to its adminiftration, any perfons but fuch as
had taken the oath of fidelity to the State.
The Quakers were by this excluded, and the
management of it fell into hands not fo pure.
The fpirit of depredation was manifeft in it,
and paper-money was ftill more injurious.
Creditors of the hofpital were paid, or rather
ruined by this operation.   About a year ago,
on the report of the infpectors of the hofpitals,
the legiflature, confidering the abufes practifed
in that adminiftration, confided that of the
bettering-houfe.again to the Quakers.   Without any refentment of the affronts they had
received during the war, and only anxious to
do good and perform their duty, the Friends
accepted the adminiftration, and exercife it,
as before, with zeal and fidelity.   This
change has produced the effect which was
expected.   Order is vifibly re-eftablifhed ;
many adminiftrators are appointed, one of
whom,

whom, by turns, is to visit the hospital every day : fix physicians are attached to it, who perform the service *gratis*.

I have seen the hospitals of France, both at Paris, and in the provinces. I know none of them, but the one at Besançon, that can be compared to this at Philadelphia. Every sick, and every poor person, has his bed well furnished, but without curtains, as it should be. Every room is lighted by windows placed opposite, which introduce plenty of light, that great consolation to a man confined, of which tyrants for this reason are cruelly sparing. These windows admit a free circulation of air : most of them open over the fields ; and as they are not very high, and are without grates, it would be very easy for the prisoners to make their escape ; but the idea never enters their heads. This fact proves that the prisoners are happy, and, consequently, that the administration is good.

The kitchens are well kept, and do not exhale that fetid odour which you perceive from the best kitchens in France. The eating-rooms, which are on the ground floor, are equally clean, and well aired : neatness and good air reign in every part. A large garden

garden at the end of the court, furnifhes vegetables for the kitchen. I was furprifed to
find there, a great number of foreign fhrubs
and plants. The garden is well cultivated.
In the yard they rear a great number of hogs;
for, in America, the hog, as well as the ox,
does the honours of the table through the
whole year.

I could fcarcely defcribe to you the different fenfations which, by turns, rejoiced and
afflicted my heart, in going through their different apartments. An hofpital, how well fo-
ever adminiftered, is always a painful fpectacle to me. It appears to me fo confoling
for a fick man to be at his own home, attended by his wife and children, and vifited
by his neighbours, that I regard hofpitals as
vaft fepulchres, where are brought together
a crowd of individuals, ftrangers to each other,
and feparated from all they hold dear. And
what is man in this fituation?—A leaf detached from the tree, and driven down by the
torrent—a fkeleton no longer of any confift-
ence, and bordering on diffolution.

But this idea foon gives place to another.
Since focieties are condemned to be infefted
with great cities, fince mifery and vice
are

are the neceſſary offspring of theſe cities, a
houſe like this becomes the afylum of beneficence; for, without the aid of ſuch inſtitu-
tions, what would become of the greater
part of thoſe wretches who here find a refuge? ſo many women, blind, deaf, rendered
diſguſting by their numerous infirmities.
They muſt very ſoon periſh, abandoned by
all the world, to whom they are ſtrangers.
No door but that of their common mother
earth would receive theſe hideous figures,
were it not for this proviſion made by their
common friend, Society.

I ſaw in this hoſpital, all that miſery and
diſeaſe can aſſemble. I ſaw women ſuffering
on the bed of pain; others, whoſe meagre
viſages, roughened with pimples, atteſt the
effect of fatal incontinence; others, who
waited with groans the moment when Heaven would deliver them from a burden which
diſhonours them; others, holding in their
arms the fruit, not of a legal marriage, but
of love betrayed. Poor innocents! born under
the ſtar of wretchedneſs! Why ſhould men be
born, predeſtinated to misfortunes? But, bleſs
God, at leaſt, that you are in a country where
baſtardy is no obſtacle to refpectability and
the rights of citizenſhip. I ſaw with pleaſure,

fure, thefe unhappy mothers careffing their infants, and nurfing them with tendernefs. There were few children in the hall of the little orphans ; thefe were in good health, and appeared gay and happy. Mr. Shoe-maker, who conducted me thither, and another of the directors, diftributed fome cakes among them, which they had brought in their pockets. Thus the directors think of their charge even at a diftance, and occupy themfelves with their happinefs. Good God! there is, then, a country where the foul of the governor of an hofpital, is not a foul of brafs!

Blacks are here mingled with the whites, and lodged in the fame apartments. This, to me, was an edifying fight ; it feemed a balm to my foul. I faw a negro woman fpinning with activity by the fide of her bed. Her eyes feemed to expect from the director, a word of confolation—She obtained it ; and it feemed to be heaven to her to hear him. I fhould have been more happy, had it been for me to have fpoken this word : I fhould have added many more. Unhappy negroes! how much reparation do we owe them for the evils we have occafioned them—the evils we ftill occafion them ! and they love us !

The

The happinefs of this negrefs was not equal to that which I faw fparkle on the vifage of a young blind girl, who feemed to leap for joy at the found of the director's voice. He afked after her health : fhe anfwered him with tranfport. She was taking her tea by the fide of her little table—Her tea !—My friend, you are aftonifhed at this luxury in an hofpital—It is becaufe there is humanity in its adminiftration, and the wretches are not crowded in here in heaps to be ftifled. They give tea to thofe whofe conduct is fatisfactory: and thofe who by their work are able to make fome favings, enjoy the fruits of their induftry. I remarked in this hofpital, that the women were much more numerous than the men ; and among the latter, I faw none of thofe hideous figures fo common in the hofpitals of Paris—figures on which you trace the marks of crimes, mifery, and indolence. They have a decent appearance : many of them afked the director for their enlargement, which they obtained.

But what refources have they, on leaving this houfe ? They have their hands, anfwered the director, and they may find ufeful occupations. But the women, replied I, what can they do ? Their condition is not fo fortunate,

tunate, faid he. In a town where fo many men are occupied in foreign commerce, the number of unhappy and diforderly females will be augmented. To prevent this inconvenience, it has been lately propofed to form a new eftablifhment, which fhall give to girls of this defcription a ufeful occupation, where the produce of the induftry of each perfon fhall be preferved and given to her on leaving the houfe; or, if fhe fhould choofe to remain, fhe fhall always enjoy the fruit of her own labour.

This projeƈt will, without doubt, be executed; for the Quakers are ingenious and perfevering, when they have in view the fuccour of the unhappy. My friend, the author of this projeƈt is my conduƈtor. I fee him beloved and refpeƈted, conftantly occupied in ufeful things; and he is but thirty years of age! and is it aftonifhing that I praife a feƈt which produces fuch prodigies?

On our return from the hofpital, we drank a bottle of cider. Compare this frugal repaft to the fumptuous feafts given by the fuperintendants of the poor of London—by thofe humane infpeƈtors who affemble to confult on making repairs to the amount of fix fhillings, and

and order a dinner for fix guineas. You never find among the Quakers, thefe robberies upon indigence, thefe infamous treafons againſt beneficence. Blefs them, then, ye rich and poor: ye rich, becaufe their fidelity and prudence economife your money; ye poor, becaufe their humanity watches over you without ceafing.

The expences of this hofpital amount to about fivepence a-day, money of Pennſylvania, for each penfioner. You know that the beſt adminiſtered hofpital in Paris, amounts to about fourteen pence like money a-day; and, what a difference in the treatment!

LETTER

L E T T E R XII.

HOSPITAL for LUNATICS.

THIS is the hofpital fo juftly celebrated by M. de Crevecœur, and which the humane Mr. Mazzei regards only as a cu-riofity fcarcely worth feeing.

The building is fine, elegant, and well kept. I was charmed with the cleanlinefs in the halls of the fick, as well as in the particular chambers. I obferved the buft of Franklin in the library, and was told that this honour was rendered him as one of the principal founders of this inftitution. The library is not numerous; but it is well chofen. The hall on the firft floor, is appropriated to fick men: there were fix in it. About the fame number of fick women were in a like hall on the fecond floor. Thefe perfons appeared by no means miferable; they feemed to be at home. I went below, to fee the lunatics; they were about fifteen, male and female,

Each

Each one has his cell, with a bed, a table, and
a convenient window with grates. Stoves
are fixed in the walls, to warm the cell in
winter.

There were no mad perfons among them.
Moſt of the patients are the victims of religious melancholy, or of diſappointed love.
Theſe unhappy perfons are treated with the
greateſt tendernefs; they are allowed to walk
in the court ; are conſtantly viſited by two
phyſicians. Dr. Ruſh has invented a kind of
ſwing chair for their exerciſe.

What a difference between this treatment
and the atrocious regulations to which we
condemn ſuch wretches in France ! where
they are rigorouſly confined, and their diforders fcarcely ever fail to increaſe upon
them. The Turks, on the contrary, manifeſt
a ſingular refpect to perfons infane : they
are eager to adminifter food to them, to load
them with careffes. Fools in that country
are never known to be injurious ; whereas,
with us, they are dangerous, becauſe they
are unhappy.

The view of theſe perfons affected me
more than that of the ſick. The laſt of
human

human miferies, in my opinion, is confinement ; and I cannot conceive how a fick
perfon can be cured in prifon, for confinement
itfelf is a continual malady. The exercife
of walking abroad, the view of the fields, the
murmur of the rivulets, and the finging of
birds, with the aid of vegetable diet, appear
to me the beft means of curing infanity.
It is true, that this method requires too many
attendants ; and the impoffibility of following it for the hofpital of Philadelphia, makes
it neceffary to recur to locks and bars. But
why do they place thefe cells beneath the
ground-floor, expofed to the unwholefome humidity of the earth ? The enlightened and
humane Dr. Rufh told me, that he had endeavoured for a long time, in vain, to introduce a change in this particular ; and that
this hofpital was founded at a time when little
attention was thought neceffary for the accom-
modation of fools. I obferved, that none of
thefe fools were naked, or indecent ; a thing
very common with us. Thefe people preferve, even in their folly, their primitive
charaƈteriftic of decency.

I could not leave this place without being
tormented with one bitter refleƈtion.—A man
of

of the moſt brilliant genius may here finiſh his days. If Swift had not been rich, he had dragged out his laſt moments in ſuch an hoſpital. O ye who watch over them, be gentle in your adminiſtration !—perhaps a benefactor of the human race has fallen under your care.

LETTER

LETTER XIII.

On BENJAMIN FRANKLIN.

THANKS to God he ftill exifts !—This
great man, for fo many years the pre-
ceptor of the Americans, who fo glorioufly
contributed to their independence, death had
threatened his days ; but our fears are diffipated, and his health is reftored.   I have
juft been to fee him, and enjoy his converfation, in the midft of his books, which he ftill
calls his beft friends.   The pains of his cruel
infirmity change not the ferenity of his
countenance, nor the calmnefs of his converfation.   If thefe appeared fo agreeable to our
Frenchmen, who enjoyed his friendfhip in
Paris, how would they feem to them here,
where no diplomatic functions impofe upon
him that mafk of referve which was fometimes fo chilling to his guefts.   Franklin,
furrounded by his family, appears to be one
of thofe patriarchs whom he has fo well defcribed, and whofe language he has copied
with fuch fimple elegance.   He feems one
of thofe ancient philofophers, who at times
defcended

defcended from the fphere of his elevated
genius, to inftruct weak mortals, by accom-
modating himfelf to their feeblenefs.   I have
found in America, a great number of enlightened politicians and virtuous men; but I
find none who appear to poffefs, in fo high
a degree as Franklin, the characteriftics of a
real philofopher.   You know him, my friend.
A love for the human race in habitual exercife, an indefatigable zeal to ferve them,
extenfive information, fimplicity of manners,
and purity of morals; all thefe furnifh not
marks of diftinction fufficiently obfervable
between him and other patriot politicians, unlefs we add another characteriftic; it is, that
Franklin, in the midft of the vaft fcene in
which he acted fo diftinguifhed a part, had
his eyes fixed without ceafing on a more extenfive theatre—on heaven and a future life;
the only point of view which can fuftain,
difintereft, and aggrandife man upon earth,
and make him a true philofopher.   All his
life has been but a continued ftudy and practice of philofophy.

I wifh to give you a fketch of it from
fome traits which I have been able to collect,
as his hiftory has been much disfigured.
This fketch may ferve to rectify fome of
those

thofe falfe anecdotes which circulate in Europe.

Franklin was born at Bofton, in 1706, the fifteenth child of a man who was a dyer and a foap-boiler. He wifhed to bring up this fon to his own trade ; but the lad took an invincible diflike to it, preferring even the life of a failor. The father difliking this choice, placed him apprentice with an elder fon, who was a printer, and publifhed a newfpaper.

Three traits of character, difplayed at that early period, might have given an idea of the extraordinary genius which he was after-terwards to difcover.

The puritanic aufterity which at that time predominated in Maffachufetts, impreffed the mind of young Benjamin in a manner more oblique than it had done that of his father. The old man was in the practice of making long prayers and benedictions before all his meals. One day, at the beginning of win-ter, when he was falting his meat, and lay-ing in his provifions for the feafon, " Father," fays the boy, " it would be a great faving of time, if you would fay grace over all thefe

barrels

barrels of meat at once, and let that fuffice for the winter."

Soon after he went to live with his brother, he began to addrefs pieces to him for his paper, in a difguifed hand-writing. Thefe effays were univerfally admired : his brother became jealous of him, and endeavoured, by fevere treatment, to cramp his genius. This obliged him foon to quit his fervice, and go to feek his fortune at New-York.

Benjamin had read a treatife of Dr. Tryon on the Pythagorean regimen ; and, fully convinced by its reafoning, he abftained from the ufe of meat for a long time ; and became irreconcilable to it, until a cod-fifh, which he caught in the open fea, and found its ftomach full of little fifh, overturned his whole fyftem. He concluded, that fince the fifhes eat each other, men might very well feed upon other animals. This Pythagorean diet was economical to the printer's boy: it faved him fome money to lay out for books ; and reading was the firft and conftant paffion of his life.

Having left his father's houfe without recommendation, and almoft without money, depending only upon himfelf, but always confident

confident in his own judgment, and rejoic-
ing in his independence, he became the fport
of accidents, which ferved rather to prove
him, than to difcourage him. Wandering
in the ftreets of Philadelphia, with only five
fhillings in his pocket, not known to a perfon
in the town, eating a cruft of bread, and
quenching his thirft in the waters of the
Delaware; who could have difcerned in this
wretched labourer, one of the future legiflators of America, one of the fathers of modern philofophy, and an ambaffador covered
with glory in the moft wealthy, the moft
powerful, and the moft enlightened country
in the world? Who could have believed
that France, that Europe, would one day
erect ftatues to that man who had not where
to lay his head?

This circumftance reminds me of a fimilar
one of Rouffeau:—Having for his whole
fortune fix liards; harraffed with fatigue,
and tormented with hunger; he hefitated
whether he fhould facrifice this little piece
to his repofe, or to his ftomach. He decided
the conflict by purchafing a piece of bread,
and refigning himfelf to fleep in the open air.
In this abandonment of nature and men, he
ftill enjoyed the one, and defpifed the other.
The

The Lyonnefe, who difdained Rouffeau becaufe he was ill dreffed, has died unknown; while altars are now erected to the man ill-dreffed. Thefe examples ought to confole men of genius, whom fortune may reduce to the neceffity of ftruggling againft want. Adverfity but forms them, and perfeverance will bring its reward.

Arriving at Philadelphia did not finifh the misfortunes of Benjamin Franklin. He was there deceived and difappointed by governor Keith, who, by fine promifes for his future eftablifhment, which he never realized, induced him to embark for London, where he arrived without money and without recommendations. Happily he knew how to procure fubfiftence. His talent for the prefs, in which no perfon excelled him, foon gave him occupation. His frugality, the regularity of his conduct, and the good fenfe of his converfation, procured him the efteem of his comrades: his reputation in this refpect, exifted for fifty years afterwards in the printing-offices in London.

An employment promifed him by a Mr. Derham, recalled him to his country in 1726, when fortune put him to another proof.

His

His protector died ; and Franklin was obliged, for fubfiftence, to have recourfe again to the prefs. He found the means foon afterwards to eftablifh a printing-prefs himfelf, and to publifh a gazette. At this period began his good fuccefs, which never afterwards aban-doned him. He married a Mifs Read, to whom he was attached by a long friendfhip, and who merited all his efteem. She par-took of his enlarged and beneficent ideas, and was the model of a virtuous wife and a good neighbour.

Having arrived at this degree of indepen-dence, Franklin had leifure to purfue his fpeculations for the good of the public. His gazette furnifhed him with the regular and conftant means of inftructing his fellow citi-zens. He made this gazette the principal object of his attention ; fo that it acquired a vaft reputation, was read through the whole country, and may be confidered as having contributed much to perpetuate in Pennfyl-vania thofe excellent morals which ftill dif-tinguifh that State.

I poffefs one of thefe gazettes, compofed by him, and printed at his prefs. It is a precious relique, a monument which I wifh

to

to preferve with reverence, to teach men to
blufh at the prejudice which makes them
defpife the ufeful and important profeffion
of the editor of daily papers. Men of this
profeffion, among a free people, are their
firft preceptors, and beft friends ; and when
they unite talents with patriotifm and philofophy, when they ferve as the canal for
communicating truths, for diffipating prejudices, and removing thofe hatreds which prevent the human race from uniting together
in one great family, thefe men are the
curates, the miffionaries, the angels deputed
from heaven for the happinefs of men.

Let it not be faid, in ridicule of this profeffion, that an ill ufe is fometimes made of it,
for the defence of vice, of defpotifm, of
errors. Shall we profcribe eloquence and
the ufe of fpeech, becaufe wicked men poffefs
them ?

But a work which contributed ftill more
to diffufe in America the practice of frugality, economy, and good morals, was *Poor
Richard's Almanack*. You are acquainted
with it ; it had a great reputation in France,
but ftill more in America. Franklin continued it for twenty-five years, and fold annually

nually more than ten thoufand copies. In this work, the moft weighty truths are delivered in the fimpleft language, and fuited to the comprehenfion of all the world.

In 1736, Franklin began his public career. He was appointed Secretary of the General Affembly of Pennfylvania, and continued in that employment for many years.

In 1737, the Englifh government confided to him the adminiftration of the general poft-office in America. He made it at once lucrative to the revenue, and ufeful to the inhabitants. It ferved him particularly, to extend everywhere his ufeful gazettes.

Since that epoch, not a year has paffed without his propofing, and carrying into execution, fome project ufeful to the colonies.

To him are owing the companies of affurance againft fire; companies fo neceffary in countries where houfes are built with wood, and where fires completely ruin individuals; while, on the contrary, they are difaftrous in a country where fires are not frequent, and not dangerous.

To

To him is owing the eftablifhment of the Philofophical Society at Philadelphia, its library, its univerfity, its hofpitals, &c.

Franklin, perfuaded that information could not be extended but by firft collecting it, and by affembling men who were likely to poffefs it, was always extremely ardent to encourage literary and political clubs. In one of thefe clubs, which he founded, the following queftions were put to the candidate :—

" Do you love all men, of whatever religion they may be? Do you believe that we ought to perfecute or decry a man for mere fpeculative opinions, or for his mode of worfhip? Do you love truth for its own fake? and will you employ all your efforts to difcover it, and to make it known to others ?"

Obferve, again, the fpirit of this club in the queftions put to the members at their meetings.—" Know you any citizen who has lately been remarkable for his induftry? Know you in what the Society can be ufeful to its brethren, and to all the human race? Is there any ftranger arrived in town? In what can the Society be ufeful to him? Is there any young perfon beginning bufinefs, who

who wants encouragement ? Have you obferved any defects in the new acts of the
legiflature, which can be remedied ? How
can the Society be ufeful to you ?"

The attention which he paid to thefe inftitutions of literature and humanity, did not
divert him from his public functions, nor
from his experiments in natural philofophy.

His labours on thefe fubjects are well
known ; I fhall therefore not fpeak of them,
but confine myfelf to a fact which has been
little remarked : it is, that Franklin always
directed his labours to that kind of public
utility which, without procuring any great
eclat to its author, produces great advantage
to the citizens at large. It is to this popular
tafte, which characterifed him, that we owe
the invention of his electrical conductors, his
economical ftoves, his differtations, truly
philofophical, on the means of preventing
chimneys from fmoking, on the advantages
of copper roofs to houfes, the eftablifhment
of fo many paper-mills in Pennfylvania*, &c.

The

* Dr. Franklin told me, that he had eftablifhed about eighteen
paper-mills. His grandfon, Mr. T. Franklin, will doubtlefs
publifh

The circumſtances of his political career are likewiſe known to you; I therefore paſs them over in ſilence. But I ought not to omit to mention his conduct during the war of 1755. At that period he enjoyed a great reputation in the Engliſh colonies. In 1754 he was appointed one of the members of the famous Congreſs, which was held at Albany; the object of which was to take the neceſ-ſary meaſures to prevent the invaſion of the French. He preſented to that Congreſs an excellent *plan of union and defence*, which was adopted by that body; but it was re-jected in London by the department for the colonies, under the pretext that it was too democratical. It is probable that, had this plan been purſued, the colonies would not have been ravaged by the dreadful war which followed. During this war, Franklin per-formed many important functions. At one time he was ſent to cover the frontiers, to raiſe troops, build forts, &c. You then ſee him conteſting with the governor, to force him to give his conſent to a bill taxing the family of Penn, who were proprietors of

---

publiſh a collection of his uſeful letters on the ſalutary or per-nicious effects of different proceſſes in the arts. Theſe letters are ſcattered in the American gazettes. The collection of them would be curious.

one-

one-third of the lands of Pennfylvania, and
refufed to pay taxes.   He then was fent
deputy to London, where he was fuccefsful
in fupporting the caufe of the colony in the
Privy Council againft that powerful family.

The fuperior fkill and management which
he difcovered in thefe negociations, were the
forerunners of the more important fuccefs
which attended him during the war of independence, when he was fent ambaffador to
France.

On his final return to his country, he obtained all the honours which his important
fervices merited.   His great age, and his infirmities, have compelled him at laft to renounce his public career, which he has run
with fo much glory.   He lives retired, with
his family, in a houfe which he has built
on the fpot where he firft landed, fixty years
before, and where he found himfelf wandering without a home, and without acquaintance.   In this houfe he has eftablifhed a
printing-prefs and a type-foundery.   From
a printer he had become ambaffador; from
this he has now returned to his beloved
prefs, and is forming to this precious art
his grandfon, Mr. Bache.   He has placed
him

him at the head of an enterprife which will
be infinitely ufeful; it is a complete edition
of all the claffic authors, that is, of all thofe
moral writers whofe works ought to be the
manual for men who wifh to gain inftruction,
and make themfelves happy by doing good to
others.

It is in the midft of thefe holy occupations, that this great man waits for death
with tranquillity. You will judge of his
philofophy on this point, which is the touchftone of philofophy, by the following letter,
written thirty years ago on the death of his
brother John Franklin, addreffed to Mrs,
Hubbard, his daughter-in-law,

" My dear child,

" I AM grieved with you; we have loft
" a friend, who, to us, was very dear,
" and very precious. But it is the will
" of God and of nature, that thefe mortal
" bodies fhould be laid afide, when the foul
" is ready to enter into real life; for this
" life is but an embryo ftate, a preparation
" for life. A man is not completely born,
" until he is dead. Shall we complain, then,
" that a new-born has taken his place among
" the immortals? We are fpirits. It is a
                                    " proof

" proof of the goodnefs of God, that our
" bodies are lent us fo long as they can be
" ufeful to us, in receiving pleafure, in ac-
" quiring knowledge, or in doing good to
" our fellow-creatures; and he gives a new
" proof of the fame goodnefs in delivering
" us from our bodies, when, inftead of plea-
" fure, they caufe us pain; when, inftead of
" aiding others, we become chargeable to
" them. Death is then a bleffing from God;
" we ourfelves often prefer a partial death
" to a continued pain; it is thus that we
" confent to the amputation of a limb, when
" it cannot be reftored to life. On quitting
" our bodies, we are delivered from all kinds
" of pain. Our friend and we are invited
" to a party of pleafure which will endure
" eternally: he has gone firft; why fhould
" we regret it, fince we are fo foon to fol-
" low, and we know where we are to meet?"

*Appendix to the preceding chapter, written
in December* 1790.

FRANKLIN has enjoyed, this year, the
bleffing of death, for which he waited fo long
a time. I will here repeat the reflections
which I printed in my Gazette of the 13th
of June laft, on this event, and on the decree

cree of the National Aſſembly on this occaſion.

I will introduce them with the diſcourſe of
M. Mirabeau in that aſſembly.

" Gentlemen,
" Franklin is dead—he has returned to
" the boſom of God—the genius who has
" liberated America, and ſhed over Europe
" the torrents of his light!

" The ſage of two worlds—the man for
" whom the hiſtory of ſciences and the hiſ-
" tory of empires contend, ſhould doubtleſs
" hold an elevated rank in the human race.

" Too long have political cabinets been
" accuſtomed to notify the death of thoſe
" who are great only in their funeral pomp;
" too long has the etiquette of courts pro-
" claimed hypocritical mourning. Nations
" ought to mourn only for their benefactors;
" the repreſentatives of nations ought to re-
" commend to their homage, none but the
" heroes of humanity.

" The Congreſs has ordained a mourning
" of two months for the death of Franklin;
" and

" and America, at this moment, is rendering
" this tribute of veneration to one of the
" fathers of her conftitution.

" Would it not be worthy of you, gentle-
" men, to join them in this truly religious
" act, to participate in this homage rendered
" in the face of the univerfe to the rights of
" men, to the philofopher, who has contri-
" buted the moft to extend their empire over
" the face of the earth ?

" Antiquity would have raifed altars to
" that powerful genius, who, for the benefit
" of men, embracing heaven and earth, could
" have curbed the thunders of the one, and
" the tyrants of the other. Europe, enlight-
" ened and free, owes at leaft a teftimony of
" gratitude to the greateft man that ever
" adorned philofophy and liberty !

" I propofe that it be decreed, that the
" National Affembly go into mourning three
" days for Benjamin Franklin."

The Affembly received with acclamation,
and decreed with unanimity, the propofal of
M. Mirabeau.

The

The honour thus done to the memory of
Franklin, will reflect glory on the National
Affembly.   It will give an idea of the immenfe difference between this legiflature and
other political bodies ; for, how many prejudices muft have been vanquifhed, before
France could bring her homage to the tomb
of a man, who, from the ftation of a journey-
man printer, had raifed himfelf to the rank
of legiflator, and contributed to place his
country on a footing among the great powers
of the earth.

This fublime decree was pronounced, not
only without hefitation, but with that enthufiafm which is infpired by the name of a
great man, by the regret of having loft him,
by the duty of doing honour to his afhes,
and by the hope, that rendering this honour
may give rife to like virtues and like talents
in others.   And, oh ! may this Affembly, penetrated with the greatnefs of the homage
which fhe has rendered to genius, to virtue,
to the pure love of liberty and humanity ;
may fhe never tarnifh this homage, by yield-
ing to the folicitations of men who may wifh
to obtain the fame honours for the manes of
ambitious individuals, who, miftaking art for
genius,

genius, obfcure conception for profound ideas, the defire of abafing tyrants for the love of humanity, the applaufe of a volatile people for the veneration of an enlightened world, may think proper to afpire to the honour of a national mourning.

This hope fhould doubtlefs infpire the man of genius, the man of worth; but ye who fincerely indulge the wifh to place yourfelves by the fide of Franklin, examine his life, and have the courage to imitate him. Franklin had genius: but he had virtues; he was good, fimple, and modeft; he had not that proud afperity in difpute, which repulfes with difdain the ideas of others; he liftened—he had the art of liftening—he anfwered to the ideas of others, and not to his own.

I have feen him attending patiently to young people who, full of frivolity and pride, were eager to make a parade before him, of fome fuperficial knowledge of their own. He knew how to eftimate them; but he would not humiliate them, even by a parade of goodnefs. Placing himfelf at once on a level with them, he would anfwer without having the air of inftructing them. He knew that inftruction in its pompous ap-
                                            parel,

parel, was forbidding. Franklin had knowledge, but it was for the people ; he was always grieved at their ignorance, and made
it his conftant duty to enlighten them.
He ftudied for ever to leffen the price of
books, in order to multiply them. In a word,
genius, fimplicity, goodnefs, tolerance, indefatigable labour, and love for the people—
thefe form the character of Franklin ; and
thefe you muft unite, if you wifh for a name
like his.

LETTER

LETTER XIV.

Steam-boat—Reflections on the Character of the Americans, and the English.

Sept. 1. 1788.

I BREAKFASTED with Samuel Ameland, one of the richeſt and moſt beneficent of the Society of Friends. He is a pupil of Anthony Benezet; he ſpeaks of him with enthuſiaſm, and treads in his ſteps. He takes an active part in every uſeful inſtitution, and rejoices in the occaſion of doing good; he loves the French nation, and ſpeaks their language. He treats me with the greateſt friendſhip; offers me his houſe, his horſes, and his carriage. On leaving him, I went to ſee an experiment, near the Delaware, on a boat, the object of which is to aſcend rivers againſt the current. The inventor was Mr. Fitch, who had found a company to ſupport the expence. One of the moſt zealous aſſociates is Mr. Thornton, of whom I have ſpoken. This invention was diſputed be

tween

tween Mr. Fitch and M. Rumfey of Virginia *. However it be, the machine which
I faw, appears well executed, and well adapt-
ed to the defign. The fteam-engine gives
motion to three large oars of confiderable
force, which were to give fixty ftrokes per
minute.

I doubt not but, phyfically fpeaking, this
machine may produce part of the effects
which are expected from it : but I doubt its
utility in commerce ; for, notwithftanding
the affurances of the undertakers, it muft
require many men to manage it, and much
expence in repairing the damages occafioned
by the violence and multiplicity of the fric-

---

* Since writing this letter, I have feen Mr. Rumfey in
England. He is a man of great ingenuity ; and, by the explanation which he has given me, it appears that his difcovery,
though founded on a fimilar principle with that of Mr. Fitch,
is very different from it, and far more fimple in its execution.
M. Rumfey propofed then (Feb. 1789) to build a veffel which
fhould go to America by the help only of the fteam-engine,
and without fails. It was to make the paffage in fifteen
days. I perceive with pain that he has not yet executed his
project ; which, when executed, will introduce into commerce as great a change as the difcovery of the Cape of
Good Hope.   AUTHOR.

The tranflator is informed, that M. Rumfey is purfuing his
operations with greater vigour, and more extenfive expectations, than ever.

tion.

tion. Yet I will allow, that if the movements can be fimplified, and the expence
leffened, the invention may be ufeful in a
country where labour is dear, and where the
borders of rivers are not acceffible, like thofe
in France, by horfes to draw the boats. This
idea was confoling to Dr. Thornton, whom
I faw affailed by railleries on account of the
fteam-boat. Thefe railleries appear to me
very ill placed. The obftacles to be con-
quered by genius are every where fo confiderable, the encouragement fo feeble, and
the neceffity of fupplying the want of hand-
labour in America fo evident, that I cannot,
without indignation, fee the Americans difcouraging, by their farcafms, the generous
efforts of one of their fellow-citizens.

When will men be reafonable enough to
encourage each other by their mutual aid,
and increafe the general ftock of public
good, by mutual mildnefs and benevolence?
It is for republics to fet the example: you
fee more of it in America than elfewhere; it
is vifibly taking root, and extending itfelf
there. You do not find among the Americans, that concealed pride which acquits a
benefit, and difpenfes with gratitude; that
felfifh rudenefs which makes of the Englifh

a nation

a nation by themſelves, and enemies to all others. You will, however, find ſometimes veſtiges of their indifference for other peo-ple, and their contempt for ſtrangers who travel among them. For example, a ſtranger in a ſociety of Americans, if he has the miſ-fortune not to ſpeak their language, is ſome-times left alone; no perſon takes notice of him. This is a breach of humanity, and a neglect of their own intereſt; of humanity, becauſe conſolation is due to a man diſtant from his friends, and his ordinary means of amuſement; of their own intereſt, becauſe ſtrangers, diſguſted with this treatment, haſten to quit the country, and to prejudice others againſt it.

I ſay that this inattention to ſtrangers is above all remarkable in the Engliſh. I do not think that I am deceived; I have lived long among them, and am generally accuſed of too much partiality for them. This ſame fault is obſervable in the Engliſh iſlands. I have remarked it in many of them; and I fear that the vices in general of the inhabit-ants of the iſlands will corrupt the Ameri-cans, who appear to me remarkably fond of extending their connection with them. I heard one of them put the following queſtion

to

to feveral Americans, at a review of the
volunteers of Philadelphia: " Can you tell
me whether thefe brave officers are barbers or
coblers ?" This vulgar pleafantry difcovers
the man of prejudice, the infolent and bafe
European, the valet of a defpot. Such railleries tend to deftroy that idea of equality
which is the bafis of republics.

But why do not men of fenfe, who are
witneffes of thefe follies, refute them with
vigour ? Why that cowardly fupplenefs which
is decorated with the name of politenefs ? Is
it not evident that it hardens the corrupted
man, and fuffers to grow up in feeble minds,
prejudices which one vigorous attack would
deftroy ?

L E T-

LETTER XV.

The Society of Agriculture—The Library.

Sept. 2. 1788.

I WAS prefent at a meeting of the Agricultural Society.   It is not of long ftanding, but is numerous, and poffeffes a confiderable fund.   If fuch a fociety ought to
receive encouragement in any country, it is
in this.   Agriculture is the firft pillar of this
State ; and though you find many good
farmers here, yet the great mafs of them
want information ; and this information can
only be procured by the union of men well
verfed in theory and practice.

The fubject of this meeting was an important one.   The papillon, or worm, called
The Heffian Fly, had, for feveral years, ravaged the wheat in many parts of the United
States.   The King of England, fearing that
this infect might pafs into his ifland, had
juft prohibited the importation of the American wheat.   The Supreme Executive Council

til of Pennfylvania, in order to counteract
the effects of this prohibition, by gaining information on the fubject, applied to the Society of Agriculture; they defired to know if
this infect attacked the grain, and whether it
was poffible to prevent its ravages.

Many farmers prefent at this meeting,
from their own experience, and that of their
neighbours and correfpondents, declared, that
the infect depofited its eggs, not in the ear,
but in the ftalk; fo that they were well convinced, that, on threfhing the wheat, there
could be nothing to fear that the eggs would
mix with the grain; and confequently they
could not be communicated with the grain.

Mr. Polwell, and M. Griffiths, prefident
and fecretary of this fociety, do equal honour
to it; the one by the neatnefs of his compofition, and the elegance of his ftyle; the
other, by his indefatigable zeal.

Among the ufeful inftitutions which do
honour to Philadelphia, you diftinguifh the
public library; the origin of which is owing
to the celebrated Franklin. It is fupported
by fubfcription. The price of entrance into
this fociety is ten pounds. Any perfon has
the

the privilege of borrowing books. Half of
the library is generally in the hands of readers;
and I obferved with pleafure, that the books
were much worn by ufe.

At the fide of this library is a cabinet of
natural hiftory. I obferved nothing curious
in it, but an enormous thigh-bone, and fome
teeth as enormous, found near the Ohio, in
a mafs of prodigious bones, which nature
feems to have thrown together in thofe ages
whofe events are covered from the eye of
hiftory by an impenetrable veil.

LETTER

LETTER XVI.

On the Market of Philadelphia.

Sept. 3. 1788.

IF there exifts, fays Franklin, an Atheift in the univerfe, he would be converted on feeing Philadelphia—on contemplating a town where every thing is fo well arranged. If an idle man fhould come into exiftence here, on having conftantly before his eyes the three amiable fifters, Wealth, Science, and Virtue, the children of Induftry and Tempe-rance, he would foon find himfelf in love with them, and endeavour to obtain them from their parents.

Such are the ideas offered to the mind on a market-day at Philadelphia. It is, without contradiction, one of the fineft in the uni-verfe. Variety and abundance in the articles, order in the diftribution, good faith and tranquillity in the trader, are all here united. One of the effential beauties of a market,

is

is cleanliness in the provisions, and in those
who sell them. Cleanliness is conspicuous
here in every thing; even meat, whose aspect
is more or less disgusting in other markets,
here strikes your eyes agreeably. The spectator is not tormented with the sight of little
streams of blood, which infect the air, and
foul the streets. The women who bring the
produce of the country, are dressed with decency; their vegetables and fruits are neatly
arranged in handsome, well-made baskets.
Every thing is assembled here, the produce of
the country, and the works of industry; flesh,
fish, fruits, garden-seeds, pottery, iron ware,
shoes, trays, buckets extremely well made,
&c. The stranger is never wearied in contemplating this multitude of men and women
moving and crossing in every direction, without tumult or injury. You would say, that
it was a market of brothers, that it was a
rendezvous of philosophers, of the pupils of
the silent Pythagoras; for silence reigns without interruption: you hear none of those
piercing cries, so common elsewhere; each
one sells, bargains, and buys in silence. The
carts and horses which have brought in the
supplies, are peaceably arranged in the next
street, in the order in which they arrive;
when disengaged, they move off in silence:
no

no quarrels among the carmen and the por-
ters. You fee none of our fools and maca-
ronies gallopping with loofe reins in the
ftreets. Thefe are the aftonifhing effects of
habit ; a habit infpired by the Quakers, who
planted morals in this country ; a habit of
doing every thing with tranquillity and with
reafon ; a habit of injuring no perfon, and
of having no need of the interpofition of the
magiftrate.

To maintain order in fuch a market in
France, would require four Judges and a
dozen foldiers. Here, the law has no need
of mufkets ; education and morals have done
every thing. Two clerks of the police walk
in the market. If they fufpect a pound of
butter of being light, they weigh it : if light,
it is feized for the ufe of the hofpital.

You fee, here, the fathers of families go to
market. It was formerly fo in France : their
wives fucceeded to them ; thinking themfelves difhonoured by the tafk, they have refigned it to the fervants. Neither œconomy
nor morals have gained any thing by this
change.

The price of bread is from one penny to
two

twopence the pound, beef and mutton from
twopence to fourpence, veal from one penny to twopence ; hay from twenty to thirty fhillings the ton ; butter from fourpence
to fixpence the pound ; wood from feven-
pence to eightpence the cord.　Vegetables
are in abundance, and cheap.　Wines of Europe, particularly thofe of France, are cheaper
here than anywhere elfe.　I have drank the
wine of Provence, faid to be made by M.
Bergaffe, at ninepence the bottle ; but the
taverns are extremely dear.　Articles of luxury are expenfive : a hair-dreffer cofts you
eightpence a-day, or twelve fhillings the
month.　I hired a one-horfe chaife three days ;
it coft me three louis d'ors.

LETTER

LETTER XVII.

General Affembly of Pennfylvania—A Farm owned by a Frenchman,

Sept. 6. 1788.

I HAD made an acquaintance at New-York with General Miflin, who was then Speaker of the Houfe of Reprefentatives of Pennfylvania. I met him again at Philadelphia. His character was well drawn by M. de Chaftellux. He is an amiable, obliging man; full of activity, and very popular. He fills his place with dignity and firmnefs; an enemy to artifice and difguife; he is frank, brave, difinterefted, and warmly attached to democratic principles. He is no longer a Quaker: having taken arms, he was forced to quit the Society; but he ftill profeffes a great efteem for that fect, to which his wife has always remained faithful. The General had the complaifance to conduct me one day to the General Affembly. I faw nothing remarkable in it: the building is far from that magnificence attributed to it by the

Abbe

Abbe Raynal : it is certainly a fine building, when compared with the other edifices of Philadelphia ; but it cannot be put in competition with thofe public buildings which we call fine in Europe.

There were about fifty members prefent, feated on chairs inclofed by a baluftrade. Behind the baluftrade, is the gallery for fpectators. A *Petit Maître*, who fhould fall fuddenly from Paris into this Affembly, would undoubtedly find it ridiculous. He would fcoff at the fimplicity of their cloth coats, and, in fome cafes, at the negligence of their toilettes ; but every man who thinks, will defire that this fimplicity may for ever remain, and become univerfal. They pointed out to me, under one of thefe plain coats, a farmer by the name of Findley, whofe eloquence difplays the greateft talents.

The eftate of General Miflin, where we went to dine, is five miles from town, by the falls of the Skuylkill. Thefe falls are formed by a confiderable bed of rocks : they are not perceiveable when the water of the river is high. The General's houfe enjoys a moft romantic profpect. This route prefents the veftiges of many houfes burnt by the Englifh,

glifh, who had likewife deftroyed all the
trees, and left the country naked.

I faw at General Miflin's, an old Quaker,
who fhook me by my hand with the more
pleafure, as he faid he found in my air a
refemblance of Anthony Benezet. Other
Quakers told me the fame thing. There is
no great vanity in citing this fact, when I
recollect what M. de Chaftellux fays of his
figure; but he had eyes of goodnefs and
humanity.

Springmill, where I went to fleep, is a
hamlet eight miles up the Skuylkill. The beft
houfe in it is occupied Mr. L. a Frenchman.
It enjoys the moft fublime profpect that you
can imagine. It is fituated on a hill. On
the fouth-eaft, the Skuylkill flows at its foot
through a magnificent channel between two
mountains covered with wood. On the banks
you perceive fome fcattering houfes and cultivated fields.

The foil is here compofed of a great quantity of talc, granit, and a yellow gravel;
fome places a very black earth. In the neighbourhood are quarries of marble of a middling
finenefs,

finenefs, of which many chimney-pieces are made.

I fhall give you fome details refpecting this Frenchman's farm ; they will fhew you the manner of living among cultivators here, and they may be ufeful to any of our friends who may wifh to eftablifh themfelves in this country. Obfervations on the manner of extending eafe and happinefs among men, are, in the eyes of the philofopher, as valuable as thofe which teach the art of affaffinating them. The houfe of Mr. L. is very well built in ftone, two ftories high, with five or fix fine chambers in each ftory. From the two gardens, formed like an amphitheatre, you enjoy that fine profpect above mentioned. Thefe gardens are well cultivated, and contain a great quantity of *bee-hives.*

A highway feparates the houfe from the farm. He keeps about twenty horned cattle, and ten or twelve horfes. The fituation of things on this farm, proves how little is to be feared from theft and robbery in this country; every thing is left open, or inclofed without locks. His farm confifts of two hundred and fifty acres ; of which the greater

part

part is in wood; the reft is in wheat, Indian corn, buck-wheat, and meadow. He fhewed me about an acre of meadow, from which he has already taken this year, eight tons of hay: he calculates, that, including the third cutting, this acre will produce him this year ten pounds. His other meadows are lefs manured, and lefs productive.

Mr. L. recounted to me fome of his paft misfortunes—I knew them before—He was the victim of the perfidy of an intendant of Guadaloupe, who, to fupprefs the proofs of his own accomplicity in a clandeftine commerce, tried to deftroy him by imprifonment, by affaffination, and by poifon. Efcaped from thefe perfecutions, Mr. L. enjoys fafety at Springmill; but he does not enjoy happinefs. He is alone; and what is a farmer without his wife and family?

He pays from five to fix pounds taxes for all his property, confifting of an hundred and twenty acres of wood land, eighty acres of arable, twenty-five acres of meadow, three acres of garden, a great houfe, feveral fmall houfes for his fervants, his barns, and his cattle. By this fact, you may judge of the exaggerations of the detractors of the United

United States on the fubject of taxes. Compare this with what would be paid in France for a like property. Mr. L. has attempted to cultivate the vine: he has planted a vineyard near his houfe, on a fouth-eaft expofure, and it fucceeds very well.

It is a remark to be made at every ftep in America, that vegetation is rapid and ftrong. The peach-tree, for example, grows faft, and produces fruit in great quantities. Within one month after you have cut your wheat, you would not know your field; it is covered with grafs, very high, and very thick.

It will be a long time, however, before the vine can be cultivated to profit in America: *firft*, becaufe labour is dear, and the vine requires vaft labour *; *fecondly*, becaufe the wines of Europe will be for a long time cheap in America. Mr. L. furnifhed me with the proof of this. He gave me fome very good Noufillon, which coft him, by the

---

* In Orleannois, the whole operation of cultivating the vine, and making the vintage, cofts to the proprietor thirty livres, twenty-five fhillings fterling, an acre. A man cannot perform the labour of more than five acres a year; fo that he gets fix pounds five fhillings a-year, and fupports himfelf. Compare this with the price of labour in America, and that with the price of French wines.

fingle

fingle bottle, only eightpence; and I know that this fame wine, at firft hand, coft five-pence or fixpence.

We ought to regard the birds as a great dif-couragement to the culture of the vine in America. You often fee immenfe clouds of black-birds, which, fettling on a vineyard, would deftroy it in an inftant.

I have already mentioned, that the paftures and fields in America are inclofed with bar-riers of wood, or fences. Thefe, when made of rails fupported by pofts, as above de-fcribed, are expenfive, efpecially in the neighbourhood of great towns, where wood is dear. Mr. L. thinks it beft to replace them by ditches fix feet deep, of which he throws the earth upon his meadows, and borders the fides with hedges; and thus renders the paf-fage impracticable to the cattle. This is an agricultural operation, which cannot be too much recommended to the Americans.

The country here is full of fprings; we faw fome very fine ones. Mr. L. told us of one which carries a mill night and day, and ferves to water his meadows when occafion requires.

I afked

I afked him where he purchafed his meat? He fays, when a farmer kills beef, mutton, or veal, he advertifes his neighbours, who take what they choofe, and he falts the re-mainder. As he is here without his family, he has no fpinning at his houfe; makes no cheefe, keeps no poultry. Thefe parts of rural economy, which are exercifed by wo-men, are loft to him; and it is a confider-able lofs. He fows no oats, but feeds his horfes with Indian corn and buck-wheat ground. I faw his vaft corn-fields covered with pumpkins, which are profitable for cat-tle. He has a joiner's fhop, and a turning-lathe. He makes great quantities of lime on his farm, which fells very well at Philadel-phia. He has obtained leave from the State to erect a ferry on the Skuylkill, which he fays will produce him a profit of forty pounds a-year. He is about to build a faw-mill.

The lands newly cleared, produce much more than the lands of France. He had bad wheat this year, though it had promifed well: having grown to a prodigious height, the grain was fhrivelled and meagre. He fays, the *mildew* has diminifhed his crop by more than three hundred bufhels. The

caufe

caufe of the mildew is fuppofed to be this:—
That when the feafon advances, it is fometimes attended by fogs, and very heavy dews:
the fun burfting through the fog, evaporates
the drops on the ftalk; and the fudden
change from cold and wet, to warm and dry,
enfeebles and withers the plant. The mildew is an evil very general in Pennfylvania.

Mr. L. told me, that there was no other
remedy but to fow early, that the plant may
be more vigorous at the feafon of the mildew.

This farm had coft him two thoufand
pounds; and he affured me, that, allowing
nothing for fome loffes occafioned by his ignorance of the country, of the language on his
firft arrival, and for the improvements he had
made, his land produces more than the intereft of his money. He told me, that the
houfe alone had coft more than he paid
for the whole: and this is very probable.
Perfons in general who defire to make good
bargains, ought to purchafe lands already
built upon; for, though the buildings have
coft much, they are counted for little in the
fale.

Though diftant from fociety, and ftruggling
againft

againft many difadvanges, he affured me that
he was happy; and that he fhould not fail
to be completely fo, were he furrounded by
his family, which he had left in France.

He is attentive to the fubject of meteoro-
logy; it is he that furnifhes the meteorologic
tables publifhed every month in the Colum-
bian Magazine: they are certainly the moft
exact that have appeared on this continent.
He thinks there is no great difference between
the climate here and that of Paris: that here,
the cold weather is more dry; that the fnow
and ice remain but a fhort time; that there
never paffes a week without fome fair days;
that there falls more rain here than in
France, but that it rarely rains two days fucceffively; that the heat is fometimes more
intenfe, that it provokes more to fweat and
to heavinefs; finally, that the variations are
here more frequent and more rapid.

The following is the refult of the obfervations of this Frenchman for four years :——
The greateft cold in this part of Pennfylvania, is commonly from ten to twelve degrees below the freezing point of Reaumur's
thermometer: the greateft heats are from
twenty-fix to twenty-eight degrees above:
                                        the

the mean term of his obfervations for four years, or the temperature, is nine degrees and fix tenths : the mean height of the barometer is twenty-nine inches ten lines and one tenth, Englifh meafure : the prevailing wind is north-north-weft. In the year there are fifteen days of thunder, feventy-fix days of rain, twelve days of fnow, five days of tempeft with rain; thefe eighty-one days of rain, with thofe of fnow, give thirty-five inches of water, French meafure. The fky is never obfcured three days together. The country is very healthy, and extremely vegetative. Wheat harveft is from the 8th to the 12th of July. No predominant ficknefs has been remarked during thefe four years.

LETTER

LETTER XVIII.

Journey of two Frenchmen to the Ohio.

Sept. 10. 1788.

I HAVE had the good fortune to meet here a Frenchman, who is travelling in this country, not in purfuit of wealth, but to gain information. It is Mr. Saugrain, from Paris: he is an ardent naturalift; fome circumftances firft attached him to the fervice of the King of Spain, who fent him to Spanifh America to make difcoveries in minerals and natural hiftory. After the death of his protector, Don Galves, he returned to France. In 1787, he formed the project with Mr. Piguet, who had fome knowledge in botany, to vifit Kentuckey and the Ohio.

They arrived at Philadelphia, and paffed immediately to Pittfburg. There the winter overtook them, and the Ohio froze over, which rarely happens. They lodged themfelves a few miles from Pittfburg, in an open houfe, where they fuffered much from the cold.

cold. The thermometer of Reaumur defcended to 32 degrees, while at Philadelphia
it was only at 16. During their ftay here,
they made many experiments. Mr. Saugrain weighed feveral kinds of wood in an
hydroftatic balance which he carried with
him. He difcovered, likewife, which fpecies
would yield the greateft quantity, and the
beft quality of potafh. Many experiments
convinced him, that the ftalks of Indian corn
yield a greater quantity than wood, in proportion to the quantity of matter. He examined the different mines of the country.
He found fome of iron, of lead, of copper,
and of filver. He was told of a rich iron-
mine belonging to Mr. Murray; but he was
not fuffered to fee it.

On the opening of the Spring, they defcended the Ohio, having been joined by another Frenchman, Mr. Rague, and a Virginian. They landed at Mufkinquam, where
they faw General Harmer, and fome people
who were beginning a fettlement there.

At fome diftance below this place, they
fell in with a party of favages. M. Piguet
was killed, and M. Sangrain wounded and
taken prifoner; he fortunately made his efcape,
rejoined

rejoined the Virginian, and found the means of returning to Pittſburg, having loſt his money and all his effects.   He then returned to Philadelphia, where I have met him, on his way to Europe.

He has communicated to me many ob-ſervations on the weſtern country.   The im-menſe valley waſhed by the Ohio, appears to him the moſt fertile that he has ever ſeen. The ſtrength and rapidity of vegetation in that country are incredible, the ſize of the trees enormous, and their variety infinite. The inhabitants are obliged to exhauſt the firſt fatneſs of the land in hemp and tobacco, in order to prepare it for the production of wheat.   The crops of Indian corn are pro-digious ; the cattle acquire an extraordinary ſize, and keep fat the whole year in the open fields.

The facility of producing grain, rearing cattle, making whiſky, beer, and cyder, with a thouſand other advantages, attract to this country great numbers of emigrants from other parts of America.   A man in that country, works ſcarcely two hours in a day, for the ſupport of himſelf and family ; he paſſes moſt of his time in idleneſs, hunting, or or drinking. The women fpin, and make cloaths for their hufbands and families. Mr. Saugrain faw very good woollens and linens made there. They have very little money; every thing is done by barter.

The active genius of the Americans is always pufhing them forward. Mr. Saugrain has no doubt but fooner or later the Spaniards will be forced to quit the Miffiffippi, and that the Americans will pafs it, and eftablifh themfelves in Louifiana, which he has feen, and confiders as one of the fineft countries in the univerfe.

Mr. Saugrain came from Pittfburg to Philadelphia in feven days, on horfeback. He could have come in a chaife; but it would have taken him a longer time. It is a poft road, with good taverns eftablifhed the whole way *.

* Mr. Saugrain is fo enchanted with the independent life of the inhabitants of the weftern country, that he returned again in the year 1790, to fettle at Scioto.

LETTER

LETTER XIX.

*On the School for the Blacks at Philadelphia,
and the principal American Authors who
have written in their favour.*

THERE exifts, then, a country where the
Negroes are allowed to have fouls, and
to be endowed with underftanding capable
of being formed to virtue and ufeful knowledge ; where they are not regarded as beafts
of burden, in order that we may have the
privilege of treating them as fuch. There
exifts a country, where the Blacks, by their
virtues and their induftry, belye the calumnies which their tyrants elfewhere lavifh
againft them ; where no difference is perceived between the memory of a black head
whofe hair is craped by nature, and that of a
white one craped by art. I have had a proof
of this to-day. I have feen, heard, and examined thefe black children. They read well,
repeat from memory, and calculate with rapidity. I have feen a picture painted by a
young negro, who never had a mafter: it
was furprifingly well done.

I faw

I faw in this fchool, a mulatto, one-eighth negro; it is impoffible to diftinguifh him from a white boy. His eyes difcovered an extraordinary vivacity; and this is a general characteriftic of people of that origin.

The black girls, befides reading, writing, and the principles of religion, are taught fpinning, needle-work, &c.; and their miftreffes affure me, that they difcover much ingenuity. They have the appearance of decency, attention, and fubmiffion. It is a nurfery of good fervants and virtuous houfe-keepers. How criminal are the planters of the iflands, who form but to debauchery and ignominy, creatures fo capable of being fafhioned to virtue!

It is to Benezet that humanity owes this ufeful eftablifhment—to that BENEZET whom Chaftellux has not blufhed to ridicule, for the fake of gaining the infamous applaufes of the parafites of defpotifm.

The life of this extraordinary man merits to be known to fuch men as dare to think, who efteem more the benefactors of their fellow-creatures, than their oppreffors, fo bafely idolized during their life.

Anthony

Anthony Benezet was born at St. Quintin, in Picardy, in 1712. Fanaticifm, under the protection of a bigot king, directed by an infamous confeffor, and an infamous woman, fpread at that time its ravages in France. The parents of Benezet were warm Calvinifts; they fled to England, and he embraced the doctrines of the Quakers. He went to America in 1731, and eftablifhed himfelf at Philadelphia in commerce, the bufinefs to which he had been educated. But the rigidity of his principles and his tafte not agreeing with the fpirit of commerce, he quitted that bufinefs in 1736, and accepted a place in the academy of that fociety. From that time all his moments were confecrated to public inftruction, the relief of the poor, and the defence of the unhappy negroes. Benezet poffeffed a univerfal philanthropy, which was not common at that time; he regarded, as his brothers, all men, of all countries, and of all colours; he compofed many works, in which he collected all the authorities from Scripture, and from other writings, to difcourage and condemn the flave trade and flavery. His works had much influence in determining the Quakers to emancipate their flaves.

It was not enough to fet at liberty the unhappy

unhappy Blacks; it was neceffary to inftruct them—to find them fchoolmafters. And where fhould he find men willing to devote themfelves to a tafk which prejudice had rendered painful and difgufting? No obftacle could arreft the zeal of Benezet; he fet the firft example himfelf: he confecrated his little fortune to the foundation of this fchool; his brethren lent fome affiftance; and by the help of the donations of the fociety of London, the fchool for Blacks at Philadelphia enjoys a revenue of 200l. fterling.

He confecrated his fortune and his talents to their inftruction; and in 1784, death removed him from this holy occupation, to receive his reward. The tears of the Blacks, which watered his tomb, the fighs of his fraternity, and of every friend of humanity which attended his departing fpirit, muft be a prize more confoling than the laurels of a conqueror.

Benezet carried always in his pocket a copy of his works on the Slavery of the Blacks, which he gave and recommended to every one he met, who had not feen them. It is a method generally followed by the Society of Friends. They extend the works of utility;

utility; and it is the true way of gaining proselytes.

This philanthropic quaker was preceded in the same career, by many others, whom I ought to mention. The celebrated George Fox, founder of this sect, went from England to Barbadoes in the year 1671, not to preach against slavery, but to instruct the blacks in the knowledge of God, and to engage masters to treat them with mildness.

The minds of men were not yet ripe for this reform; neither were they when William Burling, of Long-Island, in 1718, published a treatise against slavery. He was a respectable quaker: he preached, but in vain; the hour was not yet come.

Ought not this circumstance to encourage the friends of the blacks in France? Sixty years of combat were necessary to conquer the prejudice of avarice in America. One year is scarcely passed since the foundation of the society at Paris; and some apostates already appear, because success has not crowned their first endeavours.

Burling was followed by Judge Sewal, a
presbyterian

prefbyterian of Maffachufetts. He prefented
to the General Affembly, a treatife intitled
Jofeph fold by his brethren. He difcovers the
pureft principles, and completely overturns
the hackneyed arguments of the traders, refpecting the pretended wars of the African
princes.

It is often faid againft the writings of the
friends of the blacks, that they have not
been witneffes of the fufferings which they
defcribe. This reproach cannot be made
againft Benjamin Lay, an Englifhman, who,
brought up in the African trade, afterwards
a planter at Barbadoes, abandoned his plantation, on account of the horror infpired by
the frightful terrors of flavery endured by
the negroes. He retired to Philadelphia,
became a quaker, and ceafed not the remainder of his life to preach and write for the
abolition of flavery. His principal treatife
on this fubject appeared in 1737. He was
thought to have too much zeal, and to have
exaggerated in his defcriptions. But thefe
defects were expiated by a life without a
ftain, by an indefatigable zeal for humanity,
and by profound meditations. Lay was
fimple in his drefs, and animated in his
fpeech; he was all on fire when he fpoke on
flavery.

flavery. He died in 1760, in the 80th year of his age.

One of the men moft diftinguifhed in this career of humanity, was a quaker named John Woolman. He was born in 1720. Early formed to meditation, he was judged by the Friends worthy of being a minifter at the age of twenty-two. He travelled much to extend the doctrines of the fect; but was always on foot, and without money or provifions, becaufe he would imitate the apoftles, and be in a fituation to be more ufeful to the poor people and to the blacks. He abhorred flavery fo much, that he would not tafte any food that was produced by the labour of flaves. The laft difcourfe that he pronounced, was on this fubject. In 1772, he undertook a voyage to England, to concert meafures with the Friends there, on the fame fubject; where he died with the fmall-pox. He left feveral ufeful works, one of which has been through many editions, intitled *Confiderations on the Slavery of the Blacks.*

I thought it my duty, my friend, to give you fome account of thefe holy perfonages, before defcribing to you the fituation of the blacks in this immenfe country.

LETTER

LETTER XX.

*The means ufed to abolifh the Slave Trade, and
Slavery, in the United States.*

WOOLMAN and Benezet had in vain
employed all their efforts to effect the
abolition of this traffic under the Englifh
government. The miftaken intereft of the
mother country caufed all the petitions to
be rejected in the year 1772; yet the minds
of men were prepared in fome of the colonies; and fcarcely was independence declared, when a general cry arofe againft this
commerce. It appeared abfurd for men defending their own liberty, to deny liberty to
others. A pamphlet was printed, in which
the principles on which flavery is founded,
were held up in contraft with thofe which
laid the foundation of the new conftitution.

This palpable method of ftating the fubject, was attended with a happy fuccefs; and
the Congrefs, in 1774, declared the flavery of
the Blacks to be incompatible with the bafis
of republican governments. Different legiflatures

latures haftened to confecrate this principle of
Congrefs.

Three diftinct epochs mark the conduct of
the Americans in this bufinefs—the prohibition of the importation of flaves—their
manumiffion—and the provifion made for
their inftruction. All the different States are
not equally advanced in thefe three objects.

In the Northern and Middle States, they
have profcribed for ever the importation of
flaves ; in others, this prohibition is limited
to a certain time. In South Carolina, where
it was limited to three years, it has lately
been extended to three years more. Georgia
is the only State that continues to receive
tranfported flaves. Yet, when General Ogle-
thorpe laid the foundation of this colony, he
ordained, that neither rum nor flaves fhould
ever be imported into it. This law, in both
its articles, was very foon violated.

We muft acknowledge, however, that the
Americans, more than any other people, are
convinced that all men are born free and
equal : we muft acknowledge, that they direct
themfelves generally by this principle of equality ; that the Quakers, who have begun,
who

who have propagated, and who ftill propagate this revolution of fentiment, have been
guided by a principle of religion, and that
they have facrificed to it their perfonal intereft.

Unhappily their opinion on this fubject
has not yet become univerfal ; intereft ftill
combats it with fome fuccefs in the Southern
States.   A numerous party ftill argue the impoffibility of cultivating their foil without
the hands of flaves, and the impoffibility of
augmenting their number without recruit-
ing them in Africa.   It is to the influence of
this party, in the late general convention,
that is to be attributed the only article which
tarnifhes that glorious monument of human
reafon, the new federal fyftem of the United
States.   It was this party that propofed to
bind the hands of the new Congrefs, and to
put it out of their power for twenty years
to prohibit the importation of flaves.   It was
faid to this auguft affembly, *Sign this article,*
or we will withdraw from the union.   To
avoid the evils, which, without meliorating
the fate of the Blacks, would attend a political fchifm, the convention was forced to
wander from the grand principle of univerfal
liberty, and the preceding declaration of
Congrefs.

Congrefs. They thought it their duty to
imitate Solon, to make, not the beft law poffible, but the beft that circumftances would
bear.

But, though this article has furprifed the
friends of liberty in Europe, where the fecret
caufes of it were not known; though it has
grieved the fociety in England, who are ready
to accufe the new legiflators of a cowardly
defection from their own principles; yet we
may regard the general and irrevocable pro-
fcription of the flave trade in the United
States, as very near at hand. This conclufion
refults from the nature of things, and even
from the article itfelf of the new conftitution
now cited. Indeed, nine States have already
done it; the Blacks, which there abound,
are confidered as free. There are then nine
afylums for thofe to efcape to from Georgia, not to fpeak of the neighbourhood of
the Floridas, where the flaves from Georgia
take refuge, in hopes to find better treatment
from the Spaniards; and not to fpeak of thofe
vaft forefts and inacceffible mountains which
make part of the Southern States, and where
the perfecuted Negro may eafily find a retreat from flavery. The communications
with the back country are fo eafy, that it is
impoffible

impoffible to ftop the fugitives; and the expence of reclaiming is difproportioned to
their value. And though the free States do not
in appearance oppofe thefe reclamations, yet
the people there hold flavery in fuch horror,
that the mafter who runs after his human
property, meets little refpe&t, and finds little
affiftance. Thus the poffibility of flight
creates a new difcouragement to the importation, as it muft leffen the value of the flave,
induce to a milder treatment, and finally
tend, with the concurrence of other circumftances, to convince the Georgian planter,
that it is more fimple, more reafonable, and
lefs expenfive, to cultivate by the hands of
freemen. We are right then in faying, that
the nature of things in America is againft
the importation of flaves.

Befides, the Congrefs will be authorifed in
twenty years to pronounce definitively on this
article. By that time, the fentiments of humanity, and the calculations of reafon, will
prevail; they will no longer be forced to
facrifice equity to convenience, or have any
thing to fear from oppofition or fchifm.

LETTER

LETTER XXI.

Laws of the different States for the Manu-
miſſion of Slaves.

SLAVERY, my friend, has never polluted
every part of the United States.   There
was never any law in New Hampſhire, or
Maſſachuſetts, which authoriſed it.   When,
therefore, thoſe States proſcribed it, they only
declared the law as it exiſted before.   There
was very little of it in Connecticut; the puritanic auſterity which predominated in that
colony, could ſcarcely reconcile itſelf with
ſlavery.   Agriculture was better performed
there by the hands of freemen; and every
thing concurred to engage the people to give
liberty to the ſlaves:---ſo that almoſt every
one has freed them; and the children of ſuch
as are not yet free, are to have their liberty
at twenty-five years of age.

The caſe of the Blacks in New-York is
nearly the ſame; yet the ſlaves there are
more numerous.

It is becauſe the baſis of the population
there

there is Dutch; that is to fay, people lefs difpofed than any other to part with their property. But liberty is affured there to all the
children of the flaves, at a certain age.

The State of Rhode-Ifland formerly made
a great bufinefs of the flave trade. It is now
totally and for ever prohibited.

In New-Jerfey the bulk of the population
is Dutch. You find there, traces of that fame
Dutch fpirit which I have defcribed. Yet the
Weftern parts of the State are difpofed to free
their Negroes; but the Eaftern part are oppofed to it.

It is probable that their obftinacy will be
overcome; at leaft it is the opinion of the
refpectable Mr. Livingfton, celebrated for the
part he has acted in the late revolution: he
has declared this opinion in a letter written
to the Society at Philadelphia. He has himfelf freed all his flaves, which are very numerous. He is one of the moft ardent
apoftles of humanity; and, knowing the character of his countrymen, he reafons, tempo-
rifes with their intereft, and doubts not of
being able to vanquifh their prejudices. The
Quakers have been more fortunate in Pennfylvania.

fylvania. In the year 1758, they voted, in their general meeting, to excommunicate every member of the Society who fhould perfift in keeping flaves. In 1780, at their requeft, feconded by a great number of perfons from other fects, the General Affembly abolifhed flavery for ever, forced the owners of flaves to caufe them to be enregiftered, declared their children free at the age of twenty-eight years, placed them, while under that age, on a footing of hired fervants, affured to them the benefit of trial by jury, &c. But this act did not provide againft all the abufes that avarice could afterwards invent. It was illuded in many points. A foreign commerce of flaves was carried on by fpeculators ; and fome barbarous mafters fold their Blacks, to be carried into foreign countries; others fent the negro children into neighbouring States, that they might there be fold, and deprived of the benefit of the law of Pennfylvania, when they fhould come of age; others fent their black pregnant women into another State, that the offspring might be flaves; and others ftole free negroes, and carried them to the iflands for fale. The Society, fhocked at thefe abufes, applied again to the Affembly, who paffed a new act in March laft, effectually to prevent them. It ordained,

ordained, that no black could be fent into a neighbouring ftate without his confent; confifcated all veffels and cargoes employed in the flave trade; condemned to the public works the ftealers of negroes, &c.

Doubtlefs we cannot beftow too much praife on the indefagitable zeal of the Society in Pennfylvania, which folicited thefe laws, nor on the fpirit of equity and humanity difplayed by the legiflature in paffing them; but fome regret muft mingle itfelf with our applaufe. Why did not this refpectable body go farther? Why did it not extend at leaft the hopes of freedom to thofe who were flaves at the time of the paffing the firft act? They are a property, it is faid; and all property is facred. But what is a property founded on robbery and plunder? What is a property which violates laws human and divine? But let this property merit fome regard. Why not limit it to a certain number of years, in order to give at leaft the cheap confolation of hope? Why not grant to the flave, the right of purchafing his freedom? What! the child of the negro flave fhall one day enjoy his liberty; and the unhappy father, though ready to leap with joy on beholding the fortune of his fon, muft roll back his eyes with aggra-

vated

vated anguiſh on his own irrevocable bond-
age! The ſon has never felt, like him, the tor-
ture of being torn from his country, from his
family, from all that is dear to man; the ſon
has not experienced that ſeverity of treatment ſo common in this country before this
revolution of ſentiment; yet the ſon is fa-
voured, and the father conſigned to deſpair.
But this injuſtice cannot long ſully the law
of a country where reaſon and humanity
prevail. We may hope that a capitulation
will be made with avarice; by which theſe
ſlaves ſhall be drawn from its hands.

Again—Why, in the act of March 1780,
is it declared that a ſlave cannot be a witneſs
againſt a freeman? You either ſuppoſe him
leſs true than the freeman, or you ſuppoſe
him differently organiſed. The laſt ſuppo-
ſition is abſurd; the other, if true, is againſt
yourſelves; for, why are they leſs conſcien-
tious, more corrupted, and more wicked?—
it is becauſe they are ſlaves. The crime
falls on the head of the maſter; and the ſlave
is thus degraded and puniſhed for the vice
of the maſter.

Finally, why do you ordain that the maſter ſhall be reimburſed from the public trea-
ſury,

fury, the price of the flave who may fuffer
death for crimes? If, as is eafy to prove, the
crimes of flaves are almoft univerfally the
fruit of their flavery, and are in proportion
to the feverity of their treatment, is it not
abfurd to recompenfe the mafter for his tyranny? When we recollect that thefe mafters
have hitherto been accuftomed to confider
their flaves as a fpecies of cattle, and that the
laws make the mafter refponfible for the damages done by his cattle, does it not appear
contradictory to reverfe the law relative to
thefe black cattle, when they do a mifchief,
for which fociety thinks it neceffary to extirpate them? In this cafe, the real author of
the crime, inftead of paying damages, receives
a reward.

No, my friend, we will not doubt but
thefe ftains will foon difappear from the code
of Pennfylvania. Reafon is too predominant
to fuffer them long to continue.

The little State of Delaware has followed
the example of Pennfylvania. It is moftly
peopled by Quakers—inftances of giving
freedom are therefore numerous. In this
ftate, famous for the wifdom of its laws, for
its good faith and fœderal patriotifm, refides
that

that angel of peace, Warner Miflin. Like Benezet, he occupies his time in extending the opinions of his Society relative to the freedom of the blacks, and the care of providing for their exiftence and their inftruction. It is in part to his zeal that is owing the formation of a fociety in that ftate, after the model of the one at Philadelphia, for the abolition of flavery.

With the State of Delaware finifhes the fyftem of protection to the blacks. Yet there are fome negroes freed in Maryland, becaufe there are fome Quakers there; and you perceive it very readily, on comparing the fields of tobacco or of Indian corn belonging to thefe people, with thofe of others; you fee how much fuperior the hand of a freeman is to that of a flave, in the operations of induftry.

When you run over Maryland and Virginia, you conceive yourfelf in a different world; and you are convinced of it, when you converfe with the inhabitants. They fpeak not here of projects for freeing the negroes; they praife not the focieties of London and America; they read not the works of Clarkfon—No, the indolent mafters behold
with

with uneafinefs, the efforts that are making
to render freedom univerfal. The Virginians are perfuaded of the impoffibility of
cultivating tobacco without flavery ; they fear,
that if the Blacks become free, they will caufe
trouble ; on rendering them free, they know
not what rank to affign them in fociety ; whether they fhall eftablifh them in a feparate
diftrict, or fend them out of the country.
Thefe are the objections which you will hear
repeated every where againft the idea of freeing them.

The ftrongeft objection lies in the character, the manners and habits of the Virginians. They feem to enjoy the fweat of
flaves. They are fond of hunting; they love
the difplay of luxury, and difdain the idea of
labour. This order of things will change
when flavery fhall be no more. It is not,
that the work of a flave is more profitable
than that of a freeman; but it is in multiplying the flaves, condemning them to a miferable nourifhment, in depriving them of
cloaths, and in running over a large quantity of land with a negligent culture, that
they fupply the neceffity of honeft induftry.

L E T-

LETTER XXII.

On the general State, Manners, and Character
of the Blacks in the United States.

THE free Blacks in the Eaſtern States,
are either hired ſervants, or they keep
little ſhops, or they cultivate the land. You
will ſee ſome of them on board of coaſting
veſſels. They dare not venture themſelves
on long voyages, for fear of being tranſported
and ſold in the iſlands. As to their phyſical
character, the Blacks are vigorous, of a ſtrong
conſtitution*, capable of the moſt painful
labour, and generally active. As ſervants,
they are ſober and faithful. Thoſe who
keep ſhops, live moderately, and never augment their affairs beyond a certain point.

The reaſon is obvious; the Whites, though
they treat them with humanity, like not to

* The married Blacks make at leaſt as many children as the
Whites ; but it is obſerved, that more of them die. This is
owing leſs to Nature, than to the want of fortune, and of the
care of phyſicians and ſurgeons.

give

give them credit to enable them to undertake any extenfive commerce, nor even to
give them the means of a common education,
by receiving them into their counting-houfes.
If, then, the Blacks are confined to the retails
of trade, let us not accufe their capacity, but
the prejudices of the Whites, which lay obftacles in their way.

The fame caufes hinder the Blacks who
live in the country, from having large plantations. Their little fields are generally well
cultivated; their log-houfes, full of children
decently clad, attract the eye of the philofopher, who rejoices to fee, that, in thefe habi-
tations, no tears atteft the rod of tyranny.

In this fituation the Blacks are indeed happy; but let us have the courage to avow,
that neither this happinefs, nor their talents,
have yet attained their perfection. There
exifts ftill too great an interval between them
and the Whites, efpecially in the public opinion. This humiliating difference prevents
thofe efforts which they might make to raife
themfelves. Black children are admitted to
the public fchools; but you never fee them
within the walls of a college. Though free,
they

they are always accuftomed to confider themfelves as beneath the Whites.

We may conclude from this, that it is un-
fair to meafure the extent of their capacity
by the examples already given by the free
Blacks of the North.

But when we compare them to the flaves
of the South, what a difference we find!---In
the South, the Blacks are in a ftate of abjection
difficult to defcribe; many of them are naked,
ill fed, lodged in miferable huts, on ftraw.
They receive no education, no inftruction in
any kind of religion; they are not married,
but coupled.   Thus are they brutalized, lazy,
without ideas, and without energy.   They
give themfelves no trouble to procure cloaths,
or to have better food; they pafs their Sunday, which is their day of reft, in total inaction.   Inaction is their fupreme happinefs;
they therefore perform little labour, and that
in a carelefs manner.

We muft do juftice to the truth.   The
Americans of the Southern States treat their
flaves with mildnefs; it is one of the effects
of the general extenfion of the ideas of liberty.

ty. The flave labours lefs; but this is all the alteration made in his circumftances, and he is not the better for it, either in his nourifhment, his clothing, his morals, or his ideas. So that the mafter lofes; but the flave does not gain. If they would follow the example of the Northern States, both Whites and Blacks would be gainers by the change.

When we defcribe the flaves of the South, we ought to diftinguifh thofe that are employed as houfe-fervants, from thofe that work and live in the field. The picture that I have given, belongs to the latter; the former are better clad, more active, and lefs ignorant.

It has been generally thought, and even written by fome authors of note, that the Blacks are inferior to the Whites in mental capacity. This opinion begins to difappear; the Northern States furnifh examples to the contrary. I fhall cite two, which are ftriking ones: the firft proves, that, by inftruction, a Black may be rendered capable of any of the profeffions: the fecond, that the head of a Negro may be organifed for the moft aftonifhing calculations, and confequently for all the fciences.

I faw

I faw at Philadelphia a black phyfician, named James Derham. The following hiftory of him was attefted to me by many phyficians:

He was brought up a flave in a family of Philadelphia, where he learned to read and write, and was inftructed in the principles of religion. When young, he was fold to Doctor John Kearfley junior, who employed him in compounding medicines, and in adminiftering them in fome cafes to the fick. At the death of Doctor Kearfley he paffed through different hands, and came to be the property of George Weft, furgeon of the Britifh army, under whom, during the war in America, he performed the lower functions in phyfic.

At the clofe of the war, he was purchafed by Doctor Robert Dove of New Orleans, who employed him as his affiftant. He gained the Doctor's good opinion and friendfhip to fuch a degree that he foon gave him his freedom on moderate conditions. Derham was, by this time, fo well inftructed, that he immediately began to practife, with fuccefs, at New Orleans: he is about twenty-fix years of age, married, but has no children. His practice brings him three thoufand livres a-year. Doctor Wiftar told me, that he converfed with him particularly

particularly on the acute difeafes of the country where he lives, and found him well verfed in the fimple methods now in practice of
treating thofe difeafes.   I thought, faid the
Doctor, to have indicated to him fome new
remedies ; but he indicated new ones to me.

He is modeft, and has engaging manners;
he fpeaks French with facility, and has fome
knowledge of Spanifh.

The other inftance has been cited by Doctor Rufh, a celebrated phyfician and writer
of Philadelphia.   It is Thomas Fuller, born in
Africa, a flave, near feventy years of age,
near Alexandria.   He can neither read nor
write, and has had no inftruction of any
kind ; but he calculates with furprifing facility, and will anfwer any queftion in arithmetic, with a promptitude that has no example.

Thefe inftances prove, without doubt, that
the capacity of the negroes may be extended
to any thing ; that they have only need of
inftruction and liberty.   The difference between thofe who are free and inftructed, and
thofe who are not, is ftill more vifible in
their induftry.   The lands inhabited by the
whites

whites and free blacks, are better cultivated, produce more abundantly, and offer every-where the image of eafe and happinefs. Such, for example, is the afpectof Connecticut, and of Pennfylvania.

Pafs into Maryland and Virginia, and, as I faid before, you are in another world;—you find not there thofe cultivated plains, thofe neat country-houfes, barns well diftri-buted, and numerous herds of cattle, fat and vigorous. No: every thing in Maryland and Virginia wears the print of flavery: a ftarved foil, bad cultivation, houfes falling to ruin, cattle fmall and few, and black walking fkeletons; in a word, you fee real mifery, and apparent luxury, infulting each other.

They begin to perceive, even in the South-ern States, that, to nourifh a flave ill, is a miftaken œconomy; and that money em-ployed in their purchafe, does not render its intereft. It is perhaps more owing to this confideration than to humanity, that you fee free labour introduced in a part of Virginia, in that part bordered by the beautiful river Shenadore. In travelling here, you will think yourfelf in Pennfylvania.

Such

Such will be the face of all Virginia, when
flavery fhall be at an end.   They think flaves
neceffary only for the cultivation of tobacco :
this culture declines, and muft decline in Virginia.   The tobacco of the Ohio and the Miffiffippi is more abundant, of a better quality,
and requires lefs labor.   When this tobacco
fhall open its way to Europe, the Virginians
will be obliged to ceafe from this culture, and
afk of the earth, wheat, corn, and potatoes ;
they will make meadows, and rear cattle.
The wife Virginians anticipate this revolution,
and begin the culture of wheat.   At their head
may be reckoned that aftonifhing man, who,
though an adored General, had the courage
to be a fincere republican ; who alone feems
ignorant of his own glory ; whofe fingular
deftiny it will be to have twice faved his country, to have opened to her the road to profperity, after having conducted her to liberty.
At prefent, wholly occupied in ameliorating
his lands, in varying their produce, in opening roads and canals, he gives his countrymen an ufeful example, which doubtlefs will
be followed.

He has neverthelefs (muft I fay it ?) a numerous crowd of flaves ; but they are treated
with

with the greateſt humanity; well fed, well
clothed, and kept to moderate labour; they
bleſs God without ceaſing, for having given
them ſo good a maſter.   It is a taſk worthy
of a ſoul ſo elevated, ſo pure, and ſo diſinte-
reſted, to begin the revolution in Virginia,
to prepare the way for the emancipation of
the negroes. This great man declared to me,
that he rejoiced at what was doing in other
States on this ſubjeƈt ; that he ſincerely deſired the extenſion of it in his own country:
but he did not diſſemble, that there were
ſtill many obſtacles to be overcome ; that it
was dangerous to ſtrike too vigorouſly at a
prejudice which had begun to diminiſh ; that
time, patience, and information, would not
fail to vanquiſh it.   Almoſt all the Virginians, added he, believe that the liberty of the
blacks cannot ſoon become general.   This is
the reaſon why they wiſh not to form a ſociety, which may give dangerous ideas to their
ſlaves.   There is another obſtacle—the great
plantations of which the State is compoſed,
render it neceſſary for men to live ſo diſperſ-
ed, that frequent meetings of a ſociety would
be difficult.

I replied, that the Virginians were in an
error,

error, that evidently fooner or later the negroes would obtain their liberty every-where.
It is then for the intereft of your countrymen to prepare the way to fuch a revolution,
by endeavouring to reconcile the reftitution
of the rights of the blacks with the intereft of
the whites. The means neceffary to be taken
to this effect, can only be the work of a fociety; and it is worthy the faviour of America
to put himfelf at their head, and to open the
door of liberty to three hundred thoufand unhappy beings of his own State. He told me,
that he defired the formation of a fociety, and
that he would fecond it; but that he did not
think the moment favourable. — Doubtlefs
more elevated views abforbed his attention,
and filled his foul. The deftiny of America
was juft ready to be placed a fecond time in
his hands.

It is certainly a misfortune that fuch a fociety does not exift in Virginia and Maryland; for it is to the perfevering zeal of thofe
of Philadelphia and New-York, that we owe
the progrefs of this revolution in America,
and the formation of the fociety in London.

Why am I unable to paint to you the im-
preffions

preffions I received in attending the meetings of thefe different focieties ? What ferenity in the countenances of the members ! What fimplicity in their difcourfes, candour in their difcuffions, beneficence and energy in their decifions ! Each feemed eager to fpeak, not to fhew his brilliance, but to be ufeful.

With what joy they learned that a like fociety was formed at Paris, in that capital fo renowned for its opulence and luxury, for its influence over a vaft kingdom, and through moft of the ftates of Europe ! They haftened to publifh it in all the gazettes, as likewife the tranflation of the firft difcourfe pronounced in that fociety. They faw with joy, in the lift of the members, the name of La Fayette, and that of other perfons known for their energy and patriotifm.

They did not doubt, if this fociety fhould brave the firft obftacles that attend it, and fhould unite itfelf with that of London, but that the information which they might give on the flave trade, and its unprofitable infamy, would enlighten the governments of Europe, and determine them to fupprefs it.

It

It is doubtlefs to this effufion of joy, and to the flattering recommendations which I carried from Europe, rather than to my feeble efforts, that I owe the honor of being received a member of thefe focieties. They did not confine themfelves to this ; they appointed committees to affift me in my labours, and their archives were opened to me.

Thefe beneficent focieties are at prefent contemplating new projects for the completion of their work of juftice and humanity. They are endeavouring to form fimilar inftitutions in other States, and they have fucceeded in the State of Delaware. The bufinefs of thefe focieties is not only to extend light and information to legiflatures, and to the people at large *, on the objects they have in view, and to form the blacks by early inftruction in the duties of citizens ; but they extend gratuitous protection to them in all cafes of individual oppreffion, and make it their duty to watch over the execution of the laws which have been obtained in their fa-

---

* In 1787, the Society of New-York offered a gold medal for the beft difcourfe, at the public commencement at the college, on the injuftice and cruelty of the flave trade, and the fatal effects of flavery.

vour. Mr. Myers Fifher, one of the firft lawyers of Philadelphia, is always ready to lend them his affiftance, which he generally does with fuccefs, and always without reward. Thefe focieties have committees in different parts of the country, to take notice of any infractions of thefe laws of liberty, and to propofe to the legiflature fuch amendments as experience may require.

Appendix to the preceding Letter, written in 1791.

MY wifhes have not been difappointed. The progrefs of thefe focieties is rapid in the United States: there is one already formed even in Virginia * ; even there, men have dared to publifh that truth which has fo often made avarice to tremble—that truth which formerly would have been ftifled in a Baftille: *God has created men of all nations, of all languages, of all colours, equally free : Slavery, in all its forms, in all its degrees, is a violation of the Divine laws, and a degradation of human nature.*

* A fimilar fociety is lately formed in the State of Connecticut, probably not known to M. de Warville. TRANSLATOR.

Believe

Believe it, my dear friend, thefe truths, conveyed in all the public papers, will complete the extirpation of that odious flavery, which the nature of things in that country is deftroying with great rapidity. For you may well imagine, that, in the rage of emigration to the weftern territory *, the negroes find it eafy to fly from flavery, and that they are well received wherever they go.

The folemn examples given by great men, will contribute much to this revolution of principle. What proprietor of human beings does not blufh for himfelf, on feeing the celebrated General Gates affemble his numerous flaves, and, in the midft of their careffes and tears of gratitude, reftore them all to liberty; and in fuch a manner as to prevent any fatal confequences that might refult to them from the fudden enjoyment of fo great a benefit?

The fociety of Philadelphia, which may be regarded as the father of thefe holy inftitutions, has lately taken more effectual meafures, both to inftruct the blacks, and to form them

* In all the conftitutions of the New States forming in the weftern territory, it is declared, that there fhall be neither flavery nor involuntary fervitude.

to different employments. " The wretch,"
fay they, in their addrefs to the public, " who
" has long been treated as a beaft of burthen,
" is often degraded fo far as to appear of a
" fpecies inferior to that of other men ; the
" chains which bind his body, curb likewife
" his intellectual faculties, and enfeeble the
" focial affections of his heart."

To inftruct and counfel thofe who are free,
and render them capable of enjoying civil liberty; to excite them to induftry; to furnifh
them with occupations fuitable to their age,
fex, talents, and other circumftances ; and to
procure to their children an education fuitable to their ftation, are the principal objects
of this fociety.

For this end they have appointed four committees : firft, a committee of infpection, to
watch over the morals and general conduct of
the free blacks ; fecond, a committee of guar-
dians, whofe bufinefs it is to place the children with honeft tradefmen and others, to acquire trades ; third, a committee of education, to overfee the fchools ; fourth, a committee of employ, who find employment for
thofe who are in a fituation to work.   What
friend

friend of humanity does not leap with joy at
the view of an object fo pious and fublime ?
Who does not perceive it is dictated by that
fpirit of perfeverance, which animates men
of dignity, habituated to good actions, not
from oftentation, but from a confcioufnefs of
duty? Such are the men who compofe thefe
American focieties. They will never abandon this good work, until they have carried it
to its laft degree of perfection ; that is to fay,
until, by gentle and equitable means, they
fhall have placed the blacks in every refpect
on a footing with the whites. Yet thefe are
the celeftial focieties which infamous avarice
blufhes not to calumniate.

The perfeverance with which thefe focieties have extended their principles in their
writings, brought forward, laft year, a debate
in Congrefs, on the fubject of procuring a re-
vocation of that article in the conftitution,
which fufpends the power of Congrefs for
twenty years on the fubject of the flave trade.

I ought to have mentioned to you, in my
letter, an eloquent addrefs to the general convention of 1787, from the fociety of Pennfylvania. I will cite to you the clofe of it :
" We

" We conjure you," fay they, " by the attributes of the Divinity, infulted by this inhuman traffic ; by the union of all the human
race in our common father, and by all the
obligations refulting from this union ; by the
fear of the juft vengeance of God in national
judgments; by the certainty of the great
and terrible day of the diftribution of rewards
and punifhments ; by the efficacy of the prayers of good men, who would infult the Ma-
jefty of Heaven, if they were to offer them
in favour of our country, as long as the ini-
quity we now practife continues its ravages
among us ; by the facred name of Chriftians ;
by the pleafures of domeftic connections, and
the anguifh of their diffolution ; by the fufferings of our American brethren, groaning in
captivity at Algiers, which Providence feems
to have ordained to awaken us to a fentiment
of the injuftice and cruelty of which we are
guilty towards the wretched Africans ; by the
refpect due to confiftency in the principles and
conduct of true republicans ; by our great and
intenfe defire of extending happinefs to the
millions of intelligent beings who are doubtlefs one day to people this immenfe continent ; finally, by all other confiderations,
which religion, reafon, policy, and humanity can fuggeft ; we conjure the Convention of
the

the United States, to make the fuppreffion of
the flave trade a fubject of ferious deliberation."

Addreffes from all parts of the United
States, figned by the moft refpectable men,
have been prefented to the new Congrefs.
Never was a fubject more warmly debated ;
and, what never happened before in America,
it gave occafion to the moft atrocious invectives from the adverfaries of humanity. You
will not doubt that thefe adverfaries were the
deputies from the South. I except, however,
the virtuous Madifon, and efpecially Mr.
Vining, brother of that refpectable woman fo
unjuftly outraged by Mr. Chaftellux. He
defended, with real eloquence, the caufe of
the blacks.

I muft not forget to name among the advocates of humanity, Meff. Scott, Gerry, and
Boudinot. You will be aftonifhed to find
among their adverfaries the firft denunçiator of
the Cincinnati, Mr. Burke ; he who unfolded, with fo much energy, the fatal confequences of the inequality which this order would
introduce among the citizens ; and the fame
man could fupport the much more horrible
inequality eftablifhed between the whites and
blacks.

You

You will be ftill more aftonifhed to learn,
that he uniformly employed the language of
invective.   This is the weapon that the partizans of flavery always ufe in America, in
England, and in France.

One of the moft ardent petitioners to Congrefs in this caufe, was the refpectable Warner Miflin.   His zeal was rewarded with
atrocious calumnies, which he always anfwered with mildnefs, forgivenefs, and argument.

LETTER

LETTER XXIII.

On replacing the Sugar of the Cane by the Sugar of Maple.

ON this continent, my friend, so polluted and tormented with flavery, Providence has placed two powerful and infallible means of destroying this evil. The means are, the focieties of which we have been speaking, and the fugar-maple.

Of all vegetables containing fugar, this maple, after the fugar-cane, contains the greatest quantity. It grows naturally in the United States, and may be propagated with great facility. All America feems covered with it, from Canada to Virginia; it becomes more rare at the fouthward, on the eaft of the mountains; but it is found in abundance in the back country.

Such is the beneficent tree which has, for a long time, recompenfed the happy colonifts, whofe pofition deprived them of the delicate fugar of our iflands.

They

They have till lately contented themfelves with beftowing very little labour on the manufacture, only bringing it to a ftate of common coarfe fugar; but fince the Quakers have difcerned in this production, the means of deftroying flavery, they have felt the neceffity of carrying it to perfection; and fuccefs has crowned their endeavours.

You know, my friend, all the difficulties attending the cultivation of the cane. It is a tender plant; it has many enemies, and requires conftant care and labour to defend it from numerous accidents: add to thefe, the painful efforts that the preparation and manufacture cofts to the wretched Africans; and, on comparing thefe to the advantages of the maple, you will be convinced, by a new argument, that much pains are often taken to commit unprofitable crimes. The maple is produced by nature; the fap to be extracted, requires no preparatory labour; it runs in February and March, a feafon unfuitable for other rural operations. Each tree, without injury to itfelf, gives twelve or fifteen gallons, which will produce at leaft five pounds of fugar. A man aided by four children, may eafily, during four weeks running

running of the fap, make fifteen hundred pounds of fugar *.

Advantages, like thefe, have not failed to excite the attention of the friends of humanity; fo that, befides the focieties formed for the abolition of flavery, another is formed, whofe exprefs object is to perfect this valuable production.

Mr. Drinker † of Philadelphia, made, laft year, fixty barrels of maple fugar on his eftate on the Delaware ; and he has publifhed a pamphlet on the beft method of proceeding in this manufacture.

Edward Pennington, of Philadelphia, for-

* M. Lanthenas, one of the moft enlightened defenders of the Blacks in France, has made fome calculations on this fubject, which cannot be too often repeated. Suppofing, fays he, that a family will produce in a feafon 1500lb. of fugar, 80,000 families will produce, and that with very little trouble, a quantity equal to what is exported from St. Domingo in the moft plentiful year, which is reckoned at one hundred and twenty millions. This fuppofes twenty millions of trees, rendering five pounds each, eftimating the acre of the United States at 38,476 fquare feet of France ; and fuppofing the trees planted at feven feet diftance, about 30,000 acres appropriated to this ufe, would fuffice for the above quantity of fugar.

† Some of the following facts took place in 1789 and 1790, as my friends have written me from Philadelphia. I thought proper to infert them in this letter, to which they belong.

merly

merly a refiner in the Weft Indies, has declared this fugar equal to that of the iflands,
in grain, colour, and tafte.

The cultivators in the State of New-York
perceive, in an equal degree, the advantages of
this production ; they have made, this year, a
great quantity of fugar, and brought it to
great perfection.

Whenever there fhall form from North to
South a firm coalition, an ardent emulation
to multiply the produce of this divine tree,
and efpecially when it fhall be deemed an
impiety to deftroy it *, not only America may
fupply herfelf, but fhe may fill the markets
of Europe with a fugar, the low price of
which will ruin the fale of that of the iflands
—a produce wafhed with the tears and the
blood of flaves.

What an aftonifhing effect it would produce,
to naturalize this tree through all Europe !
In France, we might plant them at twenty

---

* A farmer has publifhed, that no lefs than three millions
of the maple trees are deftroyed annually in clearing the lands
in the fingle State of New-York. It is certainly worthy the
care of every Legiflature in the Union, to prevent the deftruction of fo ufeful a tree, which feems to have been planted by
the hand of Heaven, for the confolation of man.

feet

feet diftance, in a kind of orchard, which would at the fame time produce pafture, fruits, and other vegetables. In this manner an acre would contain 140 trees, which, even when young, would produce three pounds of fugar a-year. This would give 420 pounds the acre, which, at threepence fterling the pound, and deducting one half for the labour, would yield annually 52l. 6s. fterling, clear profit ; befides other productions, which thefe trees would not impede. This calculation might be reafonably carried much higher ; but I chofe to keep it as low as poffible *.

Thus we fhould obtain a profitable pro-duction in Europe, and diminifh fo many ftrokes of the whip, which our luxury draws upon the blacks. Why is it, that, in our ca-pital, where the delicacy of fentiment is fome-

* The author ought to have carried the idea further. The fugar maple for fuel is equal to the beft oak ; for cabinet work, and many fimilar ufes, it is fuperior to moft of the fpecies of wood ufed in Europe ; as a tree of ornament and pleafure, it is at leaft equal to the elm or poplar. How many millions of young trees, for the above ufes, are planted every year in all parts of Europe, to renew and perpetuate the forefts, the pub-lic walks, the public and private gardens and parks, to border the great roads, &c.! for all thefe purpofes the fugar maple might be planted, and the juice to be drawn from it might be reckoned a clear profit to the world. The experiment of M. Noailles, in his garden at St. Germains, proves that this Ame-rican tree would fucceed well in Europe.—TRANSLATOR.

times

times equal to that of fenfation, no focieties
are formed, whofe object fhould be to fweeten
their coffee with a fugar not embittered by
the idea of the exceffive tears, cruelties, and
crimes, without which thefe productions have
not been hitherto procured?—an idea which
cannot fail to prefent itfelf to the imagination of every humane and enlightened man.
Our devotees, our ignorant and inhuman
priefts, who never fail to be great lovers of
coffee and fugar, would, by thefe means, be
faved from the horrible part which they take
in the moft enormous crime on which the fun
ever fhone. In confuming thefe articles, do
they not encourage thofe whofe guilt is more
direct in the operation of producing them?
and yet, with what coldnefs, with what culpable indifference, do thefe pious men look upon
our Society of the Friends of the Blacks!

LETTER

LETTER XXIV.

*On a Plan for the Re-emigration of the Blacks
of the United States, to Africa.*

I HAVE already, my friend, given you a
ſketch of the ideas of Dr. Thornton on
this ſubject. This ardent friend of the Blacks
is perſuaded, that we cannot hope to ſee a
ſincere union between them and the Whites,
as long as they differ ſo much in colour, and
in their rights as citizens. He attributes to
no other cauſe, the apathy perceivable in many
Blacks, even in Maſſachuſetts, where they
are free. Deprived of the hope of electing
or being elected repreſentatives, or of riſing
to any places of honour and truſt, the Negroes
ſeem condemned to drag out their days in a
ſtate of ſervility, or to languiſh in ſhops of
retail. The Whites reproach them with a
want of cleanlineſs, indolence, and inattention. But how can they be induſtrious and
active, while an inſurmountable barrier ſeparates them from other citizens?

Even

Even on admitting them to all the rights
of citizens, I know not if it would be poffible
to effect a lafting and fincere union ; we are
fo ftrongly inclined to love our likenefs, that
there would be unceafing fufpicions, jealoufies, and partialities, between the Whites and
Blacks. We muft then recur to the project
of Mr. Thornton—a project firft imagined
by that great apoftle of philanthropy, Doctor
Fothergill!—a project executed by the Society at London, or rather by the beneficent
Grenville Sharp!—a project for reftoring the
Negroes to their country, to eftablifh them
there, and encourage them in the cultivation
of coffee, fugar, cotton, &c. to carry on manufacture, and to open a commerce with
Europe. Mr. Thornton has occupied himfelf
with this confoling idea. He propofed himfelf to be the conductor of the American
Negroes who fhould repair to Africa. He
propofed to unite them to the new colony at
Sierra-Leona. He had fent, at his own expence, into Africa, a well-inftructed man,
who had fpent feveral years in obferving the
productions of the country, the manufactures
moft fuitable to it, the place moft convenient,
and the meafures neceffary to be taken to
fecure the colony from infults, and every
thing was prepared. He had communicated

his

his plan to fome Members of the Legiflature of Maffachufetts, who did not at firft relifh it. They liked better to give lands to their Negroes, and encourage them in the cultivation. But, fays the Doctor, what can they do with their land, unaccuftomed to war, and furrounded by favages? Suppofing them to fucceed, will you admit their reprefentatives to fit in your Affemblies, to prefide over you? ---No. Reftore them then to their native country.

The Doctor was perfuaded, that when his defign fhould be known, thoufands of the Negroes would follow him. He had remarked, as well as I, the injuftice of reproaching them with the fpirit of idlenefs. If they are lazy, fays he, why fo much expence to go and fteal them from their country for the fake of their labour?

His reafoning begins to convince men of reflexion, and his plan gives a folution to the problem of Mr. Jefferfon.---*See Notes on Virginia.*

The State of Maffachufetts has fince received a requeft from the Negroes, for the execution of the project. They have promifed

mifed to give aid to it, as foon as they fhall be affured of a fituation in Africa proper for a good eftablifhment : they have even promifed to furnifh veffels, inftruments, provifions, &c.

What advantage would refult to Africa, to Europe, and even to America, from the execution of this plan! For the Blacks of Africa would gradually civilize by the affiftance of thofe from America ; and the Whites, whom they ought to execrate, would never mingle with them. By this civilization, Europe would open a vaft market to her manufactures, and obtain, at a cheap rate, and without the effufion of blood, thofe productions which coft her at the iflands fo much money and fo many crimes. God grant that this idea may foon be realized * !

A Society is formed in England, whofe object is to follow the eftablifhment of Sierra Leona, and open a trade there for the productions of the country. This fettlement is on land belonging to the Englifh, and dependant on the Englifh Government.

* To perceive the advantages, read the work intitled *L'Amiral refuté par lui-meme ;* and fee the efforts made in England, to eftablifh colonies in Africa, and to civilize the Blacks.

Another

Another fociety is formed, whofe object is partly the fame, but who wifh to render this eftablifhment independent of every European Government. They have lately publifhed their plan, under the following title : *Plan of a free Community on the Coaft of Africa, formed under the protection of Great Britain, but entirely independent of all European Government and Laws; with an invitation, under certain conditions, to thofe who may defire to partake of the advantages of this undertaking.*

In this plan, of which every friend to humanity muft wifh the fuccefs, it is declared, that the Society is founded on the principle of univerfal philanthropy, and not fimply for the neceffities of commerce :---advantages too much prized ; as if the happinefs of all the human race confifted in the acquifition of wealth.

LETTER

LETTER XXV.

On Philadelphia, its buildings, police, &c.

IN confidering the vices which tarnifh Old Europe, and the mild fraternity that unites the Quakers, Voltaire fometimes flew off in imagination beyond the feas, and longed to go and finifh his days in the City of Brothers. What would he have faid, had he been able to have realized his dream, and to have been a witnefs of the peace which reigns in this town? I am wrong: Voltaire would have haftened to return to Europe: he burned with the love of glory; he lived upon incenfe, and he would have received but little here. The gravity of the Quakers would have appeared to him a gloomy pedantry: he would have yawned in their affemblies, and been mortified to fee his epigrams pafs without applaufe; he would have fighed for the fparkling wit of his amiable fops of Paris.

Philadelphia may be confidered as the metropolis of the United States. It is certainly the

the fineft town, and the beft built ; it is the
moft wealthy, though not the moft luxurious.
You find here more men of information,
more political and literary knowledge, and
more learned focieties. Many towns in America are more ancient ; but Philadelphia has
furpaffed her elders.

The Swedes were firft eftablifhed on the
fpot where this town has been fince built.
The Swedifh church on the banks of the Delaware is more than one hundred years old.
It is the oldeft church in the town, at prefent
under the care of Dr. Collins, a Swedifh minifter of great learning and merit. He writes
very well in Englifh, and has compofed many
works in that language ; among which is
the *Foreign Spectator*, in which he unfolds
the foundeft principles of republican policy.
He is a fervent apoftle of liberty.

Penn brought into his new colony a government truly fraternal. Brothers who
live together, have no need of foldiers, nor
forts, nor police, nor that formidable appa-
ratus which makes of European towns garri-
fons of war.

At ten o'clock in the evening all is tranquil
in

in the ftreets; the profound filence which reigns there, is only interrupted by the voice of the watchmen, who are in fmall numbers, and who form the only patrole. The ftreets are lighted by lamps, placed like thofe of London.

On the fide of the ftreets are footways of brick, and gutturs conftructed of brick or wood. Strong pofts are placed to prevent carriages from paffing on the footways. All the ftreets are furnifhed with public pumps, in great numbers. At the door of each houfe are placed two benches, where the family fit at evening to take the frefh air, and amufe themfelves in looking at the paffengers. It is certainly a bad cuftom, as the evening air is unhealthful, and the exercife is not fufficient to correct this evil, for they never walk here: they fupply the want of walking, by riding out into the country. They have few coaches at Philadelphia. You fee many handfome waggons, which are ufed to carry the family into the country; they are a kind of long carriage, light and open, and may contain twelve perfons. They have many chairs and fulkeys, open on all fides; the former may carry two perfons, the latter only one.

The

The horfes ufed in thefe carriages are neither handfome nor ftrong ; but they travel very well. I have not yet met with thofe fine horfes of which M. de Crevecœur fpeaks, and which I thought were equal to the enormous breed of Flanders. I fufpect the Americans of not taking fufficient care of their horfes, and of nourifhing them ill ; they give them no ftraw in the ftable: on returning from long and fatiguing courfes, they are fent to pafture.

Philadelphia is built on a regular plan ; long and large ftreets crofs each other at right angles : this regularity, which is a real ornament, is at firft embarraffing to a ftranger ; he has much difficulty in finding himfelf, efpecially as the ftreets are not infcribed, and the doors not numbered. It is ftrange that the Quakers, who are fo fond of order, have not adopted thefe two conveniences; that they have not borrowed them from the Englifh, of whom they have borrowed fo many things. This double defect is a torment to ftrangers. The fhops, which adorn the principal ftreets, are remarkable for their neatnefs.

The State-houfe, where the Legiflature affembles, is a handfome building: by its fide
they

they are building a magnificent houfe of juftice.

Mr. Raynal has exaggerated every thing;
the buildings, the library, the ftreets : he
fpeaks of ftreets 100 feet wide; there is
none of this width, except Market-ftreet;
they are generally from 50 to 60 feet wide.
He fpeaks of wharfs of 200 feet: there is
none fuch here; the wharfs in general
are fmall and niggardly. He fays they
have every where followed the plan laid
down by Mr. Penn in building their houfes.
They have violated it in building Water-
ftreet, where he had projeded elegant wharfs.
Raynal fpeaks likewife of houfes covered with
flate, and of marble monuments in the
churches, and in the halls of the State-houfe.
I have feen nothing of all this.

Behind the State-houfe is a public garden ;
it is the only one that exifts in Philadelphia.
It is not large ; but it is agreeable, and one
may breathe in it. It is compofed of a number of verdant fquares, interfeded by alleys.

All the fpace from Front-ftreet on the
Delaware to Front-ftreet on the Skuylkill, is
already

already diftributed into fquares for ftreets
and houfes, they build here: but not fo
brifkly as at New-York. The inhabitants
wifh for the aggrandizement of their city:
they are wrong; Philadelphia is already too
confiderable. When towns acquire this degree of population, you muft have hofpitals,
prifons, foldiers, police, fpies, and all the
fweeping train of luxury; that luxury which
Penn wifhed to avoid. It already appears:
they have carpets, elegant carpets; it is a
favourite tafte with the Americans; they receive it from the interefted avarice of their
old mafters, the Englifh.

A carpet in fummer is an abfurdity; yet
they fpread them in this feafon, and from
vanity: this vanity excufes itfelf by faying
that the carpet is an ornament; that is to fay,
they facrifice reafon and utility to fhow.

The Quakers have likewife carpets; but
the rigorous ones blame this practice. They
mentioned to me an inftance of a Quaker
from Carolina, who, going to dine with one
of the moft opulent at Philadelphia, was offended at finding the paffage from the door
to the ftaircafe covered with a carpet, and
would not enter the houfe; he faid that he
never

never dined in a houfe where there was luxury; and that it was better to clothe the poor, than to clothe the earth.

If this man juftly cenfured the prodigality of carpets, how much more feverely ought he to cenfure the women of Philadelphia? I fpeak not here of the Quaker-women; I refer my obfervations on them to the chapter which I referve for that fociety. But the women of the other fects wear hats and caps almoft as varied as thofe of Paris. They beftow immenfe expences on their toilet and head-drefs, and difplay pretenfions too affected to be pleafing.

It is a great misfortune that, in republics, women fhould facrifice fo much time to trifles; and that men fhould likewife hold this tafte in fome eftimation.

A very ingenious woman in this town is reproached with having contributed more than all others to introduce this tafte for luxury. I really regret to fee her hufband, who appears to be well informed, and of an amiable character, affect, in his buildings and furniture, a pomp which ought for ever to have been a ftranger to Philadelphia; and why?

why? to draw around him the gaudy prigs and parafites of Europe. And what does he gain by it? jealoufy; the reproach of his fellow-citizens, and the ridicule of ftrangers. When a man enjoys pecuniary advantages, and at the fame time poffeffes genius, knowledge, reflection, and the love of doing good, how eafy it is to make himfelf beloved and efteemed, by employing his fortune, and perhaps increafing it, in enterprifes ufeful to the public!

Notwithftanding the fatal effects that might be expected here from luxury, we may fay with truth, that there is no town where morals are more refpected. Adultery is not known here; there is no inftance of a wife, of any fect, who has failed in her duty.

This, I am told, is owing to what may be called the civil ftate of women. They marry without dower; they bring to their hufbands only the furniture of their houfes; and they wait the death of their parents, before they come to the poffeffion of their property.

I have been informed, however, of a Mrs. Livingfton, daughter of Doctor Shippen, who lives feparated from her hufband. This feparation

ration was made by mutual agreement. This young woman married Mr. Livingſton only in obedience to the father; obedience of this kind is very rare in this country. The father promiſed to take her again, if ſhe ſhould not be pleaſed with her huſband: ſhe was not pleaſed with him; the father received her, and ſhe lives at preſent virtuous and rc-ſpected.

You would not have ſo good an idea of the morals of this country, if you were to read a ſatire lately publiſhed, intitled *The Times.* The author is Mr. Markoe. He diſ-covers a remarkable talent for poetry; a ta-lent ſimilar to that of our ſatyriſt Guibert, who lately died in an hoſpital; but, like him, he paints with two high colours; and, like all poets, he often ſubſtitutes fable for truth. Mr. Markoe inſpires the leſs confidence, as he diſhonours his writings by an intemperate life. A ſatyriſt, to be believed, and to be uſeful, ought to exhibit the moſt unexcep-tionable morals.

The celebrated Paine, author of Common Senſe, ſo much venerated by the French, is moſt cruelly treated in this ſatire. This is not the firſt that has been publiſhed againſt him;

him; I have feen another, very fevere, by an inhabitant of North-Carolina.

Mr. Paine has enjoyed great fuccefs here; it is not therefore furprifing, that fatires fhould be written againft him. Whatever may be the caufe of it, it cannot be denied, that his writings had a great effect on the American revolution; and this circumftance ought to place him in the rank of the benefactors of America.

I have feen another author at Philadelphia, who has imagination and wit; it is Mr. Crawford. He has publifhed feveral poems; as likewife Obfervations on the Slavery of the Negroes, full of good fenfe and humanity. He has publifhed an addrefs of the famous George Fox to the Jews. Mr. Crawford has a turn for myftical ideas; this, aided by great application to ftudy, and an inflammable imagination, has led him to turns of infanity. He was formerly a deift, and has been converted by the celebrated Doctor Jebb.

There is no town on the continent where there is fo much printing done as at Philadelphia. Gazettes and book-ftores are numerous

merous in the town, and paper-mills in the
State.

Among the printers and bookfellers of this
town, I remarked Mr. Carey, an Irifh printer,
who, for having publifhed, in his journal of
The Volunteers of Ireland, an article which
wounded fome people in place, particularly
Mr. Fofter, was perfecuted, and obliged to
fly to America. Being deftitute of money,
M. de la Fayette gave him affiftance, and
enabled him to eftablifh a prefs, on condition
that this act of generofity fhould remain a
fecret. Mr. Carey kept his word; but, having a public quarrel two years afterwards with
another printer, Mr. Ofwald, who quarrels
with all the world, and who called in queftion
the origin of Mr. Carey's fortune, he was
obliged to reveal the fecret.

This printer, who unites great induftry
with great information, publifhes a monthly
collection, called *The American Mufeum*,
which is equal to the beft periodical publication in Europe. It contains every thing the
moft important that America produces in the
arts, in the fciences, and in politics. The
part that concerns agriculture, is attended to
with great care.

There

There are at prefent very few French merchants at Philadelphia. The failure of thofe who firft came, difcouraged others, and has put the Americans on their guard. I have endeavoured to difcover the caufe of thefe failures; and have found that the greater part of thefe French merchants had either begun with little property, or had made imprudent purchafes, or given themfelves up to extravagant expences. Moft of them were ignorant of the language, cuftoms, and laws of the country; moft of them were feduced by the high price which they received for their goods, in paper-money: imagining that this paper would foon rife to par, they amaffed as much as poffible of it, calculating on enormous profits; and thus fed the hopes of their correfpondents in Europe. Thefe hopes were difappointed. Some knowledge of bufinefs, of men, of politics, of revolutions, and of the country, would have taught them, that many years muft elapfe before the public debt could be paid. It became necef-fary to break the illufion, to fell this paper at a lofs, in order to meet their engagements. But they had fet up their equipages; they were in the habit of great expences, which they thought it neceffary to continue for fear of lofing their credit, for they meafured

Philadelphia

Philadelphia on the fcale of Paris. They
foolifhly imagined, that reafonable and enlightened men would fuffer themfelves, like
flaves, to be duped by the glitter of parade;
their profits ceafed, their expences multiplied, and the moment of bankruptcy arrived : they muft juftify themfelves in the
eyes of their correfpondents, and of France :
they accufed the Americans of difhonefty,
of perfidy, and of rafcality. Thefe calumniators ought to have accufed their own ignorance, their folly, and their extravagant
luxury.

Some Frenchmen paraded themfelves here
publicly with their miftreffes, who difplayed
thofe light and wanton airs which they had
practifed at Paris *. You may judge of the
offence which this indecent fpectacle would
give in a country where women are fo referved, and where the manners are fo pure.
Contempt was the confequence ; want of
credit followed the contempt ; and what is a
merchant without credit ?

* One of thefe gentlemen had the impudence to prefent in
fome of the beft families his miftrefs, not as his wife, but as
his partner in trade. This woman was afterwards publicly
kept by the ambaffador. He had not refpect enough for the
morals of the country, to induce him to conceal his tur-
pitude.

Since

Since the peace, the Quakers have returned to their commerce with great activity.
The capitals which diffidence had for a long
time locked up in their coffers, are now
drawn out to give a fpring to induſtry, and
encourage commercial fpeculations. The Delaware fees floating the flags of all nations;
and enterprifes are there formed for all parts
of the world. Manufactories are rifing in
the town and in the country; and induſtry
and emulation increafe with great rapidity.
Notwithſtanding the aſtoniſhing growth of
Baltimore, which has drawn part of the
commerce from Philadelphia, yet the energy
of the ancient capitals of this town, the univerſal eſtimation in which the Quaker-mer-
chants are held, and the augmentation of
agriculture and population, fupply this de-
ficiency.

You will now be able to judge of the
caufes of the profperity of this town. Its
fituation on a river navigable for the greateſt
fhips, renders it one of the principal places
of foreign commerce, and at the fame time
the great magazine of all the productions of
the fertile lands of Pennfylvania, and of thofe
of fome of the neighbouring States. The vaſt
rivers, which by their numerous branches
communicate

communicate to all parts of the State, give a value to the lands, and attract inhabitants. The climate, lefs cold than that of the Northern States, and lefs warm than that of the South, forms another very confiderable alteration.

But I firmly believe that it is not fimply to thofe phyfical advantages that Pennfylvania owes her profperity. It is to the manners of the inhabitants; it is to the univerfal tolerance which reigned there from the beginning; it is to the fimplicity, œconomy, induftry, and perfeverance of the Quakers, which, centering in two points, agriculture and commerce, have carried them to a greater perfection than they have attained among other fects. The cabin of a fimple cultivator gives birth to more children than a gilded palace; and lefs of them perifh in infancy.

And fince the table of population of a country appears to you always the moft exact meafure of its profperity, compare, at four different epochs, the number of inhabitants paying capitation in Pennfylvania.

1760	1770	1779	1786
31,667	39,765	45,683	66,925.

You

You fee that population has more than doubled in twenty-five years, notwithftanding the horrible depopulation of a war of eight years. Obferve in this ftating, that the blacks are not included, which form about one-fifth of the population of the State. Obferve, that by the calculation of the general convention in 1787, the number of whites in this State was carried to 360,000; which fuppofes, very nearly, a wife and four children for every taxable head.

The public fpirit which the Quakers manifeft in every thing, has given rife to feveral ufeful inftitutions in Philadelphia, which I have not yet mentioned. One of them is the *Difpenfary*, which diftributes medicines *gratis* to the fick who are not in a fituation to purchafe them.

See how eafy and cheap it is to do good. Let thofe men blufh, then, who diffipate their fortunes in luxury and in idlenefs! One thoufand fix hundred and forty-feven perfons were treated by this eftablifhment during the year 1787. By calculation this treatment coft to the eftablifhment five fhillings and nine pence for each patient. Thus, for two hundred pounds fterling, fixteen hundred and

and forty-feven perfons are rendered happy.

To this public fpirit, fo ingenious in varying its benefits, is owing the *Benevolent Inftitution*, whofe objeＣt it is to fuccour, in their own houfes, poor women in childbed.

Another fociety has for its objeＣt to alleviate the fituation of prifoners.

The Philadelphians confine not their attention to their brethren; they extend it to ftrangers; they have formed a fociety for the affiftance of emigrants who arrive from Germany. A fimilar one is formed at New-York, called the Hibernian Society, for the fuccour of emigrants from Ireland. Thefe focieties inform themfelves, on the arrival of a fhip, of the fituation of the emigrants, and procure them immediate employ.

Here is a company for infurance againft fire. The houfes are conftruＣted of wood and brick, and confequently expofed to the ravages of fire. The infurers are the infured, a method which prevents the abufes to which your company at Paris is expofed.

In

In the midſt of all theſe things which excite my admiration and my tender regard,
one trait of injuſtice gives me much pain,
becauſe it ſeems to tarniſh the glory of Pennſylvania. Penn left to his family an immenſe
property here. In the laſt war his deſcend-
ants took part with the Engliſh government,
and retired to England. The legiſlature of
Pennſylvania paſſed a law, taking from them
all their lands and their rents, and voted to
give them for the whole, one hundred and
fifty thouſand pounds. This ſum was to have
been paid in paper-money, which ſuffered then
a conſiderable depreciation. The firſt term
only has been paid.

It cannot be denied, that there was a great
injuſtice in the eſtimation, in the mode of
payment, and in the delay. The State of
Pennſylvania has too much reſpect for property, and too much attachment to juſtice,
not to repair its wrongs one day to the
family of Penn, which ſubſiſts at preſent
only at the expence of the Engliſh nation.

LETTER

L E T T E R   XXVI.

Progreſs of Cultivation in Pennſylvania.

HITHERTO, my friend, we have ſpoken only of farms already in good culture, and in the neighbourhood of towns. We muſt now penetrate farther, deſcend into the midſt of the wilderneſs, and obſerve the man, detached from ſociety, with his axe in his hand, felling the venerable oak, that had been reſpected by the ſavage, and ſupplying its place with the humble ſpire of corn. We muſt follow this man in his progreſs, obſerve the changes that his cabin undergoes, when it becomes the center of twenty other cabins which riſe ſucceſſively round it. An American farmer has communicated to me the principal traits of the rural picture which I am going to lay before you. The firſt planter *,

or

---

* As the tranſlator recollects to have ſeen this fanciful deſcription many times publiſhed in America, he was leſs anxious in re-tranſlating it, to flatter the original author, by re-
taining all his ideas, than he was to ſave the credit of M. de
Warville, by abridging the piece. Credulity is indeed a leſs
fault in a traveller than prejudice ; but it ought, however, to

be

or he who begins a fettlement in the woods,
is generally a man who has loft his fortune
and his credit in the cultivated part of the ftate.
He emigrates in the month of April. His
firft work is to build a little cabin for himfelf
and family ; the roof is of rough hewn wood,
the floor of earth. It is lighted by the door,
or fometimes by a little window with oiled
paper. A more wretched building adjoining
it gives fhelter to a cow and two miferable
horfes. This done, he attacks the trees that
furround his cabin. To extirpate them by
the root, would require too much labour. He
contents himfelf by cutting them at two or
three feet from the ground. The fpace thus
cleared is then plowed, and planted with Indian corn. The foil, being new, requires
little culture; in the month of October it
yields a harveft of forty or fifty bufhels the
acre. Even from the month of September,
this corn furnifhes a plentiful and agreeable
nourifhment to his family. Hunting and
fifhing, with a little grain, fuffice, during the
winter, for the fubfiftence of his family ;
while the cow and horfes of our planter feed

be corrected. Accounts like this put one in mind of Dr.
Franklin's romance of *Mary Baker,* fo religioufly believed
and copied by the Abbé Raynal, in his Hiftory of the Two
Indies.

on the poor wild grafs, or the buds of trees.
During the firft year, he fuffers much from
cold and hunger; but he endures it without
repining.   Being near the favages, he adopts
their manners; his fatigue is violent, but it
is fufpended by long intervals of repofe: his
pleafures confift in fifhing and hunting;
he loves fpiritous liquors; he eats, drinks,
and fleeps in the filth of his little cabin.

Thus roll away the firft three years of our
planter in lazinefs, independence, the varia-
tion of pleafure, and of labour.   But population augments in his neighbourhood, and
then his troubles begin.   His cattle could
before run at large; but now his neighbours
force him to retain them within his little
farm.   Formerly the wild beafts gave fubfiftence to his family; they now fly a country which begins to be peopled by men, and
confequently by enemies.   An increafing fociety brings regulations, taxes, and the parade of laws; and nothing is fo terrible to
our independent planter as all thefe fhackles.
He will not confent to facrifice a fingle natural right for all the benefits of government;
he abandons then his little eftablifhment, and
goes to feek a fecond retreat in the wilder-
nefs, where he can recommence his labours,

and

and prepare a farm for cultivation. Such are
the charms of independence, that many men
have begun the clearing of farms four times
in different parts of this State.

It has been remarked, that the preaching
of the Gofpel always drives off men of this
clafs. And it is not furprifing if we confider how much its precepts are oppofed to
the licentioufnefs of their manner of life.
But the labour beftowed by the firft planter
gives fome value to the farm, which now
comes to be occupied by a man of the fecond
clafs of planters. He begins by adding to
his cabin a houfe. A faw-mill in the neighbouring fettlement, furnifhes him with boards.
His houfe is covered with fhingles, and is
two ftories high. He makes a little meadow, plants an orchard of two or three
hundred apple-trees. His ftable is enlarged ;
he builds a fpacious barn of wood, and covers
it with rye-ftraw. Inftead of planting only
Indian corn, he cultivates wheat and rye ;
the laft is deftined to make whifky. But
this planter manages ill ; his fields are badly
plowed, never manured, and give but fmall
crops. His cattle break through his fences,
deftroy his crops, and often cut off the hopes
of the year. His horfes are ill fed, and feeble ;

ble; his cattle often die with hunger in the
Spring; his houfe and his farm give equal
proofs of the want of induftry; the glafs of
his windows has given place to old hats and
rags. This man is fond of company; he
drinks to excefs; paffes much of his time in
difputing about politics. Thus he contracts
debts, and is forced, after fome years, to fell
his plantation to a planter of the third and
laft clafs.

This is ordinarily a man of property, and
of a cultivated mind. His firft object is to
convert into meadow all his land, on which
he can conduct water. He then builds a
barn of ftone, fometimes a hundred feet in
length, and forty in breadth. This defends
his cattle from cold, and they eat lefs when
kept warm, than when expofed to the froft.
To fpare the confumption of fuel, he makes
ufe of economical ftoves, and by this he
faves immenfe labour in cutting and carting
wood. He multiplies the objects of culture;
befides corn, wheat, and rye, he cultivates
oats and buck-wheat. Near his houfe he
forms a garden of one or two acres, which
gives him quantities of cabbage, potatoes,
and turnips. Near the fpring which furnifhes him with water, he builds a dairy-
house.

houfe.   He augments the number, and im-
proves the quality of his fruit-trees.   His
fons are always at work by his fide; his wife
and daughter quit their wheels for the labours of the harveft.   The laft object of induftry is to build a houfe for his own ufe.
This building is generally of ftone; it is vaft,
well diftributed, and well furnifhed.   His
horfes and cattle, by their good appearance,
their ftrength, and fecundity, prove that they
are well fed, and well attended.   His table
abounds with delicate and various difhes.
His kitchen flows with milk and honey.
The ordinary drink of his family, is beer,
cyder, and wine; his wife and daughters
manufacture their cloathing.   In proportion
as he grows rich, he perceives the value of
the protection of the laws; he pays his taxes
with punctuality; he contributes to the fupport of churches and fchools, as the only
means of infuring order and tranquillity.

Two-thirds of the farmers of Pennfylvania
belong to this third clafs.   It is to them that
the State owes its ancient reputation and im-
portance.   If they have lefs of cunning than
their neighbours of the South, who cultivate
their lands by flaves, they have more of the
republican virtues.   It was from their farms
that

that the American and French armies were principally fupplied during the laft war; it was from their produce that came thofe millions of dollars brought from the Havanna after the year 1780—millions which laid the foundation of the bank of North-America, and fupported the American army till the peace.

This is a feeble fketch of the happinefs of a Pennfylvania farmer; a happinefs to which this State calls men of all countries and of all religions. It offers not the pleafures of the Arcadia of the poets, or thofe of the great towns of Europe; but it promifes you independence, plenty, and happinefs—in rereturn for patience, induftry, and labour. The moderate price of lands, the credit that may be obtained, and the perfect fecurity that the courts of juftice give to every fpecies of property, place thefe advantages within the reach of every condition of men.

I do not pretend here to give the hiftory of all the fettlements of Pennfylvania. It often happens, that the fame man, or the fame family, holds the place of the firft and fecond, and fometimes of the third clafs of planters above defcribed. In the counties near Philadelphia,

delphia, you fee vaft houfes of brick, and farms well cultivated, in the poffeffion of the defcendants, in the fecond or third degree, of the companions of William Penn.

This paffion for emigration, of which I have fpoken, will appear to you unaccountable:---that a man fhould voluntarily abandon the country that gave him birth, the church where he was confecrated to God, the tombs of his anceftors, the companions and friends of his youth, and all the pleafures of polifhed fociety---to expofe himfelf to the dangers and difficulties of conquering favage nature, is, in the eyes of a European philofopher, a phenomenon which contradicts the ordinary progrefs and principles of the actions of men. But fuch is the fact; and this paffion contributes to increafe the population of America, not only in the new fettlements, but in the old ftates; for, when the number of farmers is augmented in any canton beyond the number of convenient farms, the population languifhes, the price of land rifes to fuch a degree as to diminifh the profits of agriculture, encourage idlenefs, or turn the attention to lefs honourable purfuits. The beft preventative of thefe evils is the emigration of part of the inhabitants. This part generally con-

fifts

fifts of the moft idle and diffipated, who neceffarily become induftrious in their new fettlement; while the departure augments the means of fubfiftance and population to thofe left behind ; as pruning increafes the fize of the tree, and the quantity of its fruit.

The third clafs of cultivators which I have defcribed, is chiefly compofed of Germans. They make a great part of the population of Pennfylvania. It is more than a century fince the firft Germans were eftablifhed here. They are regarded as the moft honeft, the moft induftrious and œconomical of the farmers. They never contract debts ; they are, of all the Americans, the leaft attached to the ufe of rum and other ardent fpirits. Thus their families are the moft numerous. It is very common to fee them have twelve or fourteen children*. It is faid, they have not fo much information as the other Americans; and information is the foul of a Republican Government: but yet you find many men refpectable for their knowledge and underftanding amongft them, fuch as Rittenhoufe, Kuhn, Mulhenberg, &c.

* According to M. Moheau, one family in 25,000 in France has thirteen children ; two have twelve.

A principal

A principal caufe of emigration in the back parts of Pennfylvania, is the hope of efcaping taxes; yet the land-tax is very light, as it does not exceed a penny in the pound of the efti-mation; and the eftimation is much under the value of the lands.

There is much irregularity in the land-tax, as likewife in the capitation, or poll-tax; but I fee with pleafure, that batchelors pay more than married men.

LETTER

LETTER XXVII.

Climate and Difeafes of Pennfylvania.

I HAVE already fpoken to you, my friend, of the climate of this happy town. The refpectable Doctor Rufh has juft communicated to me fome new and curious details, which I will communicate.

This enlightened obferver, in one energetic phrafe, has pictured to me the variations incident to Philadelphia. We have, faid he, the humidity of Great Britain in the Spring, the heat of Africa in Summer, the temperance of Italy in June, the fky of Egypt in Autumn, the fnows of Norway and the ice of Holland during the Winter; the tempefts, to a certain degree, of the Weft Indies in each feafon, and the variable winds of Great Britain in every month of the year.

Notwithftanding all thefe changes, the Doctor thinks, that the climate of Philadelphia is one of the moft healthful in the world.

In

In dry weather, the air has a peculiar elaf-
ticity, which renders heat or cold lefs infup-
portable than they are in places more humid.
The air never becomes heavy and fatiguing,
but when the rains are not followed by the
beneficent North-weft.   During the three
weeks that I have paffed here (in Auguft and
September) I have felt nothing of the languor of body, and depreffion of fpirits, which
I expected : though the heat has been very
great, I found it fupportable; nearly like that
of Paris, but it caufed a greater perfpiration.

Doctor Rufh has obferved, as have many
phyficians of Europe, that the ftate of mind
influences much on the health.   He cited to
me two ftriking examples of it.   The Englifh
feamen wounded in the famous naval battle
of the 12th of April 1782, were cured with
the greateft facility.   The joy of victory gave
to their bodies the force of health.   He had
made the fame obfervations on the American
foldiers wounded at the battle of Trenton.

Variability is the characteriftic of the climate of Pennfylvania.   It has changed by
the clearing of lands, and the diminution of
waters, which formerly abounded in this part
of America.   Many creeks, and even rivers,
have

have difappeared by degrees; and this is to be expected in a country where forests give place to cultivated fields.

Thefe changes have produced happy effects on the health of the people. An old man of this country has obferved to me, that the health of the Pennfylvanians augments in proportion to the cultivation of the country; that their vifages are lefs pale than they were thirty or forty years paft; that for fome time the number of centenaries has increafed, and that the feptuagenaries are very numerous.

In 1782, there was fuch an extraordinary drought, that the Indian corn did not come to perfection, the meadows failed, and the foil became fo inflammable, that in fome places it caught fire, and the furface was burnt.—This year it has been exceffively rainy. On the 18th and 19th of Auguft, there fell at Philadelphia feven inches of water. Wheat has fuffered much this year from the rains.

Happily all parts of the country are not fubject to the fame variations of the atmof-phere; fo that a general fcarcity is never known. If the harveft fails here, at fifty

miles

miles diſtance it abounds.   You ſee that the
heat here is about the ſame as at Paris, and
that it is never ſo great as at Rome, ſince at
the latter place the thermometer of Reaumur riſes to 30 degrees.   You ſee, that the
Winter here is not much colder than at Paris,
as it rarely deſcends more than to twelve degrees below the freezing point.   There falls
much more rain here than at Paris.   The
common quantity there is twenty inches in
the year, and it has not been known but once
in ſixty years to riſe to twenty-five, while
the common quantity at Philadelphia is thirty-
five inches.   By comparing the climate of
Philadelphia with that of Pekin, nearly in the
ſame latitude, you will find, from the tables
of Kirwan, that the Winters are much colder,
and the Summers much warmer, in that part
of China, than at Philadelphia.   Doctor Ruſh
attributes the difference to this circumſtance,
that Pennſylvania is bordered with a vaſt extent of foreſt, and that the country about Pekin
is generally and highly cultivated.

My friend Myers Fiſher, who endeavours
to explain the characters of men from the
phyſical circumſtances that ſurround them,
has communicated to me an obſervation
which he has made in that reſpect ; it is, that
the

the activity of the inhabitants of a country may be meafured by the rapidity of its rivers, and the variations in its atmofphere.

He could fee the dulnefs and indecifion of the Virginians in the flow movement of the Potowmac; while the rapid current of the rivers of the North painted to him the activity of the people of New-England.

He told me, likewife, that the health of the people might very well confift with the variations of the air, provided that wife precautions were taken. This, as he affured me, was a part of the difcipline of the Quakers. Thus, according to him, you may meafure the longevity of the people of Pennfylvania by the fect to which they belong. That of the Quakers ought to be placed at the head of this table of longevity; that of the Moravians next; the Prefbyterians next, &c.

Doctor Rufh, whofe obfervations in this refpect are numerous, has told me, that fudden variations caufed more difeafes and deaths than either heat or cold conftantly exceffive. He inftanced the vigorous winter of 1780, the burning fummer of 1782, and the rainy fummer of 1788. There were then few or

no

no difeafes; and thofe that happened were occafioned by imprudence, fuch as cold water drunk in heat, or fpiritous liquors in cold. Plurifies and inflammatory diforders are much diminifhed within fifty years. The months of May and June are confidered as the moft falubrious, and the valetudinarians are obferved to be better in Summer and in Winter.

LETTER

LETTER XXVIII.

Difeafes the moft common in the United States.
Longevity.

AMONG the difeafes of the United States,
the confumption doubtlefs makes the
greateft ravages. It was unknown to the
original inhabitants of the country; it is then
the refult of European habits of life tranfported to this new Continent. It is more
common in the towns than in the country;
it deftroys more women than men; it is a
languid diforder, which drags, by flow fteps,
its victim to the tomb; each day plunges the
dagger deeper in his breaft, and renders more
vifible the incurable wound. Death, without
ceafing, ftares him in the face, and throws a
funeral fhrowd over the remainder of his
days. The world and its pleafures difappear; the ties of friendfhip are the only ones
that are ftrengthened and endeared, and which
double the bitternefs of his approaching diffolution. The confumption, in a word, is a
long continued agony, a flow tormenting
death.

The

The phyficians of this country attribute
it to different caufes ; to the exceffive ufe
of hot drinks, fuch as tea and coffee; to
the habit of remaining too long in bed, and
the ufe of feather-beds, for they know not
the ufe of matraffes; to the cuftom of eating
too much meat, and of drinking too much
fpiritous liquors. Women are more fubject
to it than men; becaufe, independently of
the above caufes, they take but little exercife, which is the only powerful remedy
againft the ftagnation of humours, the great
principle of the marafma: they tafte but little
the pleafures of walking; a movement which,
varying the fpectacle of nature, gives a
refrefhment to the fenfes, a new fpring to the
blood, and a new vigour to the foul.

A particular caufe of confumptions a-
mongft the Quaker women is doubtlefs the
habit of gravity and immobility which they
contract in early life, and which they preferve for hours together in their filent meetings. The women of the other fects are
equally attacked by confumptions, but it is
attributed to different caufes: they are fond
of exceffive dancing; heated with this, they
drink cold water, eat cold unripe fruits,
drink

drink boiling tea, go thinly clad in winter, and give no attention to the fudden changes of weather. The Quakers are more reafonable in thefe refpects ; but they balance thefe advantages by a fatal neglect of exercife. To preferve good health, a female fhould have the gaiety of a woman of fafhion, with the prudence and precaution of a Quaker.

A moral or political caufe may likewife aid us in explaining why women are more fubject to confumptions than men. It is the want of a will, or a civil exiftence. The fubmiffion to which women are habituated, has the effect of chains, which comprefs the limbs, caufe obftructions, deaden the vital principle, and impede the circulation. The depreffion of the mind has a tendency to enfeeble the body. This fubmiffion to fathers and hufbands is more remarkable among the Quakers, than among the other fects. The time will doubtlefs come, when we fhall be convinced that phyfical health, as well as political happinefs, may be greatly promoted by equality and independence of opinions among all the members of fociety.

Confumptions,

Confumptions, however, are not fo numerous in America as is generally imagined. This name is ignorantly given to many other diforders, which reduce the body to the fame meagre ftate which follows a decay of the lungs. This appearance deceives, and may eafily deceive the attendants of of the fick, who give information to thofe who keep the bills of mortality.

Another difeafe very common here, is the fore-throat; when putrid, it is mortal. It generally proceeds from exceffive heats, cold drinks, and careleffnefs in cloathing.

When we reflect that Europe was formerly fubject to thefe epidemical difeafes, and that they have difappeared in proportion to the progrefs of cultivation, we are tempted to believe that they belong to new countries in the infancy of cultivation.

The difeafe known in Europe by the name of influenza, is likewife common in America: it made great ravages in 1789. It began in Canada, paffed through New-York, and very foon infected Pennfylvania

and

and the Southern States. Its fymptoms are laffitude, feeblenefs, chills, heats, and the head-ache. It refpeḑs no age or fex, and efpecially precipitates to the tomb thofe who were attacked by the confumption.

The fever and ague may be ranked in the clafs of thefe cruel epidemics; but it is more terrible, as its returns are annual. It not only vifits the marfhy countries and the fea-coaft, but it is feen even in the healthy region of Albany. It is combated by the Peruvian bark; but the moft fuccefsful remedy, is a journey among the mountains, or into the northern States. This fever, more humane than men, fubjeḑs not to its empire the black flaves. This exemption is attributed to a cuftom they preferve with obftinacy, of keeping fires always in their cabbins, even in the hotteft feafon. The negroes are accuftomed to confider exceffive heat as a guarantee of health; and you will fee a negrefs, while fhe labours in the field, in the ardour of a burning fun, expofe her infant to its fires, rather than lay it under the refrefhing fhade of a tree. This negrefs has not heard of the curious experiments of

Dr.

Dr. Inginhoufe on the fatal effects of fhades
and the night air, but you fee that fhe knows
their effects.

Among the maladies common in the
United States, muft be reckoned the pleurify
and the peripneumony, though they are lefs
frequent than formerly. The fmall-pox,
which formerly made fuch havocks in
the United States, is lefs formidable fince
the general practice of inoculation.

There are many phyficians at Philadelphia,
and you will perhaps affign this as the caufe
of fo many difeafes. You will be wrong.
They are faid to be fkilful; they are generally ftrangers to quackery. I know fome of
them who are highly refpectable, as well for
their virtues, as for their knowledge; fuch as
Rufh, Griffiths, Wifneer; the two laft are
Quakers.

The greateft part of thefe phyficians are,
at the fame time, apothecaries. They continue to unite thefe two fciences, out of refpect to the people, who wifh that the man
who orders the medicine fhould likewife
prepare it. There are, however, other apothecaries,

thecaries, of whom the phyſicians purchaſe their drugs.

The practice of this country is the Engliſh practice ; that is, they are much in the uſe of violent remedies. Laxatives are little in uſe. Almoſt all the phyſicians of this country are formed at the ſchool of Edinburgh, and this is the cauſe of their predilection for the Engliſh practice.

I know a Dr. Baily of this country, a man of good abilities, but perhaps too inflammable and too cauſtic, who, much irritated at the preference given by his countrymen to the Engliſh practice, was reſolved to open a communication between this country and the ſchools of France. This reſolution did him the more honour, as he was known in politics for an Anglican, and a decided royaliſt.

LETTER

LETTER XXIX.

Longevity, and Calculations on the Probabilities of Life in the United States.

YOU may think, perhaps, after the account that I have given you of the maladies which afflict America, that human life is fhorter here than in Europe. It is a prejudice; and as it has been accredited by many writers, and by fome even who have travelled in America, it becomes a duty to deftroy it.

The Abbe Robin, one of thefe travellers, has declared, that after the age of twenty-five, the American women appear old ; that children die here in greater proportion than in Europe ; that there are very few old people, &c. &c. M. Paw, I believe, had uttered thefe fables before him. Nothing is more falfe. I have obferved with care the women between thirty and fifty years of age : they have generally a good appearance, good

health,

health, and are even agreeable. I have feen
them of fifty, with fuch an air of frefhnefs,
that they would not have been taken by an
European for more than forty.   I have feen
women of fixty and feventy, fparkling with
health.   I fpeak here efpecially of the women
of New Hampfhire, Maffachufetts, and Connecticut.

In Pennfylvania you do not fee the fame
tints adorn the interefting vifages of the
daughters and wives of the Quakers ; they
are generally pale.

I have paid attention to their teeth.   I
have feen of them that are fine ; and where
they are otherwife, it is, as in England, more
owing to hot drinks than to the climate.

Not only the number of aged perfons are
more confiderable here than in Europe, as I
am going to prove to you, but they preferve generally their faculties, intellectual and
phyfical.

I was told of a minifter at Ipfwich in
Maffachufetts, who preached very well at
ninety years of age ; another, of the fame
age, walked on foot to church on Sunday
                                          twenty

twenty miles. A Mr. Temple died at the age of an hundred in 1765, and left four daughters and four fons of the following ages, 86—85—83---81---79—77—75—73.

But I will not confine myfelf to fuch light obfervations. I will give you fome tables of mortality, and of the probabilities of life, in this country. This is the only method of conveying to you certain information.

Tables of longevity may be every where confidered as the touchftone of Governments; the fcale on which may be meafured their excellencies and their defects, the perfection or degradation of the human fpecies.

The general caufes of longevity are,

1. The falubrity of the atmofphere and of the country.

2. The abundance and goodnefs of the aliments.

3. A life regular, active, and happy.

We muft, then, confider the exterior circumftances as relative to the occupations of

men,

men, to their morals, to their religion, and their government,

Wherever property is centered in a few hands, where employment is precarious and dependent, life is not fo long; it is cut off by grief and care, which abridge more the principle of life than even want itfelf. Wherever the Government is arbitrary, and tyranny defcends in divifions from rank to rank, and falls heavy on the lower claffes, life muft be fhort among the people, becaufe they are flaves; and a miferable flave, trampled on at every moment, can enjoy neither that eafe, nor that regularity, nor that interior fatisfaction, which fuftains the principles of life. The exceffes and mortifications attending on ambition, abridge, in an equal degree, the life of the clafs which tyrannizes.

On applying thefe moral and political confiderations to the United States, you may conclude, that there can be no country where the life of man is of longer duration; for, to all the advantages of nature, they unite that of a liberty, which has no equal on the Old Continent; and this liberty, let us not ceafe to repeat it, is the principle of health.

If

If any Government fhould wifh to revive the fpeculation of life annuities on felected heads, I fhould advife to felect them in the North of the United States.

It is difficult here to obtain regular tables of births and deaths.　There are fome fects who do not baptife their children, and whofe regifters are not carefully kept; others who baptife only their adults.　Some of the fick have no phyficians or furgeons, and their attendants who give the information are not exact.　The conftant fluctuations occafioned by emigrations and immigrations, ftill increafe the difficulty.　Yet we may approach near the truth, by taking for examples fuch fea-ports as are more occupied in the coafting trade than in long voyages; it is for this reafon that I have chofen the towns of Sa-lem and Ipfwich in Maffachufetts.　I take thefe tables from the Memoirs of the Aca-demy of Bofton—Memoirs little known in France.

Doctor Halley, for the ftandard of his tables of mortality, chofe Breflaw in Ger-many, on account of its interior fituation and the regular employment of its inhabitants. By the calculations of thefe political arith-
meticians,

meticians, five persons in twelve die at Breflaw
before the age of five years.

At Ipfwich, a village at the Northward of
Bofton, fix only in thirty-three die within
that age. At Breflaw, one in thirty attains
the age of eighty years; at Ipfwich, one in
eight. This difproportion is enormous; and
this longevity is found in many other parts
of Maffachufetts and New Hampfhire.

At Woodftock, in Connecticut, one hundred and thirteen perfons have died in eleven
years; of thefe twenty-one were feventy
years old and upwards, and thirteen were
eighty and upwards. This gives fomething
more than the proportion of an octogenary
in nine. Thefe facts are taken from authentic regifters.

The minifter of Andover in New Hampfhire, a refpectable and well informed man,
has affured me, that more than one in eight
males and females in his neighbourhood, pafs
the age of feventy years; and that this obfervation is the refult of long experience in that
and the neighbouring parifhes.

Compare thefe facts to thofe ftated by M.
Moheau,

A COMPARATIVE TABLE

OF THE

PROBABILITIES OF LIFE IN NEW ENGLAND AND IN EUROPE.

To face p. 359.

	NEW ENGLAND			ENGLAND						SWEDEN				GERMANY		HOLLAND.	FRANCE.
							CHESTER.			STOCKHOLM.		In the Kingdom.					
Ages.	Graduates of Harvard College.	Hingham, in Maffachufetts.	Dover, in New Hampfhire.	London, Simpfon's Tables.	Norwich.	Northampton.	Males.	Females.	Holy Crofs, near Shrewfbury.	Males.	Females.	Males.	Females.	Breflaw.	Brandenburg.	Kerfeboom's Tables of Annuitants.	M. De Parcieux's Table of Annuitants.
25	36.07	35.46	37.89	26.1	31.56	30.85	32.00	34.78	35.58	21.40	26.80	33.63	35.58	30.88	31.76	33.27	37.01
30	33.40	33.81	34.97	23.6	28.93	28.27	29.25	32.27	32.66	19.42	23.98	30.34	32.17	27.80	28.70	30.92	33.96
35	30.70	30.83	31.89	21.5	26.05	25.68	25.97	29.26	29.43	17.58	21.62	27.09	29.03	24.92	25.56	28.36	30.73
40	26.45	28.28	28.74	19.6	23.18	23.08	22.92	26.37	26.40	15.61	19.21	23.75	25.21	22.13	22.65	25.49	27.30
45	22.9	25.11	25.80	17.8	20.78	20.52	20.20	23.35	23.35	13.78	17.17	20.72	22.57	19.56	19.65	22.34	23.77
50	19.86	22.08	22.79	16.0	17.55	17.99	17.64	20.62	20.49	11.95	15.12	17.72	19.26	17.07	16.55	19.41	20.24
55	17.75	18.47	19.22	14.2	14.87	15.58	15.14	17.52	17.47	10.36	12.89	14.98	16.15	14.77	13.68	16.72	16.88
60	14.63	15.20	15.49	12.4	12.36	13.21	12.36	14.20	14.86	8.69	10.45	12.24	13.08	12.30	11.28	14.10	13.86
65	11.31	12.29	12.98	10.5	10.05	10.88	10.79	11.94	12.30	7.39	8.39	9.78	10.49	9.86	9.15	11.56	11.07
70	10.01	9.68	10.46	8.8	8.12	8.60	8.05	8.81	10.00	5.81	6.16	7.60	7.91	7.45	7.48	9.15	8.34
75	8.39	7.63	8.40	7.2	6.44	6.54	7.00	7.14	5.75	4.09	4.39	5.89	6.03	5.51	6.17	6.81	5.79
80	6.96	6.03	6.87	5.0	5.14	4.75	5.43	5.20				4.27	4.47	4.08	5.06	5.05	4.73
85	3.06	5.02	4.96		3.50	3.37	4.25	4.85				3.16	3.40	2.36	4.18	3.38	3.45

EXPLANATION.

The firft column gives the ages; the following ones give, by years and decimal parts of a year, the probabilities of life among the inhabitants of the different places mentioned. The fecond column regards the Graduates of Harvard College, at Cambridge, near Bofton: Hingham, which forms the third, is in Maffachufetts; and Dover, which forms the fourth, is in New Hampfhire. The other columns are taken from the work of Dr. Price.

Moheau *. He fays, that in the Ifland of Oerlon, of 14,000 inhabitants, there are but five or fix octogenaries, and but one for forty-two in the lift of deaths in the Ifle of Rhe, which is reckoned remarkably healthful.

The minifter of Andover made to me another obfervation, which tends to confirm a fyftem advanced by an author whofe name I forget—It is, that men of letters enjoy the greateft longevity. He told me, that the oldeft men were generally found among the Minifters. This fact will explain fome of the caufes of longevity; fuch as regularity of morals, information, independence of fpirit, and eafy circumftances.

But you will be better able to judge of the longevity in the United States, by the table of the probabilities of life given to me by the refpectable Doctor Wiglefworth, of the Univerfity of Cambridge. It contains a comparifon of thefe probabilities in New England, in England, in Sweden, in Germany, in Holland, and in France.

The firft column gives the ages; the fol-

* See *Recherches et Confiderations fur la Population de la France*, page 192.

lowing

lowing one gives, by years, and decimal parts
of a year, the probabilities of life among the
inhabitants of the different places mentioned.
You will fee in this table, that the probabilities
of life in this part of the United States, furpafs thofe of England and Sweden, even thofe
of the annuitants whofe lives ferved for the
bafis to the tables of Kerfboom ; and that
they almoft equal thofe of the annuitants
which ferved as the bafis to the calculations of
M. de Parcieux, for the eftablifhment of life
annuities *.

The fecond column is appropriated to the
graduates of the Univerfity of Cambridge,
the nurfery of minifters and ftatefmen for
that part of the country. The probabilities
in this column are calculated on the whole
lift of graduates, received fince the year 1711.

Hingham, which forms the third column,
is at the South-eaft of Bofton. The occupations and manners of life in this place, are
much the fame as in the reft of Maffachufetts.
The probabilities in this column are taken
from the lift of deaths, made with great care
for fifty years, by Doctor Gay.

* We readily conceive that the probabilities of common life
in France and Holland, are much inferior to thefe tables of annuitants.

The

The column for Dover, fituated on the river Pifcutuay, twelve miles from the fea, in New Hampfhire, is formed from the lift of deaths kept for ten years, by Doctor Belknap, minifter of that place.

The other columns, which regard the countries in Europe, are taken from the work of Doctor Price.

This comparative table will fix your ideas on the fubject of longevity in the United States. And it is to be hoped that from the care of Doctor Wiglefworth of the academy of Bofton, and that of the members of the other academies in the feveral States, we may foon have regular and complete tables for the thirteen States.

To fatisfy your curiofity more completely, I will now give you a lift of births, mar-riages, and deaths in a particular town; that you may fee the proportion between the births and deaths, and the ages of the deceafed. I will take Salem, which is con-fidered as a very unhealthful town. It is a fea-port, in the forty-fecond degree of la-titude, five leagues north-eaft of Bofton, fituated between two rivers, on a flat piece

of

of land, elevated but twenty feet above the level of the fea at high water: two little hills in the neighbourhood; foil light, dry, and fandy, without marfhes; the inhabitants not fubject to epidemical difeafes. They complain at prefent of fome nervous and hyfterical diforders, which were formerly unknown to them.

Mr. Holyoke fent to the Academy of Bofton the two following tables for this town of Salem.

TABLE for 1781.

Deaths, - - - - - - -	175
Births, - - - - - - -	317
Baptifms, - - - - - -	152
Marriages, - - - - - -	70
Taxable polls; that is, males above the age of fixteen, and refiding in the town, - -	897
Tranfient perfons, - - - -	200

AGES of the DECEASED.

In being born, - - - -	6
Within the firft month, - -	6
Between one month and one year, - - - - -	30

AGES

AGES of the DECEASED Continued.

Between one and two years, -	20
—— two and five, - - -	2
—— five and ten, - - -	7
—— ten and fifteen, - -	3
—— fifteen and twenty, -	6
—— twenty and twenty-five,	5
—— twenty-five and thirty,	7
—— thirty and forty, - -	24
—— forty and fifty, - -	10
—— fifty and fixty, - - -	7
—— fixty and feventy, -	2
—— feventy and eighty, -	7
—— eighty and ninety - -	6
Ages unknown, - - - -	27

———————

TABLE for 1782.

Deaths, - - - - - - -	189
Births, about - - - - -	385
Baptifms, - - - - - -	158
Marriages, about - - - -	84
Taxable polls, - - - - -	1000
Number of inhabitants, about	9000

AGES

AGES of the DECEASED.

In being born, - - - - - 14

In the firſt month, - - - - 11

Between one month and one }
    year, - - - - - }   27

Between one and two years, - 29

———— two and five, - - - 28

———— five and ten, - - 12

———— ten and fifteen, - - 5

———— fifteen and twenty, - 2

———— twenty and twenty-five, 8

———— twenty-five and thirty, - 8

———— thirty and forty, - - 9

———— forty and fifty, - - 8

———— fifty and ſixty, - - 7

———— ſixty and ſeventy, - - '6

———— ſeventy and eighty, - 6

———— eighty and ninety, - - 2

Ages unknown - - - 9*

You will recollect that Salem is one of the moſt unhealthful towns in America. You do not find in the above two liſts the pro-

---

* In the American journals they give the liſts of deaths. The following is one that I took at hazard in the American Muſeum for May, 1790:—Deaths, N. Hampſhire, one at 70 years. Maſſachuſets, many at 71—one at 106—one at 92—one at 87. Connecticut, one at 98—one at 91. New-York, one at 104. New-Jerſey, one at 80. Pennſylvania, one at 84—ſeveral at 76.

portion of great ages that I have mentioned in other places.

The year 1781 gives 175 deaths. [If
you look for the population of Salem by
the general rule of thirty living for one dead,
the number of inhabitants would appear to
be 5250—whereas it was 9000. You muſt
then count for Salem fifty living for one
deceaſed. In London there dies one for
twenty-three; and in the country in England,
one in forty; in Paris, one in thirty; in the
country, one in twenty-four.

In 1781, at Salem, the births are as one
to twenty-ſeven of the inhabitants. In common years in France it is as one to twenty-
ſix.

As to marriages, M. Moheau reckons for
the country in France one for 121, and for
Paris one for 160. In Salem, you muſt
count, for 1781, only one for 128. But
this is far from being the proportion for
the country in America. We have no exact table for this purpoſe. We muſt wait.

I cannot terminate this long article on
longevity without giving you the table of
births

births and deaths in the Lutheran congregation at Philadelphia for fourteen years, from 1774 to 1788. The proportion is curious.

	Births.	Deaths.
From 1774 to 1775	379	156
1775 — 1776	338	175
1776 — 1777	389	124
1777 — 1778	298	169
1778 — 1779	303	178
1779 — 1780	348	186
1780 — 1781	320	158
1781 — 1782	323	162
1782 — 1783	398	219
1783 — 1784	389	215
1784 — 1785	426	153
1785 — 1786	420	157
1786 — 1787	419	150
1787 — 1788	425	178
	5175	2369

You will obferve, that in years of the war the births were lefs numerous. This is a natural reflexion, which ought always to be made by any one who makes calculations on the population of America.

Finally, my friend, to give you a further idea of the rapidity of population in America,

rica, take the tables of Rhode-Ifland and New-Jerfey, and compare them with the one I gave you on Pennfylvania.

Population of Rhode-Ifland.

Years.	Whites.	Blacks.
1730 —	15,312 —	2,603
1742 —	29,755 —	4,375
1761 —	35,939 —	4,697
1774 —	54,435 —	5,243
1783 —	48,538 —	3,361

New Jerfey.

1738 —	43,388 —	3,981
1745 —	56,797 —	4,606
1784 —	139,934 —	10,501

You obferve by thefe tables, that the population of Rhode-Ifland, which had almoft doubled in twelve years, from thirty to forty-two, has diminifhed during the war. But with what pleafure do you fee the population in New Jerfey more than tripled in forty years, notwithftanding the obftructions occafioned by the fame bloody war! And with what pleafure do you, who are the defender of the blacks, obferve

that

that their number has more than doubled in
the fame fpace of time in New Jerfey: though
the importation of them was prohibited in
1775, though the war coft the life of a great
number of negroes, and though many of
them were ftolen by the Englifh and fold in
their iflands!

From all the facts and all the tables which
I have given you, it muft be concluded that
the life of man is much longer in the
United States of America, than in the
moft falubrious countries of Europe.

LETTER

LETTER XXX.

The Prison of Philadelphia, and Prisons in general.

AND Philadelphia likewise has its prison! I love to believe, that for the first thirty or forty years, when the Quakers were the magistrates, or rather, when there was no need of magistrates, I love to indulge the belief that there was no prison. But since the English, to deliver themselves from the banditti that infested their island, have practised letting them loose upon the colonies,—since great numbers of foreign adventurers have overspread the country, especially since the last war, which has augmented their number, reduced many to misery, and habituated others to crimes—it has been necessary to restrain them by prisons. One fact does honour to this State; which is, that among the prisoners of Philadelphia, not one in ten is a native of the country. During my stay in this town, one robbery only has been committed; and this was by a French sailor.

Almost

Almoſt all the other priſoners are either Iriſhmen or Frenchmen.

This priſon is a kind of houſe of correction. The priſoners are obliged to work; and each enjoys the profit of his own labour. This is the beſt method of ameliorating men; and it is a method uſed by the Quakers.

Thoſe who govern the houſe of correction in New York, on conſenting to take charge of criminals condemded by the law, have obtained leave to ſubſtitute to whips and mutilation their humane method of correction; and they daily ſucceed in leading back to induſtry and reaſon theſe deluded men.

One of theſe Quakers was aſked, by what means it was poſſible to correct men who diſhonour human nature, and who will not work. " We have two powerful inſtru-" ments," (replied the Quaker,) " hunger " and hope."

By the ſmall number of Pennſylvanians contained in the priſon of Philadelphia, we may conclude, that, were it not for the ſtrangers, the government of this town, like
that

that of Nantucket, might have a prifon with open doors, of which honor and repentance are the only keepers.

But, after all, what is the ufe of prifons? why thofe tombs for living men? the Indians have them not; and they are not the worfe for it. If there exifts a country where it is poffible, and where it is a duty to change this fyftem, it is America; it is therefore to the Americans that I addrefs the following re-flexions:

Prifons are fatal to the health, liberty, and morals of men. To preferve health, a man has need of a pure air, frequent exer-cife, and wholefome food. In a prifon, the air is infected, there is no fpace for exercife, and the food is often deteftable.

A man is not in health, but when he is with beings who love him, and by whom he is beloved. In prifon, he is with ftrangers and with criminals. There can exift no fo-ciety between them; or, if there does, he muft either be obliged to ftruggle without ceafing againft the horrid principles of thefe wicked men, which is a torment to him; or he adopts their principles and becomes like them.—

them.—A man by living conſtantly with
fools, becomes a fool himſelf; every thing
in life is contagion and correſpondence.

By impriſonment, you ſnatch a man from
his wife, his children, his friends; you de-
prive him of their ſuccour and conſolation;
you plunge him into grief and mortification;
you cut him off from all thoſe connections
which render his exiſtence of any import-
ance. He is like a plant torn up by the
roots and fevered from its nouriſhing ſoil;
and how will you expect it to exiſt?

The man who has for a long time vegetated
in a priſon, who has experienced frequent
convulſions of rage and deſpair, is no longer
the ſame being, on quitting this abode, that
he was when he entered it. He returns to
his family, from whom he has been long ſe-
queſtered; he no more meets from them, or
experiences in himſelf, the ſame attachment
and the ſame tenderneſs.

In putting a man in priſon, you ſubject
him to the power of the gaoler, of the turn-
key, and of the commiſſary of the priſon.
Before theſe men he is obliged to abaſe himſelf, to diſguiſe his ſenſations, to conſtrain
his

his paffions, in order that his mifery may not be increafed. This ftate of humiliation and conftraint is horrible to him; and befides, it renders his mafters imperious, unjuft, vexatious, and wicked.

To oblige a freeman to ufe fupplication to obtain juftice, is to do him a lafting injury. The tree that is once bent from its natural form never acquires it again.

The laws which ordain the *habeas corpus* are wife and natural. But they do not ordain it in all cafes. A prifoner for debt, who cannot obtain furety, muft remain a prifoner. A man accufed of a capital offence, who will be probably acquitted on trial, cannot enjoy the benefit of this law. Thefe are abufes.

Is it not much more fimple to imitate the Indians, to grant every man the privilege of his own houfe for a prifon, though you are obliged to put a fentinel at his door? and for thofe that have no houfe of their own, eftablifh a public houfe, where they can purfue their occupations.

If fuch regulations are neceffary for any fociety, it is furely for the one which has
good

good morals, and wifhes to preferve them: if they are any where practicable, it is among a people where great crimes are rare. Recollect, my friend, that but within a few years before the laft war, no capital punifhment had ever been inflicted in Connecticut.

I am furprized then that the penalty of death is not totally abolifhed in this country. Manners here are fo pure, the means of living fo abundant, and mifery fo rare, that there can be no ·need of fuch horrid pains to prevent the commiffion of crimes.

Doctor Rufh has juft given force to all thefe arguments in favour of the abolition of the punifhment of death. He has not yet fucceeded; but it is to be hoped that the State of Pennfylvania, and even all the States, difengaging themfelves from their ancient fuperftition for the Englifh laws, will foon dare to give to Europe a great example of juftice, humanity and policy. Any objections that may be made againft this reform in Europe will not apply in this country.

LETTER

LETTER XXXI.

The Quakers. Their private Morals, their Manners, &c.

I HAVE promifed you, my friend, a particular article on this refpectable fociety. I this day perform my promife.

You remember with what infulting levity M. de Chaftellux has treated them in the very fuperficial journal which he has publifhed. You recollect the energetic cenfure * which I paffed on his errors, his falfehoods, and his calumnies. You have not forgot the ftupid perfecution that this cenfure brought on me, and the monœuvres employed to ftifle my work by that fame witty Marquis, and by other academicians, who wifhed to tyrannize public opinion, and monopolize reputation.

And now, my friend, I have been able to compare the portrait which I had made of them with the original; and I am convinced

---

* See *Examen critique des Voyages dans l'Amérique Septentio-nale de M. le Marquis de Chaftellux.*

that

that it is very nearly juft.   At leaft the portrait does not flatter them.   I endeavoured to
guard myfelf from the prejudices which their
flattering reception of me might have occafioned.   The way was prepared for this reception by the Apology which I had publifhed
in their favour; it was tranflated into Englifh
even here, by fome refpectable members of
the fociety, and diftributed every where with
profufion; and I find to my fatisfaction,
that it has contributed to diffipate the unhappy
prejudices which the indifcretions, boafts and
farcafms of our frivolous academician had
excited againft the French nation.

Simplicity, candour, and good faith, characterize the actions as well as the difcourfes
of the Quakers.   They are not affected, but
they are fincere; they are not polifhed, but
they are humane; they have not that wit,
that fparkling wit,—without which a man is
nothing in France, and with which he is
every thing; but they have good fenfe, a
found judgement, an upright heart, and an
obliging temper of mind.   If I wifhed to live
in fociety, it would be with the Quakers: if
I wifhed to amufe myfelf, it would be with
my countrymen.   And their women---you
afk, what are they?   They are what they
                                                fhould

fhould be, faithful to their hufbands, tender
to their children, vigilant and œconomical
in their houfehold, and fimple in their ornaments. Their principal charaðeriftic is, that
they are not eager to pleafe all the world:
negleðful of the exterior, they referve all
their accomplifhments for the mind. Let us
fay it, let us not ceafe to repeat it, it is
among manners like thefe that we are to look
for good houfeholds, happy families, and
public virtues. But we, miferable wretches!
gangrened with our own civilization and politenefs, we have abjured thefe manners. And
who among us is happy? unlefs you can find
a man who has the courage to content himfelf with a life of nature, and to live like
people of former ages. *If you conform to nature*, fays Seneca, *you will never be poor;
if to opinion, you will never be rich.*

I will not recal to your mind all that
M. Crevecœur has faid of the Quakers: I
only wifh to fay to you what he has not faid.

Simplicity is a favorite virtue with the
Quakers; and the men ftill follow, with fome
exaðnefs, the counfel of Penn: " Let thy gar-
ments be plain and fimple; attend to cove-
nience and decency, but not to vanity. If
thou

thou art clean and warm, thy end is accomplifhed; to do more, is to rob the poor*."

I have feen James Pemberton, one of the moft wealthy Quakers, and one whofe virtues have placed him among the moft refpectable of their chiefs; I have feen him wear a thread-bare coat, but it was neat. He likes better to clothe the poor, and to expend money in the caufe of the blacks, than to change often his coats.

You know the drefs of the Quakers—a round hat, generally white; cloth coat; cotton or woollen ftockings; no powder on their hair, which is cut fhort and hangs round. They commonly carry in the pocket a little comb in a cafe; and on entering a houfe, if the hair is difordered, they comb it without ceremony before the firft mirror that they meet.

The white hat which they prefer, has

---

* See *Fruits of Solitude*, &c. by William Penn. In thefe inftances of re-tranflation, it is fcarcely poffible to preferve exactly the expreffions of the original author. Any deviations of this fort are therefore to be imputed not to a defire of changing his phrafeology, but to the misfortune of not having at hand the original work.

become

become more common here, fince Franklin has proved the advantages which it poffeffes, and the inconveniencies of the black.

The Quakers in the country generally wear cloth made in their own houfes. And at their general meeting here, in September this year, which confifted of more than fifteen hundred, nine-tenths of the number were clothed in American cloth. This is an example to the other fects.

There are fome Quakers who drefs more like other fects; who wear powder, filver buckles, and ruffles. They are called *wet quakers*. The others regard them as a kind of fchifmaticks, or feeble men. They are admitted, indeed, into their churches on Sunday, but never to their monthly or quarterly meetings.

It is not more than fifteen years fince it was a kind of crime in all fects in America to wear powder. In general, manners have changed fince the war, by the intercourfe of European armies. But to the honor of the Quakers, theirs have not changed. This is to be attributed to the rigor of their difcipline, and to their difcarding thofe who violate it.

They

They put on woollen ſtockings the 15th
of September; it is an article of their diſ-
cipline, which extends to their clothing;
and to this is to be attributed their remarkable longevity. Among the few companions
of William Penn in 1693, ſix are now alive—
Edward Drinker, born in 1680, has been
dead but two years. It is from the intimate
conviction of the advantages of their maxims,
that they perſevere in them with ſingular
conſtancy. Their ſingularities are the effect
of reaſon and long experience.

The Quaker women dreſs more comfort-
ably than thoſe of the other ſects; and this
renders them leſs ſubject to ſickneſs. Age
and fortune, however, cauſe much greater
diſtinctions in their dreſs than in that of the
men. The matrons wear the graveſt colours,
little black bonnets, and the hair ſimply
turned back. The young women curl their
hair with great care and anxiety; which coſts
them as much time as the moſt exquiſite toi-
lette. They wear little hats covered with
ſilk or ſattin. Theſe obſervations gave me
pain. Theſe young Quakereſſes, whom nature has ſo well endowed, whoſe charms have
ſo little need of the borrowed hand of art,
are remarkable for their choice of the fineſt
linens,

linens, muflins, and filks. Elegant fans play
between their fingers. Oriental luxury itfelf,
would not difdain the linen they wear. Is
this agreeable to the doctrine of Penn?
" Modefty and mildnefs," fays he, " are the
richeft and fineft ornaments of the foul.
The more fimple the drefs, the more will
beauty and thefe qualities appear."

I fay it with freedom, and I ought to fay
it to my friends the Quakers, (for I am fure
they will read me ; and I would not flatter
my friends ; a hint of good advice is always
well received by them,) that if any thing can
difcredit their principles abroad, it is the re-
laxation infenfibly introduced into their manners and cuftoms. Their tafte in linens and
filks is regarded by others as a hypocritical
luxury, ill-difguifed ; which is abfurd, at leaft
among men fo apparently devoted to fimplicity and aufterity.

Luxury begins where utility ends. Now,
where is the utility to the body in the ufe of
the fineft of linen? And how ufefully might
the money be employed, which is now applied to this luxury! There are fo many
good actions to be done! fo many perfons
in want !

Luxury

Luxury difplayed in fimple things announces more vanity than when difplayed in
an ordinary manner ; for it feems to be confidered as the meafure of wealth, of which
they affect to defpife the oftentation. Indeed,
it announces a mind not truly penetrated
with the great principles of morality---a
mind that places its happinefs, not in virtue,
but in appearance.

And what an ill example is thus given to
the other Americans by the Quakers, who
have been to them the models of fimplicity ?
Their country does not, and will not for a
long time, manufacture thefe fine linens,
thefe delicate muflins, of which the texture
is fcarcely perceptible. They muft be purchafed in foreign countries, to which they
have recourfe for fo many articles of neceffity. Thus, this luxury drains from their
country the money fo much wanted for the
extenfion of agriculture and other ufeful
enterprifes. Let the Quakers who read this
article, meditate upon it ; let them reflect,
that the ufe of rum, againft which they raife
their voice with great energy and juftice,
cannot make more ravages in America than
the introduction of luxury in their fociety.
I made the fame remark on the houfehold
furniture

furniture of thofe who are rich among them. It has the appearance of fimplicity; but in many inftances it is certainly ex-penfive.

Happily, this luxury has not yet found its way to the tables of the Quakers. Their dinners are folid, fimple, and elegant, en-livened by ferene and fenfible converfation, and endeared by hofpitality. They drink beer, Philadelphia porter, cider, and finifh with a glafs of wine. None of thofe fa-tiguing toafts, which are rather provocatives to intoxication than accents of patriqtifm.

Thofe who reproach the Quakers with fadnefs and morofenefs, are unacquainted with their true character, and have never lived with them. I, who have been received by them as a child, and domefticated as a friend, judge them very differently. I have found among them moments of gaiety, of effufions of the heart, of fprightly and agree-able converfation. They are not buffoons, but they are ferene; they are happy, and, if gaiety confifts in the expreffion of heart-felt happinefs, they are gay.

We Frenchmen have the reputation of
being

being gay, of laughing at every thing, of ba-
lancing a misfortune by a pun. This is a
folly. To laugh is the fign of gaiety, and
gaiety is the fign of agreeable fenfations. To
be gay, therefore, in the depth of mifery is
a falfhood or a folly; to be ferene and un-
moved, is wifdom. We ought not to be
depreffed by misfortunes; neither ought we
to laugh at them: the one is a weaknefs of
mind, the other is madnefs or ftupidity.

The calmnefs which characterizes the
Quakers in their joy, accompanies them
likewife in their grief, in their difcuffions,
and in all their affairs. They owe it to their
education; they are early taught to curb
their paffions, efpecially that of anger; to
render themfelves, as they call it, *immoveable*;
that is, inacceffible to fudden emotions: it
refults from this, that on all occafions, they
preferve an empire over themfelves; and
this gives them a great advantage in difcuffion over thofe who do not preferve the fame
temper. " The greateft fervice," fays Penn,
that thou canft render to reafon, is to
clothe her in calmnefs; and he that defends truth with too much heat, does her
more injury than her adverfaries themfelves." I faw an example of the effects
of

of this coolnefs in debate, in my friend
Myers Fifher, who is a learned and virtuous
practitioner of the law. I heard him before
the legiflature defend the caufe of the Pitots,
againft a bill, the object of which was, to
reduce their pay. Clearnefs, clofe reafoning,
and deep erudition, diftinguifhed his difcourfe; which was followed by fuccefs. He
preferved conftantly his calmnefs of temper,
amidft the frequent attacks and fudden inter-
ruptions on the part of the members of the
Affembly.

The Quakers carry to the borders of the
tomb this fame tranquillity of mind; and it
even forfakes not the women at this diftreffing
moment. This is the fruit of their religious
principles, and of a regular virtuous life.
They confider Heaven as their country;
and they cannot conceive why death, which
conducts to it, fhould be a misfortune.

This habitual ferenity does not diminifh
their fenfibility. The refpectable Pemberton
recounted to me the death of a beloved
daughter, which happened the day before.
I could fee the tear fteal down his cheek,
which a moment's reflexion caufed to difappear. He loved to fpeak to me of her virtues

tues and her refignation during her long
agony.   " She was an angel," (fays he,)
" and fhe is now in her place."

This good father did not exaggerate. You
will find in this Society, many of thefe
cœleftial images, clothed in ferenity, the
fymbol of internal peace and confcious virtue.

I cannot explain to you the fact; but it is
true, that I feel an expanfion of foul in their
fociety.   I meet a man of a pure mind,—I
am at once at my eafe,—we are like intimate and old acquaintance,—we underftand
each other without fpeaking. A corrupted
man, a fharper, a man of the world, produces on me a contrary impreffion.   My
foul contracts and recoils upon itfelf, like
the fenfitive plant.

The portrait which I have given you of
the Quakers, is not only the refult of my
own obfervations, but what has been told
me by enlightned men of the other fects.

I afked one day, in company, the following queftion: " Is there a greater purity of
morals, more fimplicity, more integrity,
more honefty among the Quakers, than any
                                                    other

other fects?" A man diftinguifhed for his
information and his attachment to the new
conftitution, anfwered me: " I am a Prefby-
terian; but I muft declare, that the Quakers
excel all fects in the qualities you mention."
It is not that they are all pure and irreproachable; it is not, that there are not
fome fharpers among them. The reputation
of the fect, and the advantage that may be
made of it, have naturally brought into it
fome hypocritical profelytes and rafcals. A
man would counterfeit a guinea rather than
a halfpenny; but the Quakers are very ftrict
in expelling from their fociety thofe who are
found guilty, I do not fay of crimes, but of
thofe breaches of delicacy and probity, which
the laws do not punifh. The public is often
ignorant of this excommunication; becaufe
the excommunicated member continues to go
to their public meetings on Sunday. He
cannot be hindered from this; but he is never
admitted to their monthly or quarterly meetings.

LETTER

LETTER XXXII.

*On the Reproaches made against the Quakers
by different Writers.*

THE fpectacle of virtue gives pain to the
wicked; and they avenge themfelves
by decrying it. You muft not then be furprized that writers have endeavoured to injure this fanctified body. One of thofe
who attempted, it with the moft bitternefs, is
the author of *Recherches fur les Etats Unis*,
publifhed the beginning of this year. He
has dilated, in a long chapter, all the calumnies which he had before uttered in a letter
under the name of one of his countrymen,
printed in the Paris Journal of the fixteenth
of November, 1786.

This author is Mr. Mazzei, an Italian, who
refided fome years in Virginia, and has fince
fettled in France. He might naturally, among
the planters in Virginia contract prejudices
againft the Quakers; friends of diffipation,
of luxury, of flavery, of pleafure, and of
oftentation, regard with an evil eye, a fociety

ciety who preach and practice œconomy and
simplicity. Mr. Mazzei is, besides, unacquainted with the Quakers, having never
lived in their intimacy: his testimony then
ought to have little weight. He cites as his
authority, the Virginians and the French military officers.

The French, and especially the French
officers, cannot in general be good judges in
this matter; some of them sacrifice too much
to the rage of ridicule; others have principles too different from the Quakers; and
almost all of them are superficial observers.

Yet I must say, in praise of the French
army, that they always respected the Quakers.
The commander in chief had made of their
meeting-house at Newport, a magazine of
arms. He gave it up to them on their re-
quest. An English general would have conducted very differently.

In another instance, a French officer had
quartered some soldiers at the house of a
Quaker; out of respect to their principles,
he did not suffer them to deposite their arms
in the house.

M. de

M. de Chaftellux was far from thefe principles. The caufe of his prejudice was, that
at the time when he travelled in America, the
Quakers were not treated with refpect, becaufe they refufed to take part in the war.
He caught the general contagion of diflike,
without ever hearing or feeing any of them:
And it was to pleafe the pretty graceful women of Paris, that he ridiculed the interior
grace of the Quakers.

Among the writers in their favour, are
Voltaire, Raynal, M'Auley, Crevecœur.
What names on this fubject can be placed
in oppofition to them?

In abufing the Quakers, he is obliged to
confefs that their fingular ideas have raifed
them in certain points much above other
men.

He pretends, likewife, that they have defects; and where have I denied it? *Ubi ho-
mines, ibi erunt vitia,* fays Tacitus. And
the Quakers are men. But I fay that their
principles guard them more from vice than
thofe of other men.

Mr. Mazzei confefses, that for œconomy
and

and application to bufinefs, their conduct is truly *exemplary and worthy of praife.* It is from thefe two fources that flow all the private and civil virtues; for a man, who by principle is œconomical and attentive to his bufinefs, has nothing to fear from a numerous family. If he has many children, he loves them; for he fees the means of providing for them with eafe. Such a man is neither a gambler nor a debauchee. Such a man is a good hufband; for, placing all his happinefs in domeftic life, he is forced to be good, in order to be beloved; and he cannot be happy, but by rendering thofe happy who are round him. Why did not this critic fee the confequences that muft follow from the truth which he admits? Why did he not fee that it effaced all the ill that he fays afterwards of the Quakers? Why did he not fee that it raifed them above every other fect? For, with others, example, habit, or other variable circumftances, may render men œconomical and vigilant in bufinefs; while every Quaker is fo, from a principle in his religion; a principle from which he cannot deviate, without ceafing to be a Quaker. Œconomy and induftry are with them an effential part of their religion; how much ftronger is fuch

a motive

a motive than all thofe which produce thefe in other men!

Mr. Mazzei acknowledges, that in hofpipitality and beneficence they are not inferior to other men. He ought to have faid they were fuperior; for charity and hofpitality flow from œconomy and eafy circumftances. The man that has more means, lefs real wants, and no fantaftical ones, and who really loves his fellow creatures, is neceffarily benefieent and hofpitable; and fuch is the fituation and fuch the charaɗer of the Quakers.

But the great reproach that Mr. Mazzei brings upon them is, that they are fuperior in *hypocrify.* To judge of this accufation, let us fee in what hypocrify confifts.

For a man to pretend to fentiments which he does not poffefs, to virtues which he does not praɗice—or, in a word, to appear what he is not, is what is meant by hypocrify.

Now are not the Quakers what they appear to be? This is the point to be proved. To conviɗ them of *religious hypocrify,* you muft prove that they do not believe in the Holy Spirit, and in the Gofpel; you muft
prove

prove them to be Infidels or Atheifts under the mafk of Chriftianity.

If *moral* hypocrify is intended, you muft prove that they conceal libertinifm, diffipation, and cruelty to their families, under the veil of aufterity, œconomy, and apparent tendernefs. Is it *political* hypocrify? you muft then prove that they wifh fecretly for places and dignities, which they have renounced; that they long to maffacre their fellow creatures, while they profefs a horror for the effufion of human blood; that they are really felfifh, under the mafk of friends and benefactors to the human race; that they are proud and haughty, under the appearance of fimplicity.

In a word, hypocrify is a vague term; and as long as it is not applied to facts, it fignifies nothing. It does not fuffice for its juftification, to fay, that the Quakers are *Proteftant Jefuits.*

This is but a new calumny, as vague as the other. I afk for facts. If the Quakers refemble the Jefuits in mildnefs, indulgence, tolerance, and the art of perfuafion, it is to refemble them on the virtuous fide. M. Mazzei

zei fays, they do not refemble them in every thing, and he thus effaces what M. de Chaftellux had wantonly advanced on this charge.

I am not aftonifhed that the Quakers have the art of perfuafion. They have poffeffed it for a hundred and fifty years; which is a proof, that they merit the public confidence; they muft have loft it had they been charletans or hypocrites.

The cry of hypocrify is generally fet up againft the moft grave and religious fects, and by thofe men who are feeking to juftify their own corruption. It feems, that having renounced all virtues, they like not to take the trouble to feign them; or perhaps to get rid of the weight of efteem which is due to virtue, they calculate, that it is eafier to deny its exiftence.

M. Mazzei accufes the Quakers of want of *punctuality* and *equity* in their commerce; he adds, that it is their *national character*. Obferve, my friend, that neither Mazzei nor Chaftellux adduces a fingle fact, nor a fingle authority for this affertion. It muft then be a pure calumny. If this was the character of
the

the Quakers, would facts be wanting to prove it?

I have too often heard repeated this accufation of knavery againſt them; I have, with the greateſt care, confulted Engliſh and Americans of all fects, and French merchants who have dealings with them; and I have not been able to hear of a fingle fact as an inſtance of diſhoneſty. The worſt that has been told me, is, that they are cunning, ſtrict, and inflexible; that they have no refpect for perfons or fects. I was told too, as M. Mazzei has printed, that they underſtand very well how to fell, that they fell dear. I have ſhowed in my anfwer to Chaſtellux, the abfurdity of any reproach like this. To underſtand the art of felling, does not fuppofe a want of probity; it is the fpirit of commerce; I will fay more, it is the general character of the Americans; they are artful: I will explain the caufe of it hereafter.

Mr. Bingham, one of the moſt opulent citizens of Philadelphia, and one who, from his oſtentation and luxury, cannot be very favourable to the Quakers, fpoke of them to me in the higheſt praife. He faid, that they were extremely punctual in fulfill-

ing

ing their engagements, and that they never live beyond their income.

And this will explain the common faying that you fo often hear repeated at Philadelphia, that the Quakers are fo cunning that the Jews themfelves cannot live among them. Ufurious Jews can never live among œconomical men, who have no need of borrowing money at enormous intereft; for a fimilar reafon, a feller of pork cannot live among Jews.

M. Mazzei accufes the Quakers of a *defire of gain*; though he is not fo formal in this accufation as M. de Chaftellux. I will take this opportunity to make a remark on this common reproach, with which it is fo fafhionable to revile, not only the Quakers, but commercial people in general.

The author of *Philofophical Travels in England* fays, " We are luckily exempted in France from that fpirit of avarice, that defire of gain; and we owe this exemption to the pride of a numerous body of nobles."— More luckily, however, we are at prefent exempted from this very ufeful body. But I would afk this noble traveller, with what

fpirit

ſpirit theſe honourable nobles beg and fawn
for lucrative places and penſions? With what
ſpirit do they engage, under borrowed names,
in all ſpeculations and ſtock-jobbing? With
what ſpirit do they require large gratifi-
cations for their patronage, ſecret bribes
from the Farmers-General, and a covered
intereſt in every enterprize that is carried on
in the kingdom? Is this the ſame ſpirit; or
is it better or worſe than the deſire of gain
which appears to them ſo vile in a merchant?
In two reſpeᴄts theſe men are infinitely below
the merchant; in the hypocriſy of pretending
to deſpiſe a metal which they burn to poſſeſs,
and in the uſe which they make of it. Money
gained in commerce, is generally employed
in extending commerce and uſeful ſpeculations; money gained by a noble, is ſpent in
luxury, vanity, debauchery, and creating
new poiſons in ſociety.

The deſire of gain in a merchant, conſiſts
in amaſſing wealth, in preſerving it, and in
watching over his affairs with a conſtant attention. Such then is the crime of the
Quakers. But in reproaching them with it,
we ought to conſider attentively the circumſtances of that ſociety: their religious principles exclude them from all ambitious views,
from

from all places and employments; they muſt
then attend wholly to their induſtry, to the
ſupport and eſtabliſhment of their children.
They have, therefore, more need of amaſſing
property than other citizens, who may find
the means of placing their children in public
offices, in the army, the navy, or the church.

Finally, the Quakers, having renounced
the occupations of intrigue, of amuſements,
and even of literature and the ſciences, muſt
be occupied wholly in buſineſs; and con-
ſequently appear more vigilant, that is, in the
language of lazy nobility, *more avaricious.*

M. Mazzei agrees, that the Quakers are
virtuous; but does not allow them to rank
in this reſpect above other ſects. He
believes, that other ſects have produced men
as perfect as this. I believe it as well he: the
image of Fenelon gives me as agreeable an
impreſſion as that of Fothergill or Benezet.
But I maintain,—1ſt, that the ſect of the
Quakers, in proportion to their number,
has produced more of theſe prodigies. 2d,
that no ſect preſents to us a totality ſo perfect and harmonious, and an aſſemblage of
men ſo pure and virtuous, or ſo conſtant a
ſeries of great and good actions. To prove
this

this laſt aſſertion, I will only call to your
mind the emancipation of ſlaves, executed
by them with unanimity, with the ſame
ſpirit, and followed by numerous efforts to
aboliſh ſlavery, and to meliorate and edu-
cate the blacks. Let any one cite to me in
all other ſects a ſimilar inſtance of diſintereſt-
edneſs and humanity. Let a ſect be mentioned, which, like this, has made it a law
never to take any part either in privateering *,
or in contraband trade, even in a foreign
country; for they will not tempt a foreigner
to violate the laws of his own country.

During the laſt war, the Quakers paſſed
a reſolution, that whoever of their ſociety
ſhould pay a debt in paper money (then depreciated) ſhould be excommunicated; while,
at that time, it was a crime to doubt of the
goodneſs of this paper; and the Quakers,
like all other citizens, were obliged to receive
it from their debtors at the nominal value.

* I ought to mention the conduct of a Quaker, who in the
laſt war reſtored to the original owner, his part of a prize
accidentally taken by a merchant's ſhip, in which he was inte-
reſted.

LETTER

LETTER XXXIII.

The Extent of the Society of Quakers, their
religious Principles, &c.

A Society, fimple in its manners, œconomical, and devoted principally to agriculture and commerce, muft neceffarily increafe with great rapidity. Pennfylvania may
be confidered as the mother country of the
Quakers, who form a majority of its population. They are numerous in the States of
New-York, New-Jerfey, Maryland, and
Rhode-Ifland; fome in New-Hampfhire and
Maffachufets. Many of the Quakers have
planted their tabernacles in that delightful
valley which is wafhed by the Shenadore,
beyond the firft chain of mountains. They
have no flaves; they employ negroes as hired
fervants, and have renounced the culture of
tobacco: and this valley is obferved as the
beft cultivated part of Virginia.

They have pufhed their fettlements likewife into the two Carolinas and Georgia.
They

They are beginning eftablifhments near the Ohio, and have a confiderable one already at Redftone, on the Monongahela.

It is to be wifhed, for the happinefs of the Indians, and the peace of America, that all the planters of the frontiers poffeffed the pacific principles of the Quakers: a lafting union would foon be formed between them; and blood would no longer ftain the furrows which American induftry traces in the forefts.

The religion of the Quakers is the fimpleft imaginable. It confifts in the voice of confcience, the internal fentiment, the divine inftinct, which, in their opinion, God has imparted to every one. This inftinct, this light, this grace, which every perfon brings into the world with him, appears to them the only guide neceffary for the conduct of life. But to underftand the guide, it is neceffary to know it; to be known, it fhould often be interrogated. Hence the neceffity of frequent meditations; hence the nullity of all formal worfhip, and the miniftration of priefts: for they confider forms as fo many obftacles, which turn the attention from the voice within; and priefts poffeffing no more

of

of the Divine Spirit than other men, cannot
fupply the want of meditation.

I have fhown in my Critique on the Travels
of Chaftellux, how much this meditative worfhip of the Deity is fuperior to the mechanical worfhip of other fects. I have proved
that the man who adores his Creator by me-
ditating on his own duties, will neceffarily
become good, tolerant, juft, and beneficent.
You have here the key both of the moral
character of the Quakers, and of its extraordinary duration. Their virtue is an habit,
a fecond nature.

The Quakers have been much ridiculed
for their belief in this interior principle.
For their calumniators, fome of whom have
called themfelves philofophers, are ignorant
that this belief is not peculiar to the Quakers.
We find it in a great number of fages, who
have merited the homage of mankind. With
Pythagoras, it was *the Eternal Word, the
Great Light,*—with Anaxagoras, *the Divine
Soul,*—with Socrates, *the Good Spirit, or De-
mon,*—with Timeus, *the Uncreated Principle,*—with Hieron, *the Author of Delight,
the God within the Man,*—with Plato, *the
eternal ineffable and perfect Principle of
Truth,*—

Truth,—with Zeno, *the Creator and Father of all,*—and with Plotinus, *the Root of the Soul.* When thefe philofophers endeavoured to characterife the influence of this principle within us, they ufed correfpondent expreffions. Hieron called it a *domeftic God,* an *internal God.*—Socrates and Timeus, *the Genius,* or *Angel,*—Plotinus, the *Divine Principle in Man,*—and Plato, *the Rule of the Soul, the Internal Guide, the Foundation of Virtue.*

I do not pretend to explain to you all the religious principles of the Quakers; this would lead me too far; not that their dogmas are very numerous, for their doctrine is more fimple and more concife than their morals. But this article, as well their hiftory, ought to be treated at large. I can affure you, that all the French authors who have written on them, without excepting Voltaire, have been ignorant of the true fources of information. They have contented themfelves with feizing the objects to which they could give a caft of ridicule, and have thrown afide every thing that could render that fociety refpectable.

One inviolable practice of theirs, for inftance, is, never to difpute about dogmas. They

They have cut off an endlefs chain of difpu-
tations, by not admitting the authority either
of the Old or New Teftament to be fuperior
to that of the internal principle, and by not
hiring a clafs of men for the fole purpofe of
difputing and tyranizing, under the pretext
of inftructing. What torrents of blood
would have been fpared, if the Catholics
and Proteftants had adopted a rule of conduct
fo wife; if inftead of quarrelling about un-
intelligible words, about writings that may
be changed, about the authority of the Church
and the Pope, they had believed in the internal Spirit, which for each individual
may be the fecret guide! This guide has
little concern with dogmas, and much with
morals.

Among the political principles of the
Quakers, the moft remarkable are, never to
take an oath, and never to take arms. I
fhall fpeak of the latter in an article by itfelf;
as to their refufing to take an oath, it may
be faid, that an oath adds no weight to
the declaration of an honeft man; and per-
jury has no terrors for a knave.

Their difcipline is as fimple as their doctrine. In their marriages, their births, and
interments,

interments, they use only the forms necessary to verify the existence of the fact.

A Quaker cannot marry a person of another sect; I asked the reason of this; as it appeared to me a sign of intolerance. " The preservation of our society," (replied a Quaker,) " depends on the preservation of the customs which distinguish us from other men. This singularity forces us to be more honest; and and if we should unite our families with strangers, who are not of our society, individuals would swerve from our usages, and confound them with others. A Quaker woman who should marry a Presbyterian, submits herself to the authority of a man over whom we have no influence; and the society subsists only by this domestic, voluntary, and reciprocal influence."

This influence is directed by their different assemblies. The monthly assemblies are in general composed of several neighbouring congregations. Their functions are to provide for the subsistence of the poor, and the education of their children; to examine the new converts, and prove their morals; to sustain the zeal and the religion of others; to hear and judge their faults by

means

means of fuperintendants appointed for this purpofe; to decide and fettle any difpute that may arife either between Quakers, or between a Quaker and a ftranger, provided the latter will fubmit to their arbitrament. This laft object is one of the moft important; it prevents that cruel fcourge fo ravaging in other countries, the fcourge of lawyers, the fource of fo much corruption, and the caufe of fuch fcandalous divifions. This cuftom muft be of great advantage to ftrangers who live in the neighbourhood of Quakers. The fociety excommunicates a member who will not fubmit to this arbitration.

Appeals are fometimes carried from the monthly to the quarterly affemblies; the principal bufinefs of the latter, is to fuperintend the operations of the former.

But the fuperintendance of the whole fociety belongs to the annual affemblies. Thefe receive reports from the inferior bodies refpecting the ftate of all parts of the fociety, give their advice, make regulations, judge definitively on the appeals from the lower affemblies, and write letters to each other,

other, in order to maintain a fraternal correfpondence.

There are feven annual affemblies. One
at London, to which the Quakers in Ireland
fend deputies; one in New-England, one at
New-York, one for Pennfylvania and New-
Jerfey, one in Maryland, one in Virginia,
one for the two Carolinas and Georgia.

As the Quakers believe that women may
be called to the miniftry as well as men,
and as there are certain articles of difcipline
which only concern the women, and the ob-
fervance of which can be fuperintended only
by them, they have likewife their monthly,
quarterly, and annual meetings. But they
have not the right to make regulations. This
method is much more proper to maintain
morals among women, than that of our Catholic Confeffors; which fubjeds the feeble
fex to the artifice, the fancies, and the empire of particular men; which opens the
door to the moft fcandalous fcenes, and often
carries inquifition and diffenfion into the bofom of families.

The Quakers have no falaried priefts;
their minifters are fuch men as are the moft
remarkable

remarkable for their zeal; they fpeak the moft frequently in their meetings; but all perfons, male and female, have an equal right to fpeak whenever they feel an inclination.

Thefe minifters, with fome approved elders, hold monthly meetings, by themfelves, for their own inftruction. In thefe meetings they revife, and order to be printed, fuch works as they choofe to have diftributed; and they never fail to take fuch meafures, as that ufeful works fhould be fold at a low price.

In all thefe affemblies, fome of which are very numerous, they have no prefident, and no perfon who has the leaft authority. Yet the greateft order and harmony are always obferved. You never hear two perfons fpeak at once in any of their moft interefting deliberations.

But what will furprize you more is, that in their numerous affemblies, nothing is decided but by unanimity. Each member has a kind of fufpenfive negative. He has only to fay, *I have not clearnefs*; the quef

tion

tion is then adjourned, and not decided till every member is agreed.

This ufage appears to me highly honorable to the fociety; it proves a wonderful union among this band of brothers; it proves that the fame fpirit animates them, the fpirit of reafon, of truth, and of the public good. Deliberative affemblies in general, would not be fubject to fuch long and violent difcuffions, if, like the Quakers, they were difengaged from all perfonal ambition, and if, to refolve doubts, the members addreffed themfelves only to the confciences of men.

You will, perhaps, conclude from this, that this fociety can do but little bufinefs. This will be a miftake; no fociety does more for the public good. It is owing to them, that Philadelphia has hitherto been preferved from the danger of theatres. Their petition this year, to prevent permiffion being obtained to erect one, has been fuccefsful.

A thorough knowledge of the Quakers, my friend, is not to be obtained by going, like Chaftellux, for an hour into one of their churches. Enter into their houfes; you will find them the abodes of peace, harmony,

harmony, gentlenefs, and frugality; tendernefs to children, humanity to fervants. Go into
their hofpitals; you will there fee the more
touching effects of charity, in their unex-
ampled cleanlinefs, in their aliments, in their
beds, and in their fcrupulous attentions.
Vifit the afylums of old age and decrepitude;
you will find the cloth and linen of the poor,
as decent as that of their benefactors. Each
one has his chamber, and enjoys not only
the neceffaries, but many of the agreeables
of life.

If you would quit the town, and run
over the farms of the Quakers, you will
difcover a greater degree of neatnefs, order,
and care, among thefe cultivators, than
among any other. If you examine the
interior organization of the fociety, you will
find, in every church, a treafury for charity,
containing more or lefs money, according
to the wealth of the congregation. This
is employed in affifting young tradefmen, in
fuccouring thofe who have failed in bufinefs
through misfortune, thofe who have fuffered
by fire and other accidents. You will find
many rich perfons among them, who make
it a conftant rule to give to this treafury one-
tenth of their revenue.

I am

I am perfuaded, my friend, that, after having well examined this fociety under all thefe details, you would cry out, If to-morrow I were reduced to poverty, and to be deftitute of the fuccour of my friends, GOD grant that I might finifh my days in a Quaker hofpital: if to-morrow I were to become a farmer, let me have members of this fociety for my neighbours; they would inftruct me by their example and advice, and they would never vex me with law-fuits.

LETTER

LETTER XXXIV.

The Refusal of Quakers to take any Part in War.

THESE wise men have seen that the great basis of universal happiness must be universal peace; and that to open the way to that peace, we must pronounce an anathema against the art of war. Sacred writings have taught us to believe, that the time will come when nation shall no more lift the sword against nation; and to lead to the accomplishment of so consoling a prophecy, this people believe that example is more powerful than words; that kings will always find the secret of perpetuating wars, as long as they can hire men to murder each other; and that it is their duty, as a society, to resolve never to take arms, or contribute to the expences of any war. They have been tormented, robbed, imprisoned, and martyred; they have suffered every thing; till tyranny itself, wearied with their perseverance, has exempted them from military service, and has been driven to indi-

rect

rect meafures, to force contributions from
their hands.

What then would become of our heroes
and our conquerors, our Fredericks and our
Potemkins, if all religious fects had adopted
the fame pacific fpirit, and no man could
be found, who would confent to be trained
like an automaton to the infernal act of
killing his fellow creatures.

If we wifh for the happinefs of mankind,
let us pray, that this fociety may cover the
whole globe; or let us endeavour, at leaft,
that their humane principles be adopted by
all men. Then would be realifed that univerfal peace, which the Quakers have already
realifed in countries where they have borne
the fway.

In Pennfylvania, they found the fecret of
defending themfelves from the fcourge of
military flaughter, till the war of 1755, between France and England. Though mingled with the Indians, never any quarrels
rofe among them, which led to the fpilling
of blood.

The government of England, with all its
manœuvres,

manœuvres, could never engage the Quakers to give any affiftance in this war. They not only refufed this, but they refigned all the places which they had held in the government of the colony; for it was before almoft entirely in their hands; and fuch was their œconomy, that the produce of the cuftom-houfe, and a fmall excife, were always fufficient to defray the public expences; fo that no other tax was known in the colony.

The war of 1755 changed this order of things, and occafioned heavy expences, which the colonies were obliged to pay. The Quakers were fubjected to them, as well as others; but they not only refufed, as a fociety, to pay taxes, of which war was the object, but they excommunicated thofe who paid them. They perfevered in this practice in the laft war.

At this time an animofity was kindled againft them, which is not yet extinguifhed. Faithful to their principles, they declared, that they would take no part in this war, and they excommunicated all fuch as joined either the American or the Britifh army.

I am well convinced of the facred and divine

divine principle which authorifes refiftance
to oppreffion; and I am well convinced, that
oppreffion was here manifeft; I muft therefore blame the neutrality of the Quakers on
this occafion, when their brethren were fight-
ing for independence. But I believe, likewife, that it was wrong to perfecute them
fo violently for their pacific neutrality.

If this inftance of refufal had been the
firft of the kind, or if it had been dictated
by a fecret attachment to the Britifh caufe,
certainly they would have been guilty, and
this perfecution would perhaps have been
legitimate. But this neutrality was commanded by their religious opinions, conftantly profeffed, and practifed by the fociety
from its origin.

No perfon has fpoken to me with more
impartiality refpecting the Quakers than General Wafhington, that celebrated man, whofe
fpirit of juftice is remarkable in every thing.
He declared to me, that, in the courfe of
the war, he had entertained an ill opinion
of this fociety; he knew but little of them;
as at that time there were but few of that
fect in Virginia; and he had attributed to
their political fentiments, the effect of their
religious

religious principles. He told me, that having fince known them better, he acquired an
efteem for them; and that confidering the
fimplicity of their manners, the purity of
their morals, their exemplary œconomy,
and their attachment to the conftitution, he
confidered this fociety as one of the beft
fupports of the new government, which requires a great moderation, and a total banifhment of luxury.

It was not under this point of view that
they were regarded by the Congrefs, which
laid the foundation of American independence. This Congrefs joined their perfecutors,
and banifhed fome of their moft noxious
leaders to Staunton, in Virginia, two hundred miles from their families. My friend,
Myers Fifher, was of the number. M. Mazzei quotes the violent Addrefs publifhed by
Paine againft them, but takes care not to
quote the Anfwer made to it by Fifher. But
fuch is the logic of this calumniator of the
Quakers. Since the peace, they have been
fubjected to another kind of vexation. Each
citizen, from fixteen to fifty-five years of
age, is obliged by law to ferve in the militia,
or to pay a fine. The Quakers will not
ferve nor pay the fine. The collector, whofe
duty

duty it is to levy it, enters their houfes, takes their furniture, and fells it; and the Quakers peaceably fubmit.

This method gives great encouragement to knavery. Collectors have been known to take goods to the amount of fix times the fine, to fell for a fhilling what was worth a pound, never to return the furplus, nor even to pay the ftate, but afterwards become bankrupts. Their fucceffors would then come and demand the fine already paid; but the Quakers have complained of thefe abufes to the legiflature, and an act is paffed fufpending thefe collectors till September 1789.

It would be very eafy to reconcile the wants of the ftate, and the duty of the citizen, with the religious principles of the Quakers. You might fubject them only to pacific taxes, and require them to pay a larger proportion of them. This is already done in Virginia, in abolifhing, with refpect to them, the militia fervice.

With this view of their character, you will agree with me, my friend, that our government ought to haften to naturalize this purity in France. Their example might

ferve

ferve to regenerate our manners; without
which we cannot certainly preferve our liberty for a long time, though we fhould
be able to acquire it.   The Catholic religion, which predominates in France, can
be no objection to it; for the Quakers hate
no fect, but are friendly to all.   They have
ever lived in particular harmony with the
Catholics of Pennfylvania and Maryland.
James Pemberton told me, that in the war
of 1740, he knew a mob of fanatical Prefbyterians, with axes in their hands, going
to deftroy a Catholic chapel.   Ten or twelve
Quakers ftopped them, exhorted them, and
they difperfed without effecting their defign.

Living in harmony with all other fects,
they preferve no refentment againft the apof-
tates from their own, notwithftanding the
troubles which they experienced from them.
Reafon is the only weapon which they ufe.

Poftfcript written in 1790.

IF the old government had an intereft in
inviting Quakers to France, this intereft is
doubled fince the Revolution.   The fpirit of
                                        that

that fociety agrees with the fpirit of French liberty in the following particulars:

That Society has made great eftablifhments without effufion of blood; the National Af-fembly has renounced the idea of conqueft, which is almoft univerfally the caufe of war. That Society practifes univerfal tolerance; the Affembly ordains it. The Society ob-ferves fimplicity of worfhip; the Affembly leads to it. The Society practifes good mo-rals, which are the ftrongeft fupports of a free government; the political regeneration of France, which the Affembly is about to confummate, conducts neceffarily to a rege-neration of morals.

If the French are armed from North to South, it is for liberty, it is for the terror of defpotifm, it is to obey the commands of God; for God has willed that man fhould be free, fince he has endowed him with rea-fon; he has willed that he fhould ufe all efforts to defend himfelf from that tyranny which defaces the only image of Deity in man, his virtues and his talents.

But notwithftanding this ardor in the French to arm themfelves in fo holy a caufe; they

they do not lefs refpect the religious opinions of the Quakers, which forbid them to
fpill the blood of their enemies. This error
of their humanity is fo charming, that it
is almoft as good as a truth. We are all
ftriving for the fame object, univerfal fraternity; the Quakers by gentlenefs, we by
refiftance. Their means are thofe of a fociety, ours thofe of a powerful nation.

LETTER

LETTER XXXV.

Journey to Mount Vernon in Virginia.

ON the 15th of November, 1788, I set out from Philadelphia for Wilmington, diftance twenty-eight miles, and road tolerably good. The town of Chefter, fifteen miles from Philadelphia, is a place where ftrangers like to reft. It ftands on a creek, which falls into the Delaware. It enjoys fome commerce, and the taverns here are good.

Wilmington is much more confiderable; it ftands likewife on a creek near the Delaware; the bafis of its commerce is the exportation of flour. One mile above Wilmington, you pafs the town of Brandywine; the name of which will call to your mind a famous battle gained by the Englifh over the Americans, eight miles from this town, on a river of the fame name. This town is famous for its fine mills; the moft confiderable of which is a paper-mill belonging to Mr. Gilpin and Myers Fifher, that worthy

orator

orator and man of ſcience, whom I have often mentioned. Their proceſs in making paper, eſpecially in grinding the rags, is much more ſimple than ours. I have ſeen ſpecimens of their paper, both for writing and printing, equal to the fineſt made in France.

Wilmington is a handſome town, well-built, and principally inhabited by Quakers. I have ſeen many reſpectable perſons among them, particularly Doctor Way. The celebrated Mr. Dickinſon, who reſides here, was, unfortunately for me, out of town.

I paſſed two evenings in company with Miſs Vining, that amiable woman, whom the licentious pen of Chaſtellux has calumniated, as having too much taſte for galantry. If we believe the teſtimony of all her acquaintance, this trait which he has given her is an inexcuſable libel. The Quakers themſelves, to whom her gaiety cannot be pleaſing, delare that her conduct has been uniformly irreproachable. But I believe, that this malicious and cowardly ſhaft, hurled in ſecurity from the other ſide of the Atlantic, has eſſentially injured her.

At

At nine miles from Wilmington, I paſt
Chriſtine-Bridge, a place of ſome commerce.
From thence to the head of Elk, you ſee but
few plantations, you run through eight miles
of woods, only meeting with a few log-
houſes, when you arrive at Henderſon's
tavern, a very good inn, alone in the midſt
of vaſt foreſts.   It is twenty-two miles from
thence to the ferry of the Suſquehannah.
The town here is called Havre de Grace, a
name given it by a Frenchman who laid the
foundation of the town.   It is at preſent
an irregular maſs of about 150 houſes;
but there is no doubt, when the entrance
of the river ſhall be rendered navigable, but
this will be an intereſting ſituation, and a
populous town.   Here is a charming garden
belonging to the proprietor of the ferry,
from which I had a delicious proſpect of
that magnificent river; which in this place
is more than a mile and a half wide, inter-
ſperſed with iſlands.   From thence to Baltimore are reckoned ſixty miles.   The road
in general is frightful, it is over a clay ſoil,
full of deep ruts, always in the midſt of
foreſts; frequently obſtructed by trees over-
ſet by the wind, which obliged us to ſeek
a new paſſage among the woods.   I cannot
conceive why the ſtage does not often over-
ſet.

fet. Both the drivers and their horfes difcover great fkill and dexterity, being accuftomed to thefe roads.

But why are they not repaired? Over-
feers of the roads are indeed appointed, and
fines are fometimes pronounced on delinquencies of this kind; but they are ill collected. Every thing is here degraded; it
is one of the effects of flavery. The flave
works as little as poffible; and the mafter,
eager of vile enjoyments, finds other occupations than fending his negroes to repair
the roads.

Some vaft fields of Indian corn, but bad
cultivation, pale faces worn by the fever
and ague, naked negroes, and miferable huts,
are the moft ftriking images offered to the eye
of the traveller in Maryland.

We arrived at Baltimore in the night;
but I viewed this town on my return. It
contains near two thoufand houfes; and fourteen thoufand inhabitants. It is irregularly
built, and on land but little elevated above
the furface of Patapfco Bay, on the North
of which it forms a crefcent. The bay is
not fufficiently deep to receive the largeft
fhips;

ſhips; they anchor near Fell's Point, two miles
from the centre of the town. There are ſtill
ſtagnant waters in the town; few of the ſtreets
are paved; and the great quantities of mud
after rain, announce that the air muſt be
unhealthful; but aſk the inhabitants, and
they will tell you, no. You may ſay here,
like the Swiſs, in the heat of a battle, "If
you believe theſe people, nobody can die
here!"

Baltimore was but a village before the
war; but during that period, a conſiderable
portion of the commerce of Philadelphia
was removed to this place. The greateſt
ſhips come as far as here, and can go
no farther; vaſt quantities of proviſions
deſcend the Suſquehannah, and when that
river ſhall be navigable, Baltimore muſt be
a very conſiderable port.

The quarrel about federaliſm divided the
town at the time I was in it; and the two
parties almoſt came to blows on the election
of their repreſentatives.

We left Baltimore for Alexandria at four
in the morning; diſtant about ſixty miles,
bad roads, a rude waggon, excellent horſes,
ſkillful

skillful conductors, poor cultivation, mise-
ferable huts, and miserable negroes.

They showed me a plantation belonging
to a Quaker; there were no slaves upon it.
I saw Brushtown, a new village that the
State of Maryland has pointed out for the
feat of a college. This edifice is nearly
completed; it is on an eminence, and enjoys
a good air. We breakfasted in this village,
and dined at Bladensbury, sixteen miles from
Alexandria. It is situated on a little river,
which discharges into the Potowmack, and
which admits Bateaus of twenty or thirty
tons. We could find nothing to drink, but
brandy or rum mixed with water. In countries cultivated by slaves, there is no industry
and no domestic œconomy. The people
know not the advantage of making beer or
cider on their farms.

George-town terminates the State of Maryland: it overlooks the Potowmack, has an
agreeable situation, and a considerable commerce. Regulations and imposts, inconsi-
rately laid on commerce by the State of
Virginia, have banished to George-town a
considerable part of the commerce of Alexandria.

This

This place is eight miles below George-town, on the oppofite fide of the Potow-mack. Alexandria has grown from nothing to its prefent fize within thefe forty years. It is not fo confiderable as Baltimore, which it ought to furpafs. It is almoft as irregular and as deftitute of pavements. You fee here a greater parade of luxury; but it is a miferable luxury; fervants with filk flockings in boots, women elegantly dreffed, and their heads adorned with feathers.

The inhabitants, at the clofe of the war, imagined that every natural circumftance confpired to render it a great commercial town,—the falubrity of the air, the profundity of the river admitting the largeft fhips to anchor near the quay, an immenfe extent of back country, fertile and abounding in provifions. They have therefore built on every fide, commodious ftore-houfes, and elegant wharfs; but commerce ftill languifhes on account of the reftraints above-mentioned.

I haftened to arrive at Mount Vernon, the feat of General Wafhington, ten miles below Alexandria on the fame river. On this rout you

you traverfe a confiderable wood, and after
having paffed over two hirls, you difcover
a country houfe of an elegant and majeftic
fimplicity.   It is preceded by grafs plats;
on one fide of the avenue are the ftables,
on the other a green-houfe, and houfes for
a number of negro mechanics. In a fpacious
back yard are turkies, geefe, and other poultry.   This houfe overlooks the Potowmack,
enjoys an extenfive profpect, has a vaft and
elevated portico on the front next the river,
and a convenient diftribution of the apartments within.   The General came home in
the evening, fatigued with having been to
lay out a new road in fome part of his plantations. You have often heard him compared
to Cincinnatus: the comparifon is doubtlefs juft.   This celebrated General is nothing
more at prefent than a good farmer, conftantly occupied in the care of his farm and
the improvement of cultivation.   He has
lately built a barn, one hundred feet in length
and confiderably more in breadth, deftined
to receive the productions of his farm, and
to fhelter his cattle, horfes, affes, and mules.
It is built on a plan fent him by that famous Englifh farmer Arthur Young.   But
the General has much improved the plan.
This

This building is in brick, it coſt but three hundred pounds; I am ſure in France it would have coſt three thouſand. He planted this year eleven hundred buſhels of potatoes. All this is new in Virginia, where they know not the uſe of barns, and where they lay up no proviſions for their cattle. His three hundred negroes are diſtributed in different log houſes, in different parts of his plantation, which in this neighbourhood conſiſts of ten thouſand acres. Colonel Humphreys, that poet of whom I have ſpoken, aſſured me that the General poſſeſſes, in different parts of the country, more than two hundred thouſand acres.

Every thing has an air of ſimplicity in his houſe; his table is good, but not oſtentatious; and no deviation is ſeen from regularity and domeſtic œconomy. Mrs. Waſhington ſuperintends the whole, and joins to the qualities of an excellent houſe-wife, that ſimple dignity which ought to characterize a woman, whoſe huſband has acted the greateſt part on the theatre of human affairs; while ſhe poſſeſſes that amenity, and manifeſts that attention to ſtrangers, which render hoſpitality ſo charming. The ſame
virtues

virtues are confpicuous in her interefting niece; but unhappily fhe appears not to enjoy good health.

M. de Chaftelux has mingled too much of the brilliant in his portrait of General Wafhington. His eye befpeaks great goodnefs of heart, manly fenfe marks all his anfwers, and he fometimes animates in converfation, but he has no characteriftic features; which renders it difficult to feize him. He announces a profound difcretion, and a great diffidence in himfelf; but at the fame time, an unfhakeable firmnefs of character, when once he has made his decifion. His modefty is aftonifhing to a Frenchman; he fpeaks of the American war, and of his victories, as of things in which he had no direction.

He fpoke to me of M. de la Fayette with the greateft tendernefs. He regarded him as his child; and forefaw, with a joy mixed with inquietude, the part that this pupil was going to act in the approaching revolution of France. He could not predict, with clearnefs, the event of this revolution. If, on the one fide, he acknowledges the ardor and

and enthufiafm of the French character, on the other, he faw an aftonifhing veneration for their ancient government, and for thofe monarchs whofe inviolability appeared to him a ftrange idea.

After paffing three days in the houfe of this celebrated man, who loaded me with kindnefs, and gave me much information relative to the late war, and the prefent fituation of the United States, I returned to Alexandria.

LETTER

LETTER XXXVI.

General Obfervations on Maryland and Virginia.

THE Bay of Chefapeak divides Maryland into two parts, nearly equal. The
weftern divifion is the moft peopled. Numerous bays and navigable rivers render this
ftate fingularly commodious for commerce.
It would foon become extremely flourifhing
if flavery were banifhed from it, if a more advantageous culture were fubftituted to that of
tobacco, and if the fpirit of the Catholic religion
had not adulterated the tafte for order, regularity, and feverity of manners, which characterize the other fects, and which have fo great an
influence in civil and political œconomy.
The people of this fect were well attached
to the late Revolution.

Cotton is cultivated in Maryland, as in
Virginia; but little care is taken to perfect
either its culture or its manufacture. You
fee excellent lands in thefe two ftates; but
they

they have very few good meadows, though thefe might be made in abundance. For want of attention and labor, the inhabitants make but little hay; and what they have is not good. They likewife neglect the cultivation of potatoes, carrots, and turnips for their cattle, of which their neighbours of the north make great ufe. Their cattle are left without fhelter in winter, and nourifhed with the tops of Indian corn. Of confequence many of them die with cold and hunger; and thofe that furvive the winter, are miferably meagre.

They have much perfected in this country the Englifh method of inoculation for the fmall-pox. In the manner practifed here, it is very little dangerous. General Wafhington affured me, that he makes it a practice to have all his negroes inoculated, and that he never loft one in the operation. Whoever inoculates in Virginia, is obliged, by law, to give information to his neighbours within the fpace of two miles.

The population augments every where in thefe States, notwithftanding the great emigration to the Ohio. The horfes of Virginia are, without contradiction, the fineft in
the

the country; but they bear double the price of thofe in the northern States. The practice of races, borrowed from the Englifh by the Virginians, is fallen into difufe. The places renowned for this bufinefs are all abandoned; and it is not a misfortune; they are places of gambling, drunkennefs, and quarrels.

The General informed me, that he could perceive a great reformation in his countrymen in this refpect; that they are lefs given to intoxication, that it is no longer fafhionable for a man to force his guefts to drink, and to make it an honor to fend them home drunk; that you hear no longer the taverns refounding with thofe noify parties formerly fo frequent; that the feffions of the courts of juftice were no longer the theatres of gambling, inebriation, and blood; and that the diftinction of claffes begins to difappear.

The towns in Virginia are but fmall; this may be faid even of Richmond with its *capitol.* This capitol turns the heads of the Virginians; they imagine, that from this, like the old Romans, they fhall one day give law to the whole north.

There

There is a glafs manufactory forty miles from Alexandria, which exported laft year to the amount of ten thoufand pounds in glafs: and notwithftanding the general character of indolence in this State, the famous canal of the Potowmack advances with rapidity. Crimes are more frequent in Virginia than in the northern States. This refults from the unequal divifion of property, and from flavery.

Wherever you find luxury, and efpecially a miferable luxury, there provifions, even of the firft neceffity, will be dear. I experienced this in Virginia. At a tavern there I paid a dollar for a fupper, which in Pennfylvania would have coft me two fhillings, in Connecticut one. Porter, wine, and every article, bear an exceffive price here. Yet this dearnefs is owing in part to other caufes hereafter to be explained.

LETTER

LETTER XXXVII.

*The Tobacco of Virginia, and the Tobacco
Notes.*

I Have found, with pleasure, that your excellent article on the tobacco, inserted
in our work *de la France et des Etats Unis*,
is nearly exact in all its details. It is true
that tobacco requires a strong fertile soil, and
an uninterrupted care in the transplanting,
weeding, defending from insects, cutting,
curing, rolling, and packing.

Nothing but a great crop, and the total
abnegation of every comfort, to which the
negroes are condemned, can compensate the
expences attending this production before
it arrives at the market. Thus in proportion
as the good lands are exhausted, and by
the propagating of the principles of humanity, less hard labor is required of the slaves,
this culture must decline. And thus you
see already in Virginia fields enclosed, and
meadows succeed to tobacco. Such is the
fystem

fyftem of the proprietors who beft underftand their intereft; among whom I place
GeneralWafhington,who has lately renounced
the culture of this plant.

If the Virginians knew our wants, and
what articles would be moft profitable to
them, they would pay great attention to
the culture of cotton; the confumption of
which augments fo prodigioufly in Europe.
I will not enlarge here on the fubject of
tobacco, which many authors have explained; but I will give you fome ideas on
that kind of paper-currency called tobacco-
money; the ufe of which proves, that nations need not give themfelves fo much inquietude as they ufually do on the abfence
of fpecie. In a free and fertile country,
the conftant produce of the land may give
a fixed value to any kind of reprefentative of
property.

This State has public magazines, where
the tobacco is depofited. Infpectors are appointed to take charge of thefe magazines,
and infpect the quality of the tobacco;
which, if merchantable, is received, and the
proprietor is furnifhed with a note for the
quantity by him depofited. This note circulates

culates freely in the State, according to the
known value of the tobacco. The price is
different, according to the place where it
is infpected. The following places are ranked
according to the rigidity of the infpection:
Hanover-Court, Pittfburg, Richmond, Cabin-
Point. When the tobacco is worth fixteen
fhillings at Richmond, it is worth twenty-
one at Hanover-Court. The tobacco travels
to one place or the other, according to its
quality; and if it is refufed at all places,
it is exported by contraband to the iflands,
or confumed in the country. There are
two cuttings in a year of this crop; the firft
only is prefented for infpection, the fecond
confumed in the country or fmuggled to the
iflands.

As Virginia produces about eighty thoufand
hogfheads, there circulates in the State about
eight hundred thoufand pounds in thefe notes;
this is the reafon why the Virginians have
not need of a great quantity of circulating
fpecie, nor of copper coin. The rapid
circulation of this tobacco-money fupplies
their place.

This fcarcity, however, of fmall money
fubjects the people to great inconveniences,
and

and has given rife to a pernicious practice of cutting pieces of filver coin into halves and quarters; a fource of many little knaveries. A perfon cuts a dollar into three pieces, keeps the middle piece, and paffes the other two for half dollars. The perfon who receives thefe without weighing, lofes the difference, and the one who takes them by weight, makes a fraudulent profit by giving them again at their pretended value; and fo the cheat goes round.

But notwithftanding this pitiful refource of cutting the filver, fociety fuffers a real injury for want of a plentiful copper coin; it is calculated, that in the towns the fmall expences of a family are doubled, on account of the impoffibility of finding fmall change. It fhews a ftriking want of order in the government, and increafes the mifery of the poor. Though tobacco exhaufts the land to a prodigious degree, the proprietors take no pains to reftore its vigor; they take what the foil will give, and abandon it when it gives no longer. They like better to clear new lands, than to regenerate the old. Yet thefe abandoned lands would ftill be fertile, if they were properly manured and cultivated. The Virginians take no tobacco in

fubftance,

fubftance, either in the nofe or mouth; fome of them fmoke, but this practice is not fo general among them as in the Carolinas.

The Americans wifh for the free commerce of tobacco with France; and they complain much of the monopoly of the farmers-gene-neral. If this monopoly were removed, and the tobacco fubjected only to a fmall duty on importation into France, there is no doubt but that the Americans would make our country the ftore-houfe of thofe im-menfe quantities with which they inundate Europe. You know that they are now carried chiefly to England; where about the tenth part is confumed, and the reft is ex-ported. England pays the whole in her own merchandize. Judge then of the profit fhe muft draw from this exchange; then add the commiffion, the money expended in Eng-land by a great number of Americans whom this commerce leads thither, and the profits of other branches of bufinefs that are the confe-quence of this.

Such are the advantages which it is in the power of France to acquire over England; but we muft abolifh the farms, and content ourfelves with a fmall duty on the importa-tion.

tion. The high duty paid in England on tobacco, will prevent the Americans from giving the preference to that country. It amounts to fifteen pence fterling on the pound. Though England confumes little tobacco, fhe draws from it a revenue of 600,000 pounds fterling. The ftate of the finances of that ifland, will not admit of her diminifhing this duty in order to rival France. Continue then, my friend, to preach your doctrine.

The great confumption of tobacco in all countries, and the prohibitive regulations of almoft all governments, may engage the Americans to continue this culture; for as they can furnifh it at a low price, as they navigate at fmall expence, as no people equals them in enterprize and induftry, they may undertake to furnifh the whole earth.

Spain, for inftance, will doubtlefs become a market for them. The author of the *Nouveau Voyage en Efpagne* makes the revenue which the king draws from this article, amount to twenty millions of livres (£.833,333 ⅔ fterling.) The greater part of this tobacco is brought from Brafil by the Portuguefe, fold to the king at five pence fterling the pound, and

and then fold by him at eight fhillings and
four-pence. At the expiration of the prefent contract, fays the fame author, the Americans will offer a more advantageous one,
and it is faid they will have the preference.

This high price encourages a confiderable contraband in Spain, though interdicted
by the pains of death. The law is too rigid
to be executed.

The tobacco of the Miffiffipi and the
Ohio will, doubtlefs, one day furnifh the
greater part of the confumption of Spain as
well as of France; which, if the fyftem of
liberty fhould be adopted, will become immenfe. For it is proved, by thofe who
know the fecrets of the farm, that the confumption of the latter amounts to more
than thirty millions of pounds annually, inftead of fifteen, as we have been commanded
to believe.

LETTER

LETTER XXXVIII.

The Valley of Shenadore in Virginia.

I PROPOSED, my friend, on quitting Alexandria, to vifit that charming valley, wafhed by the Shenadore, of which Jefferfon and Crevecœur have given us fo feducing a defcription. From thence I intended to return by the vale of Lancafter, and pay my refpects to the virtuous Moravians. But the approaching Revolution in France haftening my return, I am obliged to content myfelf with giving you fome idea of that country where we have been invited to fix our tabernacles; and to borrow the obfervations of different travellers, who have this year obferved, with great attention, the lands fituated between the different chains of mountains, which feparate Virginia from the weftern territory.

The Valley of Shenadore, which lies between the fouth mountain and the north, or endlefs mountain, is from thirty to forty
miles

miles wide; chalky bottom, a fertile foil, and a good air. This fituation offers almoft all the advantages of the weftern country, without its inconveniences. It is almoft in the centre of the United States, and has nothing to fear from foreign enemies. It lies between two confiderable rivers, which fall into the Chefapeak; and though the navigation of thefe rivers is interrupted for the prefent, yet there is no doubt, from the progrefs of the works on the Potowmack, that this inconvenience will foon be removed.

The price of lands here, as elfewhere, varies according to their quality; you may purchafe at any price, from one to five guineas the acre, land of the fame quality as in Pennfylvania from four to twenty guineas.

The average diftance of thefe lands from commercial towns is as follows: fifty miles from George-town, about fifty miles from Alexandria, eighty or an hundred from Richmond and from Baltimore. But this part of the country is ftill more inviting for its future profpects. Of all the rivers that difcharge into the Atlantic, the Potowmack
offers

offers the moft direct communication with
the rivers of the weft.   This circumftance
will make it one day the great channel of
intercourfe for almoft all the United States;
and its fituation renders it fecure againft being
interrupted by war.

But to realize the advantages which the
fituation of this country feems to promife,
requires a reformation of manners, and the
banifhment of luxury, which is more confiderable here than in Pennfylvania.   You
muft banifh idlenefs and the love of the chace,
which are deeply rooted in the foul of the
Virginians; and, above all things, you muft
banifh flavery; which infallibly produces thofe
great fcourges of fociety, lazinefs and vice,
in one clafs of men, uninduftrious labour
and degrading mifery in another.   The view
of this deforming wound of humanity, will
difcourage foreigners of fenfibility from com-
ing to this ftate; while they have not to
dread this difgufting fpectacle in Pennfylvania.

But it is in a country life in America,
that true happinefs is to be found by him
who is wife enough to make it consist in
tranquillity

tranquillity of foul, in the enjoyment of himfelf, and of nature. What is the fatiguing agitation of our great cities, compared to this delicious calmnefs? The trees, my friend, do not calumniate; they revile not their benefactors; men of the greateft merit cannot always fay this of their fellow-creatures.

LETTER

LETTER XXXIX.

Journey from Boſton to Portſmouth.

October, 1788.

I LEFT Boſton the 2d of October, after dinner, with my worthy friend Mr. Bar-
ret *; to whom I cannot pay too ſincere a
tribute of praiſe for his amiable qualities, or
of gratitude for the readineſs he has manifeſted on all occaſions in procuring me information on the objects of my reſearch. We
ſlept at Salem, fifteen miles from Boſton;
an excellent gravelly road, bordered with
woods and meadows. This road paſſes the
fine bridge of Malden, which I mentioned
before, and the town of Linn remarkable
for the manufacture of womens' ſhoes. It is
calculated that more than an hundred thouſand pairs are annually exported from this
town. At Reading, not far from Linn,
is a ſimilar manufacture of mens' ſhoes.

---

* He is of a reſpectable family in Boſton. He is lately
named Conſul of the United States in France.

Salem,

Salem, like all other towns in America, has a printing prefs and a gazette. I read in this gazette the difcourfe pronounced by M. D'Epreminil, when he was arrefted in full parliament in Paris. What an admirable invention is the prefs! it brings all nations acquainted with each other, and electrizes all men by the recital of good actions, which thus become common to all. This difcourfe tranfported the daughters of my hoftefs: D'Epreminil appeared to them a Brutus *.

It was cold, and we had a fire in a Frank-lin ftove. Thefe are common here, and thofe chimneys that have them not, are built as defcribed by M. de Crevecœur: they rarely fmoke. The miftrefs of the tavern, (Robinfon,) was taking tea with her daughters; they in-vited us to partake of it with them.—I repeat it, we have nothing like this in France. It is a general remark through all the United States: a tavern-keeper muft be a refpectable man, his daughters are well dreft, and have an air of decency and civility. We had good provifions, good beds, attentive fervants; neither the fervants nor the coachmen afk any money. It is an excellent practice; for

* *Heu! quantum mutatus ab illo!*

this

this tax with us not only becomes infup-
portable on account of the perfecutions which
it occafions, but it gives men an air of bafenefs, and accuftoms to the fervility of avarice.
Salem has a confiderable commerce to the
iflands, and a great activity of bufinefs by
the cod fifhery.

In paffing to Beverly, we croffed another
excellent wooden bridge. It is over a creek
near a mile wide. The conftruction of this
bridge, and the celerity with which it was
built, gives a lively idea of the activity and
induftry of the inhabitants of Maffachufetts.
It coft but three thoufand pounds; the toll
for a horfe and carriage is eight-pence; the
opening in the middle for the paffage of
veffels, is of a fimpler mechanifm than that
of Charles-town. On the road to Beverley,
I faw a flourifhing manufacture of cotton.

At Londonderry, a town chiefly inhabited
by Irifh, is a confiderable manufacture of
linen. We dined at Newberry with Mr.
Tracy, who formerly enjoyed a great fortune, and has fince been reduced by the
failure of different enterprizes, particularly
by a contract to furnifh mafts for the marine
of France. The mifcarriage of this undertaking,

taking, was owing to his having employed agents in procuring the firft cargo who deceived him, and fent a parcel of refufe mafts that were fit only for fire-wood. Though the manner in which Mr. Tracy had been deceived was fufficiently proved; yet, for the clerks of the marine at Verfailles, whofe intereft it was to decry the American timber, this fact was fufficient to enable them to caufe it ever after to be rejected. And Mr. Tracy's firft cargo was condemned and fold at Havre for 250l. He lives retired; and with the confolation of his refpectable wife, fupports his misfortunes with dignity and firmnefs,

Newberry would be one of the beft ports in the United States, were it not for a dangerous bar at the entrance. The bufinefs of fhip-building has much declined here. In the year 1772 ninety veffels were built here, in 1788 only three. This town ftands at the mouth of the fine river Marrimak, abounding in fifh of different kinds.

Twenty-four miles of fine road brings you from Newberry to Portfmouth, the capital of New-Hampfhire. There is little appearance of activity in this town. A thin population, many houfes in ruins, women and
children

children in rags; every thing announces decline.   Yet there are elegant houses and some
commerce.   Portfmouth is on the Pifcatuay,
a rapid and deep river, which never freezes
till four miles above the town.   This was
formerly one of the greateft markets for fhip-
timber.   Colonel Wentworth, one of the
moft intelligent and efteemed citizens, was
the agent of the Englifh government and
of the Eaft-India Company for that article.
This company is now renewing its demands
for this timber.   Every thing in this town
is commerce and fhip-building.

Prefident Langdon himfelf is a merchant;
he is extremely well informed in every thing
that concerns his country.   You may recollect, that at the time of the invafion of Bur-
goyne, he was the firft to mount his horfe
and lead off his fellow citizens to fight him.
He appears well perfuaded, as well as Colonel Wentworth, that the fureft road to the
profperity of their country, is the adoption
of the new federal government.

We left Portfmouth on Sunday, and came
to dine at Mr. Dalton's, five miles from Newberry, on the Marrimak: this is one of the
fineft

fineſt ſituations that can be imagined. It preſents an agreeable proſpect of ſeven leagues. This farm is extremely well arranged; I ſaw on it thirty cows, numbers of ſheep, &c. and a well furniſhed garden. Mr. Dalton occupies himſelf much in gardening, a thing generally neglected in America. He has fine grapes, apples, and pears; but he complains that children ſteal them; an offence readily pardoned in a free country. A proprietor here, who, to prevent theſe little thefts, ſhould make uſe of thoſe infernal mantraps, invented by the Engliſh, would juſtly be execrated by his fellow creatures.

Mr. Dalton received me with that frankneſs which beſpeaks a man of worth and of talents; with that hoſpitality which is more general in Maſſachuſetts, and New-Hampſhire, than in the other States.

The Americans are not accuſtomed to what we call grand feaſts; they treat ſtrangers as they treat themſelves every day, and they live well. They ſay they are not anxious to ſtarve themſelves the week, in order to gormandiſe on Sunday. This trait
will

will paint to you a people at their eafe, who wifh not to torment themfelves for fhow.

Mr. Dalton's houfe prefented me with the image of a true patriarchal family, and of great domeftic felicity; it is compofed of four or five handfome young women, dreft with decent fimplicity, his amiable wife, and his venerable father of eighty years. This refpectable old man preferves a good memory, a good appetite, and takes habitual exercife. He has no wrinkles in his face, which feems to be a characteriftic of American old age; at leaft I have often obferved it.

From Mr. Dalton's we came to Andover, where my companion prefented me to the refpectable paftor of the parifh, Doctor Symmes, in whom I faw a true model of a minifter of religion, purity of morals, fimplicity in his manner of life, and gentlenefs of character. He chears his folitude with a refpectable wife, by whom he has had many children. And the cultivation of his farm occupies thofe moments which are not neceffarily devoted to ftudy, and to the care of the fouls committed to his charge.

LETTER

LETTER XL.

Debt of the United States.

YOU have feen, my friend, in the Encyclopedia, a ftate of the American
debt brought down to the year 1784. This
article, which I believe was furnifhed to the
compilers by the learned Mr. Jefferfon, contains fome few errors. You may, however,
draw from it fome juft ideas relative to the
origin of the continental debt. There is
no work which treats of the changes made
in it fince 1784, which is the principal object of my prefent letter *.

You who are fo verfed in finance, will
doubtlefs be ftruck with the errors committed
by the Congrefs in laying the foundation of
this debt, and with the fterility of their plants
to remedy the want of money. But your
furprize will vanifh, when you examine the
critical circumftances of that body of men to
whom America owes her independence.

* Since writing this fketch, I have incorporated into it the
operations of the new Congrefs on Mr. Hamilton's report of
September 1789.

They

They muſt be ſuppoſed ignorant of the principles of finance; a ſcience which their former ſituation had happily rendered unneceſſary. They were preſſed by the imperious neceſſity of a formidable invaſion, to ſubmiſſion, or to combat; and they muſt pay thoſe who ſhould fight their battles.

The idea of paper money was the firſt, and perhaps the only one that could ſtrike them. Its object was ſo ſublime, and patriotiſm ſo fervent, that every thing was to be expected from it. The Congreſs believed in it; and in multiplying this paper, even in the midſt of a rapid depreciation, they are not to be accuſed of ill faith; for they expected to redeem the whole.

The people manifeſted the ſame confidence. But the unexpected accumulation of the quantity, the conſequent depreciation, and the gradual diſappearance of danger, were the natural and united cauſes of a revolution of ſentiment. To believe that this paper would not be redeemed at its nominal value, was in 1777 a crime. To ſay that it ought to be ſo redeemed, was in 1784 another crime.

Since

Since the eftablifhment of the new federal fyftem, the opinion, with refpeᴄt to the debt, has undergone a third revolution. Among a free people, it is impoffible but truth and honor fhould fooner or later predominate. Almoſt all the Americans are at prefent convinced, that to arrive at the high degree of profperity, to which the nature of things invites them, and to acquire the credit neceffary for this purpofe, they muft fulfill, with the moft fcrupulous punᴄtuality, all their engagements. And this conviᴄtion has determined the new Congrefs to make the finance the firft great objeᴄt of their attention.

The debt of the United Sates is divided into two claffes, *foreign* and *domeſtic*. The foreign debt is compofed, in capital, of a loan made in France of 24,000,000 * of livres at

5 *per*

* If the fecret hiftory of this debt contraᴄted in France were publifhed, it would difcover the origin of many fortunes which have aftonifhed us. It is certain, for inftance, that M. de Vergennes difpofed of thefe loans at pleafure, caufed military ftores and merchandife to be furnifhed by perfons attached to him, and fuffered not their accounts to be difputed. It is a faᴄt, that in his accounts with Congrefs, there was one million of livres that he never accounted for, after all the demands that were made to him. It is likewife a faᴄt, that out of the forty-feven millions pretended to be furnifhed in the above
articles

5 per cent. another made in Holland, under the guarantee of France, of 10,000,000 at *4 per cent.* both amounting in dollars to 6,296,296; another in Spain, at *5 per cent.* 174,011 dollars.

In Holland, in four different
    loans - -   3,600,000

Total capital - - 10,070,307 doll.
Interest to *Dec.* 31, 1789, 1,651,257

Total, capital and Interest, 11,721,564
Domestic debt liquidated,
    capital and interest to
    the 31st *Dec.* 1790. 40,414,085
Not liquidated, estimated at 2,000,000

Total, foreign and domestic, 54,124,464 doll.
                                   In

articles by France to Congress, the employment of twenty-one millions is without vouchers. Many fortunes may be made from twenty-one millions.

M. Beaumarchais, in a memoir published two years ago, pretends to be the creditor of Congress for millions. I have, in my hands, a report made to Congress by two respectable members, in which they prove, that he now owes Congress 742,413 livres, and a million more, if the wandering million above-mentioned, has fallen into his hands. These reporters make a striking picture of the manœuvres practised to deceive the Americans.

Will not the National Assembly cause some account to be rendered of the sums squandered in our part of the American war? or rather the sums which, instead of going to succour those

In the profecution of the war, each individual State had occafion to contract a debt
of its own, which, for a variety of reafons,
it was thought beft that the Congrefs fhould
affume and add to the general mafs of the
debt of the United States.

The fums thus affumed, which are fuppofed to abforb nearly the whole of all the
State debts, amount in the whole to

25,000,000 doll.

So that the total amount of
the prefent debt of the
United States is   -   79,124,464 doll.

Annual intereft of this fum,
as ftipulated   -   -   4,587,444

To complete the lift of what is annually

thofe brave ftrugglers for liberty, went to adorn the bed-cham-
bers of an actrefs? Adeline did more mifchief to the Americans, than a regiment of Heffians. Where are the accounts
of her favourite Veymerange? Why has not M. Neckar
drawn the impenetrable veil which fcreens them from the
public? And he himfelf, has he nothing to anfwer for the
choice he made of corrupted, weak, and wicked agents, and
the facility with which he ratified their accounts?

Mr. Morris and Dr. Franklin have been cenfured in the
American papers on account of thefe robberies. I am far
from joining in the accufations againft the latter; but I could
wifh he had given pofitive anfwers to the writer under the
fignature of Centinel.

to

to be paid, we muſt add the annual expences of the federal government. The following is the amount of the year 1790:

Civil liſt - - - 254,892
Department of war - 155,537
Military penſions - - 96,979

507,408

You ſee, my friend, from theſe details, that the expences of government among a free people, are far from that extravagance and pomp which are pretended to be neceſſary in other governments to delude the people, and which tend but to render them vicious and miſerable.

You ſee, that with one hundred and ten thouſand ſterling, a government is well ad-miniſterd for four millions of people, inha-biting an extent of country greater than Germany, Flanders, Holland, and Switzer-land united *. And finally, you ſee that the Americans pay leſs than a million ſterling a year for having maintained their liberty; while the Engliſh pay more than four mil-

* I ſpeak only of the ſettled parts of the United States.

lions

lions fterling additional annual expence, for having attempted to rob them of it.

By the meafures taken by the new government, the Americans are in a fair way not only to pay their intereft, but to fink the principal of their debt; and that without direct taxation.

LETTER

LETTER XLI.

Importations into the United States.

IF you doubt, my friend, of the abilities
of the United States to pay their debt,
and the expences of their government, your
doubts will be diffipated on cafting your eye
over the tables of their annual exportations.

Many publications give, as an inconteflible
maxim, " *A nation muſt import as little as
poſſible, and export as much as poſſible.*" If
they mean by this that fhe ought to produce
as much as poffible at home, it is true; but
if they underftand that a nation is neceffarily
poor when fhe imports much, it is falfe.
For if fhe imports, fhe either confumes, and
of confequence has wherewith to pay, or
fhe re-exports, and confequently makes a
profit. This maxim, like moft of the dogmas of commerce, fo confidently preached
by the ignorant, is either trivial or falfe. The
importations into the United States have
much increafed fince the peace, as you will
fee

fee by the following account of them, compared with the tables of Lord Sheffield,
which reprefent periods antecedent to the
war.

The following is the ftatement of the principal articles:

Rum, brandy, and other fpirits -	4,000,000 gall.
Wine - - - - - - -	1,000,000
Hyfon tea - - - - -	125,000 lb.
Sugar - - - -	20,000,000
Coffee, cocoa, and chocolate -	1,500,000
Molaffes - - . - -	3,000,000 gall.
Salt - - - - - -	1,000,000 barrl.

Befides the above articles, the importations
of dry goods amount to more than twenty
millions of dollars annually.

This general eftimate is calculated from
the cuftom-houfe books at New-York for
three years. Taking for bafis that New-York
makes one-fifth of the general importations
of the United States, it is believed that moft
of thefe articles are eftimated much too low;
and this idea is fupported by the amount of
duties collected fince the new federal fyftem
has begun its operations.

A great proportion of thefe articles, you
will

will be convinced, might be better imported
from France than from any other country;
and they will be, whenever we fhall underftand our intereft. Mr. Swan fays, that a
million and a half of gallons of brandy might
be brought annually from France; that it is
cheaper than the rum of Jamaica, and alto-
gether preferred by the Americans to the rum
of our iflands. He is likewife of opinion,
that French wines might be introduced in
abundance; but he recommends to our merchants, to obferve good faith in this particular, as they have inundated the United
States with bad Bourdeaux wine, which has
reflected general difcredit on all the wines of
France. He gives the preference to the
white wines of *Grave, Pontac, St. Brife:* and
then to the *Sauterne, Prignac, Barfac:* among
the red wines, he prefers the *Chateau Maigol,*
the *Segur,* the *Haut Heifs,* the *La Fite,* &c.
I drank excellent Champagne at Bofton and
New-York; and Burgundy at Philadelphia;
which is a proof that thefe wines will bear
the fea. The quantity of twenty millions of
imported fugar, is thought to be five millions below the reality: we may add to this,
five millions of maple fugar made in the
United States. What a difference between
this confumption and ours! According to a
calculation

calculation on the comparative number of inhabitants, France ought to confume two hundred millions; whereas our confumption is but eighty millions. By this fact you may judge of the difference between the inhabitants of the two continents. In America, even fervants ufe fugar in abundance. In France, the artifans and peafants cannot enjoy this neceffary article; which is confequently regarded as a fuperfluity. This circumftance will lead you to another obfervation, very important: this twenty millions of fugar is brought from our iflands; from whence the exportation is rigidly prohibited. For what purpofe then thefe prohibitions for two neigh-bouring people, who have reciprocal wants? Is not this an invitation to governments to remove barriers which are fo eafily broken over?

LETTER

LETTER XLII.

Exportations and Manufactures.

IF any thing can give an idea of the high degree of profperity, to which thefe confederated republics are making rapid ftrides, it is the contemplation of thefe two fubjects. It is impoffible to enumerate all the articles to which they have turned their attention; almoft one-half of which were unknown before the war. Among the principle ones are fhip-building, flour, rice, tobacco, manufactures in woollen, linen, hemp, and cotton; the fifheries, oils, forges, and the different articles in iron and fteel; inftruments of agriculture, nails, leather, and the numerous objects in which they are employed; paper, pafteboard, parchment, printing, pot-afh, pearl-afh, hats of all qualities, fhip-timber, and other wood of conftruction; cabinet work, cordage, cables, carriages; works in brafs, copper, and lead; glafs of different kinds; gunpowder, cheefe, butter, callicoes, printed linen, indigo, furrs, &c.

Ship-

Ship-building is one of the moft profitable branches of bufinefs in America. They built fhips here before the war; but they were not permitted to manufacture the articles necef-fary to equip them; every article is now made in the country. A fine fhip, called the *Maf-fachufetts*, of eight hundred tons, belonging to Mr. Shaw, had its fails and cordage wholly from the manufacture of Bofton; this fingle eftablifhment gives already two thou-fand yards of fail-cloth a week.

Breweries augment every where, and take place of the fatal diftilleries. There are no lefs than fourteen good breweries in Phila-delphia. The infant woollen manufactory at Hartford, from September 1788 to Sep-tember 1789, gave about five thoufand yards of cloth, fome of which fells at five dollars a yard; another at Watertown, in Maffachu-fetts, promifes equal fuccefs, and engages the farmers to multiply their fheep.

Cotton fucceeds equally well. The fpin-ning machines of Arkwright are well known here, and are made in the country.

We have juftly remarked in our work on the United States, that nature invites the
Americans

Americans to the labours of the forge, by the profuse manner in which she has covered their soil with wood, and intersperfed it with metal and coals. Pennsylvania, New-Jerfey, and Delaware, make annually three hundred and fifty tons of steel, and six hundred tons of nails and nail rods. These articles are already exported from America; as are machines for carding wool and cotton, particularly common cards, which are cheaper than the English, and of a superior quality. In these three States are sixty-three paper-mills, which manufacture annually to the amount of 250,000 dollars. The State of Connecticut last year made five thousand reams, which might be worth nine thousand dollars.

The prodigious confumption of all kinds of glafs, multiplies the eftablishment of glafs works. The one on the Potowmack employs five hundred perfons. They have begun with fuccefs, at Philadelphia, the printing of callicoes, cotton, and linen. Sugar refiners are increasing every where. In Pennsylvania are twenty-one powder-mills, which are fuppofed to produce annually 625 tons of gunpowder.

Among

Among the principal articles of exporta‑
tion are wheat and flour. To form an idea
of the augmentation of exports in the article
of flour, take the following facts : Philadelphia
exported in the year 1786 - 150,000 barrels.

$$1787 - 202,000$$
$$1788 - 220,000$$
$$1789 - 360,000$$

Many well-informed men in America, have
written different pamphlets on the augmenta‑
tion of the commerce and manufactures in
the United States, which deserve attention;
fuch as, " *Enquiries into the Principles of a
commercial Syftem. By Tench Coxe.*" " *Let‑
ter on the Work of Lord Sheffield. By Mr.
Bingham.*" " *National Arithmetic. By Mr.
Swan,*" author of the work cited in my laft
letter.

LETTER

LETTER XLIII.

American Trade to the East-Indies.

IN this commerce, my friend, you may fee
difplayed the enterprizing fpirit of the
Americans; the firft motive to it, was the
hope of œconomizing in the price of Eaft-India
goods, which they formerly imported from
England, and this œconomy muft be immenfe, if we judge of it by the great confumption of tea in America, and the high
price it bears in England. In the year 1761,
the Englifh American colonies fent to England 85,000*l.* fterling in Spanifh dollars for
this fingle article, and fince that time the confumption of it has at leaft tripled.

Another motive which encouraged them
to pufh this commerce, was the hope of
being able to fupply South-America, the
Spanifh and other iflands, and even the
markets of Europe, with the goods of the
Eaft; and to obtain every where the preference, by the low price at which they might
be afforded. And this projed is not without
foundation.

foundation. The nature of things invites the Americans to become the firft carriers in the world. They build fhips at two-thirds of the expence that they are built at in Europe: they navigate with lefs feamen, and at lefs expence, although they nourifh their feamen better: they navigate with more fafety, with more cleanlinefs, and with more intelligence, becaufe the fpirit of equality, which reigns at home, attends them likewife at fea. Nothing ftimulates men to be good failors like the hope of becoming captains.

The productions of their country are more favourable to this commerce than thofe of Europe. They carry ginfeng to China; plank, fhip-timber, flour, and falted provifions to the Cape of Good Hope, and to the ifles of France and Bourbon. They are not, therefore, obliged to export fo great a proportion of fpecie as the Europeans, who have eftablifhments in the Eaft. They are not obliged, like them, to maintain, at an enormous expence, troops, forts, fhips of war, governors, intendants, fecretaries, clerks, and all the tools of defpotifm, as ufelefs as they are expenfive; of which the price muft be added to that of the articles of this commerce.

No

No fea is impenetrable to the navigating genius of the Americans. You fee their flag every where difplayed; you fee them exploring all iflands, ftudying their wants, and returning to fupply them.

Our languifhing colony of Cayenne, would have perifhed ten times with famine, if it depended on the regular promifed fupplies of the mother country! But it is provifioned by the Americans; who remedy thus the murderous calculations of European mafters.

A floop from Albany, of fixty tons and eleven men, had the courage to go to China. The Chinefe, on feeing her arrive, took her for the cutter of fome large veffel, and afked where was the great fhip? We are the great fhip; anfwered they to the Chinefe, ftupified at their hardinefs.

Our public papers vaunt the magnificence of the European nations, who make difcoveries and voyages round the world: the Americans do the fame thing; but they boaft not of their exploits with fo much emphafis. In September, 1790, the fhip *Columbia*, Captain Gray, failed to difcover the north-weft of this continent; this is his fecond

fecond voyage round the world: the brig
Hope has failed for the fame object. Our
papers have refounded with the quarrels of
the Englifh and Spaniards for the commerce
of Nootka Sound. The Americans make no
quarrels; but they have already made a confiderable commerce on the fame coaft in furrs
and peltry. They were there trading in the
year 1789, in good intelligence with both
parties. In the fame year, no lefs than forty-
four veffels were fent from the fingle town of
Bofton to the north-weft of America, to
India, and to China. They bound not their
hopes here: they expect, one day, to open
a communication more direct to Nootka
Sound. It is probable that this place is not
far from the head waters of the Miffifippi;
which the Americans will foon navigate to
its fource, when they fhall begin to people
Louifiana and the interior of New Mexico.

This will be a fortunate epoch to the
human race, when there fhall be a third great
change in the routes of maritime commerce.
The Cape of Good Hope will then lofe its
reputation, and its afflux of commerce, as
the Mediterranean had loft it before. The
paffage which the free Americans are called
upon to open, which is ftill unknown, which
however

however, is eafy to eftablifh, and which will place the two oceans, the Atlantic and Pacific, in communication, is by the paffage by the lake of *Nicaragua**. Nature fo much favours this communication, which is deftined to fhorten the route to the Eaft-Indies, that the obftinacy of the nation which now poffeffes the country, cannot long withftand its being opened. The Spaniards wifh to monopolize every thing. The free Americans, on the contrary, feek the advantages of the great family of the human race.

* This projeft exifts; its length prevents my giving it here. The Americans expeft one day to open this paffage.

LETTER

LETTER XLIV.

The Weſtern Territory.

I Have not the time, my friend, to deſcribe
to you the new country of the Weſt;
which, though at preſent unknown to the
Europeans, muſt, from the nature of things,
very ſoon merit the attention of every commercial and manufacturing nation. I ſhall
lay before you at preſent only a general view
of theſe aſtoniſhing ſettlements, and refer
to another time the details which a ſpecula-
tive philoſopher may be able to draw from
them. At the foot of the Alleganies, whoſe
ſummits, however, do not threaten the hea-
vens, like thoſe of the Andes and the Alps,
begins an immenſe plain, interſected with
hills of a gentle aſcent, and watered every
where with ſtreams of all ſizes; the ſoil is from
three to ſeven feet deep, and of an aſtoniſhing
fertility: it is proper for every kind of culture, and it multiplies cattle almoſt without
the care of man.

It is there that thoſe eſtabliſhments are
formed,

formed, whofe profperity attracts fo many
emigrants; fuch as Kentucky, Frankland,
Cumberland, Holfton, Mufkingum, and
Scioto.

The oldeft and moft flourifhing of thefe
is Kentucky, which began in 1775, had
eight thoufand inhabitants in 1782, fifty
thoufand in 1787, and feventy thoufand in
1790*. It will foon be a State.

Cumberland, fituated in the neighbourhood of Kentucky, contains 8000 inhabitants, Holfton 5000, and Frankland 25,000.

On beholding the multiplication and happinefs of the human fpecies in thefe rapid
and profperous fettlements, and comparing them with the languor and debility
of colonies formed by defpots, how auguft
and venerable does the afpect of liberty
appear! Her power is equal to her will:
fhe commands, and forefts are overturned,
mountains fink to cultivated plains, and nature prepares an afylum for numerous gene-

---

* By a letter from Colonel Fowler, a réprefentative in the
legiflature of Virginia from Kentucky, of the 16th of December, 1790, which the tranflator has feen, it appears, that the
inhabitants of Kentucky at that time amounted to one hundred and feventy-three thoufand.

rations;

rations; while the proud city of Palmyra
perifhes with its haughty founder, and its
ruins atteft to the world that nothing is durable, but what is founded and foftered by
freedom. It appears that Kentucky will preferve its advantage over the other fettlements
on the fouth; its territory is more extenfive,
its foil more fertile, and its inhabitants more
numerous: it is fituated on the Ohio, navigable at almoft all feafons, this laft advantage
is equally enjoyed by the two fettlements of
which I am going to fpeak. The eftablifhment at the Mufkingum was formed in 1788,
by a number of emigrants from New-England, belonging to the Ohio company. The
Mufkingum is a river which falls into the
Ohio from the Weft. Thefe people have an
excellent foil, and every profpect of fuccefs.

From thefe proprietors is formed another
affociation, whofe name is more known in
France; it is that of the *Scioto Company* *,
a name

* This company has been much calumniated. It has been
accufed of felling lands which it does not poffefs, of giving
exaggerated accounts of its fertility, of deceiving the emigrants, of robbing France of her inhabitants, and of fending them to be butchered by the favages. But the title of this
affociation is inconteftible; the proprietors are reputable men;
the defcription which they have given of the lands is taken
from the public and authentic reports of Mr. Hutchins, Geo-
grapher

a name taken from a river, which after having traverſed the two millons of acres which they poſſeſs, falls into the Ohio.

This ſettlement would ſoon riſe to a high degree of proſperity, if the proper cautions were taken in the embarkation and the neceſſary means employed to ſolace them, and to prepare them for a kind of life ſo different from that to which they are accuſtomed.

The revolution in the American government, will, doubtleſs, be beneficial to the ſavages;

grapher of Congreſs. No perſon can diſpute their prodigious fertility.

Certainly the ariſtocrats of France, who may emigrate thither under the fooliſh idea of forming a monarchy, would be fatally deceived in their expectations. They would fly from the French government, becauſe it eſtabliſhes the equality of rights, and they would fall into a ſociety where this equality is confecrated even by the nature of things; where every man is ſolicited to independance by every circumſtance that ſurrounds him, and eſpecially by the facility of ſupplying his wants; they would fly to preſerve their titles, their honors, their privileges; and they would fall into a new ſociety, where the titles of pride and chance are deſpiſed, and even unknown.

This enterprize is ſuitable to the poor of Europe, who have neither property nor employment, and who have ſtrength to labour. They would find at Scioto the means of ſupplying their wants; the ſoil would give them its treaſures, at the expence of a ſlight cultivation; the beaſts of the foreſts would

favages; for the government tends effentially
to peace. But as a rapid increafe of population muft neceffarily be the confequence of
its operations, the favages muft either blend
with the Americans, or a thoufand caufes will
fpeedily annihilate that race of men.

There is nothing to fear, that the danger
from the favages will ever arreft the ardour
of the Americans for extending their fettlements. They all expect that the navigation
of the Miffifippi becoming free, will foon
open to them the markets of the iflands, and
the Spanifh colonies, for the productions

would cover their tables, until they could rear cattle on their
farms.   It would be then rendering a fervice to the unfortu-
nate people, who are deprived of the means of fubfiftence
by the Revolution, to open to them this afylum, where they
could obtain a property.

But, fay the oppofers, the poor may find thefe advantages
in France. We have great quantities of uncultivated land :
yes ; but will the proprietors fell it for almoft nothing ? will it
produce equally with that of Scioto? are provifions as cheap
here as there? No; why then declaim fo much againft an
emigration, ufeful at the fame time to France, to the individuals, and to the United States? The man who without much
expence, and in a manner that fhould make it voluntary,
could find the means of tranfporting to the forefts of America the thirty thoufand mendicants, whom fear, as well as humanity, obliges us to fupport in idlenefs in the neighbourhood
of Paris, that man would merit a ftatue. For he would at
once cure the capital of a leprofy, and render thirty thoufand
people to happinefs and good morals.

with

with which their country overflows. But
the queſtion to be ſolved is, whether the
Spaniards will open this navigation willingly,
or whether the Americans will force it. A kind
of negociation has been carried on, without ef-
feᷮ for four years; and it is ſuppoſed, that certain States, fearing to loſe their inhabitants by
emigration to the Weſt, have, in concert
with the Spaniſh miniſter, oppoſed it; and
that this concert gave riſe to a propoſition,
that Spain ſhould ſhut up the navigation for
twenty-five years, on condition that the
Americans ſhould have a free commerce with
Spain. Virginia and Maryland, though they
had more to fear from this emigration than
the other States, were oppoſed to this propoſition, as derogatory to the honor of the
United States; and a majority of Congreſs
adopted the ſentiment.

A degree of diffidence, which the inhabitants of the Weſt have ſhewn relative to
the ſecret deſigns of Congreſs, has induced
many people to believe, that the union
would not exiſt a long time between the
old and new States; and this probability of
a rupture they ſay, is ſtrengthened by ſome
endeavours of the Engliſh in Canada, to attach

tach the Weſtern ſettlers to the Engliſh government,

But a number of reaſons determine me to
believe, that the preſent union will for ever
ſubſiſt. A great part of the property of the
Weſtern land belongs to people of the Eaſt;
the unceaſing emigrations ſerve perpetually
to ſtrengthen their connexions; and as it is
for the intereſt both of the Eaſt and Weſt, to
open an extenſive commerce with South-
America, and to overleap the Miſſiſippi; they
muſt, and will, remain united for the accom-
pliſhment of this object.

The Weſtern inhabitants are convinced
that this navigation cannot remain a long
time cloſed. They are determined to open
it by good will or by force; and it would
not be in the power of Congreſs to moderate
their ardour. Men who have ſhook off the
yoke of Great-Britain, and who are maſters
of the Ohio and the Miſſiſippi, cannot conceive that the inſolence of a handful of Spaniards can think of ſhutting rivers and ſeas
againſt a hundred thouſand free Americans.
The ſlighteſt quarrel will be ſufficient to throw
them into a flame; and if ever the Americans ſhall march towards New Orleans, it
will

will infallibly fall into their hands. The Spaniards fear this moment; and it cannot be far off. If they had the policy to open the Miffifippi, the port of New Orleans would become the centre of a lucrative commerce. But her narrow and fuperftitious policy will oppofe it; for fhe fears, above all things, the communication of thofe principles of inde- pendance, which the Americans preach where- ever they go; and to which their own fuccefs gives an additional weight.

In order to avert the effects of this enter- prizing character of the free Americans, the Spanifh government has adopted the pitiful project of attracting them to a fettlement on the weft of the Miffifippi*; and by granting to thofe who fhall eftablifh themfelves there, the exclufive right of trading to New Orleans. This colony is the firft foundation of the conqueft of Louifiana, and of the civiliza- tion of Mexico and Peru.

How defirable it is for the happinefs of the human race, that this communication fhould extend! for cultivation and population here, will augment the profperity of the manufac-

* Colonel Morgan is at the head of this fettlement.

turing

turing nations of Europe. The French and
Spaniards, fettled at the Natches, on the moſt
fertile ſoil, have not, for a century, cultivated a ſingle acre; while the Americans,
who have lately made a ſettlement there, have
at preſent three thouſand farms of four hundred acres each; which furniſh the greater
part of the proviſions for New Orleans. O
Liberty! how great is thy empire; thou
createſt induſtry, which vivifies the dead.

I tranſport myſelf ſometimes in imagination to the ſucceeding century. I ſee this
whole extent of continent, from Canada to
Quito, covered with cultivated fields, little
villages, and country houſes*. I ſee Happineſs and Induſtry, ſmiling ſide by ſide, Beauty
adorning the daughter of Nature, Liberty
and Morals rendering almoſt uſeleſs the coercion of Government and Laws, and gentle
Tolerance taking place of the ferocious In-
quiſition. I ſee Mexicans, Peruvians, men
of the United States, Frenchmen, and Cana-
dians, embracing each other, curſing tyrants,

---

* America will never have enormous cities like London and
Paris ; which would abſorb the means of induſtry and vitiate
morals. Hence it will reſult, that property will be more
equally divided, population greater, manners leſs corrupted,
and induſtry and happineſs more univerſal.

and

and blefling the reign of Liberty, which leads to univerfal harmony. But the mines, the flaves, what is to become of them? The mines will be clofed, and the flaves will become the brothers of their mafters. As to gold, it is degrading to a free country to dig for it, unlefs it can be done without flaves: and a free people cannot want for figns to ferve as a medium in exchanging their commodities. Gold has always ferved more the caufe of defpotifm than that of liberty; and liberty will always find lefs dangerous agents to ferve in its place.

Our fpeculators in Europe are far from imagining that two revolutions are preparing on this continent, which will totally overturn the ideas and the commerce of the old: the opening a canal of communication between the two oceans, and abandoning the mines of Peru. Let the imagination of the philofopher contemplate the confequences. They cannot but be happy for the human race.

F I N I S.

CONTENTS.

CONTENTS.

CONTENTS.

N. B. *This Volume comprifes* M. de Warville's *two firft Volumes. His third, on the Commerce of America, has been before publifhed in Englifh.*

E R R A T A.

Page 12, *laſt line, for* Curius *read* Curios.

28, *line* 7, *for* ſelf *r.* leſs.

39, —— 3, *for* bonlevard *r.* boulevard.

102, —— 8, *for* really *r.* rarely.

116, —— 3 *from the bottom, for* have *r.* has.

118, —— 2 *from the bottom, for* modern *r.* modeſt.

160, —— 17, *for* poſterity *r.* proſperity.

172, —— 3, *for* to *r.* at.

246, —— 6, *for* pence *r.* ſhillings.

249, —— 14, *after* occupied *r.* by.

305, —— 9, *for* £. 52 6s. *r.* 52s. 6d.

326, —— 5, *for* alteration *r.* attraction.

344, —— 3 *from bottom, for* vigorous *r.* rigorous.

398, —— 18, *after* well *r.* as.

413, —— 8, *for* act *r.* art.

416, —— 15, *for* noxious *r.* noted.

417, —— 14, *for* collectors *r.* collections.

454, —— 15, *for* plants *r.* plans.